Stardom, Italian Style

New Directions in National Cinemas

Jacqueline Reich, editor

STARDOM

ITALIAN STYLE

Screen Performance and Personality in Italian Cinema

Marcia Landy

Indiana University Press
Bloomington & Indianapolis

This book is a publication of

Indiana University Press
601 North Morton Street
Bloomington, IN 47404-3797 USA

http://iupress.indiana.edu

Telephone orders	800-842-6796
Fax orders	812-855-7931
Orders by e-mail	iuporder@indiana.edu

The paper used in this publication meets the minimum requirements of American National Standard for Information Sciences—Permanence of Paper for Printed Library Materials, ANSI Z39.48-1984.

Manufactured in the United States of America

Library of Congress Cataloging-in-Publication Data

Landy, Marcia, date-
  Stardom, Italian style : screen performance and personality in Italian cinema / Marcia Landy.
    p. cm. -- (New directions in national cinemas)
  Includes bibliographical references and index.
  ISBN-13: 978-0-253-35108-1 (cloth : alk. paper)
  ISBN-13: 978-0-253-22008-0 (pbk. : alk. paper)
  1. Motion pictures—Italy. 2. Motion picture actors and actresses—Italy—Biography. 3. Motion picture producers and directors—Italy—Biography. I. Title.
  PN1993.5.I88L39 2008
  791.430945—dc22
                                    2007041968

1 2 3 4 5   13 12 11 10 09 08

Contents

Acknowledgments

When I was invited to present a paper at the Popular European Cinema conference in Stockholm, 2003, I did not realize that the presentation was to be the basis for this book. I am grateful to the organizers and particularly to Tytti Soila for that opportunity. Since that time, I have accumulated more debts as this book has taken shape. I thank the sponsoring editors at Indiana University Press, Michael Lundell and now Jane Kathleen Quinet, for their encouragement, graciousness, and generosity with time. After writing several drafts, I prevailed on Lucy Fischer, Director of Film Studies at the University of Pittsburgh, to read my latest draft, and I am extremely grateful for her careful and rigorous reading. Giuseppina Mecchia of the French and Italian department read the manuscript in its early stages, and she too made me aware of what was yet ahead of me: I hope that the present version addresses their comments and repays their hard work.

In the process of writing, I contributed essays to journals on related topics, and segments from them appear in the book albeit in considerably changed form, and I thank W. W. Norton and Company for permission to draw on relevant sections of my essay *"Rome Open City:* From Movie to Method" in *Film Analysis: A*

Norton Reader (2005), edited by Jeffrey Geiger and R. L. Rutsky, though drastically revised. Similarly, I am grateful to Yoram Allon, editorial director at Wallflower Press, for permission to incorporate (with drastic changes) segments of my essay *"Gli uomini che mascalzoni"* in *The Cinema of Italy* (2004), edited by Giorgio Bertellini. I have also drawn on an essay on film versions of *Malombra* published in the *Journal of Romance Studies* 4 (Spring 2004).

Thanks to the staff of the motion picture division of the Library of Congress, especially Madeline Matz, I was able to locate and screen important films. Also, Michael Prosser, media specialist at the University of Pittsburgh Media Resource Center, was able to locate a number of hard-to-find films on video or DVD that were essential to the study. My graduate student assistant, Joshua Zeleznick, found necessary but often elusive critical books, articles, and reviews with the aid of the interlibrary loan division of the Hillman Library. My secretary, Carol Mysliwiec, has been an invaluable support in bringing the book to completion. I am also indebted to the staff at Photofest for their patience and cooperation in finding me desired stills and saving me the time and trouble to get permissions for their use. By the same token, I acknowledge the use of stills from the Museum of Modern Art, New York, that I purchased in 2000. In relation to my use of stills from the British Film Institute, I want to thank the BFI staff for providing information on permissions, and Dean John N. Cooper and Associate Dean James A. Knapp of the Faculty and College of Arts and Sciences for providing me financial support. As always, I want to express my deep gratitude and affection to Stanley Shostak, who has survived all the drafts of the book as critical reader, technology advisor, and friend.

Introduction

[H]uman beings do not perceive things whole; we are not gods but wounded creatures, cracked lenses capable only of fractured perceptions . . . meaning is a shaky edifice we build out of scraps, dogmas, childhood injuries, newspaper articles, chance remarks, old films, small victories, people hated, people loved . . .

Salman Rushdie, *Imaginary Homelands*

Tracking Stars

Stars continue to be a subject of fascination, generating numerous studies in the popular press, journals, and magazines, and numerous book-length biographies. Many of these studies have been descriptive, focusing on the origins, rise to fame, career accomplishments, peccadilloes, or eccentricities of famous or infamous individuals who are the recipients of adulation, imitation, fanatic devotion, and fetishism.[1] Through media (cinema, and now TV and the Internet), the politician/demagogue also became a star. While curiosity about and fascination with the famous and infamous preceded cinematic culture, exemplified in epic literature, heroic drama, biography, operas, ballads, and journalism, the photographic and movie camera made possible the overcoming of regional, national, and social class boundaries, opening new social and cultural landscapes. Increasingly the star moved to center stage in the creation of new narratives of beauty, wealth, status, and desirability.

Walter Benjamin reflected on the changing perceptions of society wrought by visual technology, writing, "for the film, what matters primarily is that the actor represent himself to the public before the camera, rather than representing someone else. . . . What matters is that the part is not acted for an audience but for a mechanical contrivance . . . the projector will play with his shadow before the public and he himself must be content to play before the camera."[2] This statement is an invitation to think of this "shadow" as inviting different reflections of the "world viewed,"[3] if not lived, by a spectator in relation to specific "real" or imagined figures. In this context, the phenomenon of stardom raises questions about the nature of cinematic representation as a literal reproduction of reality.[4] Not invented by the movies but altered to suit the gaze of the age, the fascination with the star invites far-reaching explorations into social history, culture, economics, and various art forms to gain a sense of its power and persistence. My book connects the cinema in Italy to the role that stars have played in its development. The stakes and methods entailed in such a study involve philosophical (and political) considerations of language, subjectivity and objectivity, mechanical reproduction, and history making.

The faces and bodies of stars are revealing of standards of beauty; tendencies in the culture to elevate certain individuals by virtue of birth, breeding, moral attributes, and standards of success and failure; and prevailing conceptions of gender, sexuality, ethnicity, and social class. Stardom is often described as having affinity with religion, ritual, and myth. The notion of a star or diva pertains to the metamorphosis of certain humans into superhuman, if not divine, beings, and entails a form of worship replete with icons, fetishes, and other expressions of attachment, involving the star's ritual and economic value in systems of exchange. The nexus of commercial, affective, and aesthetic value is central to the phenomenon, designating and validating the prominence of an individual in terms of the qualities that this figure comes to represent in the public imagination. Hence, stardom is dependent on a host of factors integral to the culture and to its uses of the image in cinema, TV, and digital media and the forms of labor that have gone into its material production and its reception. Cinematic reproduction has been tied to realism, to correspondences between the photographic image and the world it is assumed to reproduce and reflect. Yet stardom gives the lie to cinema's prerogative to reproduce reality as it is or was. Rather than a "reflection of reality," the star is "the reality of a reflection," the consummate fabrication of an industry that plunders images and offers the illusion that they are authentic.

Reversing the traditional conception of art as imitating life, André Bazin asserted that "nature at last does more than imitate art: she imitates the artist."[5] And Gilles Deleuze, in his two books on cinema, affirms Bazin's concern with the nature of the cinematic image. Through his distinctions between what he terms the movement-image and the time-image, Deleuze offers a philosophic position for changing conceptions of cinematic form and hence of thinking about what is seen and heard from the screen and registered on brain and body.[6] His studies address significant aspects of perception that are relevant not only to a rethinking of cinematic forms but also to the role of stardom within those forms. The star is an integral part of a regime of vision in which the changing figures of thought inherent to the cinematic image from early cinema to the end of the twentieth century can be located.

An understanding of the character of stars in the first decades of the silent cinema can be profitably understood by reference to what Deleuze has termed the "movement-image." This type of image incites a perception of continuity, unity, and wholeness through the uses of framing and montage, emphasizing linkages between parts and whole. Whether exemplified by American filmmakers such as D. W. Griffith, French filmmakers such as Abel Gance, German expressionist filmmakers such as F. W. Murnau or G. W. Pabst, and Russian filmmakers such as Sergei Eisenstein, in their use of organic or inorganic metaphors—light and dark, water, machines—the image draws on movement for its overall effect, relying on images of perception, affect, and action. The most striking characteristic of the movement-image is its reliance on sensory-motor and automatic forms of response that imply "a special relationship with belief . . . [T]he cinematographic image . . . showed us the link between man and the world. Hence it developed in the direction of a transformation of the world by man, or the discovery of an internal and higher world that man himself was."[7] And the star was the bridge to that world.

The time-image works differently. This cinema of time involves the fragmentation of instants in time, a creation of characters who are, as we shall see, "'actor mediums' capable of seeing and showing rather than acting,"[8] and situations that are not extraordinary but everyday, though often ceremonial, where the cinema "becomes an analytic of the image."[9] These philosophic distinctions account for changes in the style of stardom that rely on the different relation to cinema initiated by such filmmakers as Hitchcock and Orson Welles as well as filmmakers identified with neorealism and beyond, such as Rossellini, Antonioni, and Pasolini. In the course of my discussion of stardom, I shall try to indicate where there are continuities with the movement-image and where the time-image has implications for changing spectacles of stardom in relation to configurations of the body, gesture, and faciality, and I will rely on montage, framing, music, and camera distance and proximity for determining the nature and effects of the star image.

While the writings of Deleuze are less pointedly and specifically historical, they are governed by a broad overview of twentieth-century history and politics and their relation to media, and other technological, historical, and critical perspectives that have played a role in altering conceptions of cinematic culture. An examination of the role of stardom involves considerations of acting and connections to theater, mime, and dance as well as painting; its multiple authorship includes technicians, fashion experts, musicians, studios, producers, and scriptwriters. More than a mere matter of "documenting" the attributes and influences that contribute to the production of stars, studies of multiple "authorship" serve to extricate stardom from "the belief that stars are a special category, differentiated from other actors by some ineffable 'star quality.'"[10]

Furthermore, star studies challenge ethnocentric conceptions of national cinemas. Thanks to writings by such critics as Gian Piero Brunetta, Alberto Farassino, Tim Bergfelder, Antonio Costa, Andrew Higson, Richard Dyer, and Susan Hayward, among others, the international and geopolitical character of the medium has been charted, altering the history of cinema and thereby the role of stardom. *Stardom, Italian Style* is indebted to this scholarship. My interest lies less in delineating how the "actual" lives of performers inform their stardom than in underscoring the fusion of "biography" and performance. Nor do I intend to cover star reception by way of reviews, movie magazines, tabloids, etc., except where such information illuminates changing perspectives on the star persona. My primary focus concerns on-screen performances where commerce, industry, aesthetics, cultural values, acting, and direction can be seen to converge. Stardom is my window through which to gaze on relations between the national and international dimensions of technological media, their uses of time and space to evaluate the changing spectacle of human and machinic bodies.[11] My decision to concentrate on the filmic text would seem to run counter to studies that focus on the construction and reception of stars and are based on extra-filmic sources. This study is not primarily sociological or psychoanalytic. My choice to privilege screen performance was based on several conceptual and pragmatic criteria. I sought to find a means of situating stars within certain theoretical formulations pertaining to cinema history that involve reflections on the changing character of the medium. I regard the genealogy of star images as integrally tied not only to social history but also to considerations of relations between politics and aesthetics. As to my selection of stars, I have largely (though not exclusively) chosen to focus on those individuals that have attained international attention. Inevitably, my choice of stars to discuss in the vast constellation of Italian cinema is also based on personal predilection. Given the steep decline in film production in the last decade of the twentieth century and in the new millennium, I offer a tentative discussion of the character and future of current stardom.

Italian Stardom

In undertaking an examination of the evolution of Italian film stardom over the course of a century, I ask: What is the character and fate of Italian stardom at the end of the twentieth century and in the first decade of the twenty-first century? Is it at all possible today to speak of stardom, whether in an Italian or an international framework? Not only has the life span of stars been shortened but also television, video, and tabloid media have profoundly altered public reception of stars. Stardom as a constantly changing phenomenon is inherent to the century-long history of cinema. I take a retrospective look at expressions of stardom in relation to changes in the Italian cultural and political milieu. I focus on four moments in the life of stardom: the silent cinema, the sound cinema of the fascist era, postwar neorealism, and the period beyond that to the uncertain present. I am attentive to the treatments of tradition and modernity, landscape and geography, femininity and masculinity, regionalism, technology, and leisure life that have preoccupied recent writers on Italian cinema. Where relevant, I examine theoretical writings on spectatorship and reception, data on production and exhibition, and pertinent information on the cross-cultural and international developments that involve the influx of European, Hollywood, and Asian forms into Italy as well as the movement of Italian stars and cinematic forms internationally.

The first chapter, "Eloquent Bodies: The Cinema of *Divismo*," presumes that the early cinema in Italy was not unique to that country. It was already part of the international circuit of cinematic forms and images. I distinguish the *diva*, a term derived from opera, from the star to demarcate more clearly the artistic world of the teens and twenties. In the teens, the dramatic figure of writer and political activist Gabriele D'Annunzio contributed significantly to the flourishing of *Divismo*. I explore how the world of the *divo* and *diva* was situated in a Janus-faced relation to tradition and modernity, to theater and cinema. Cinema too assisted in the creation of the divo in the figure of Mussolini, Il Duce.[12] His image was generated, disseminated, and sustained by the movie camera[13] that capitalized on his bodily image as virile and mobile leader of the people, sportsman, politico, paterfamilias, and military leader.[14]

While the divo, as represented by Bartolomeo Pagano, enjoyed extreme popularity as mythic strong man in the teens and early twenties, it was the divas that were not only nationally but also internationally prominent. Tied to images

of aristocracy, romance, strong affect, stylization, and theatricality, the diva was
not only an actor; she was in many instances, given the more informal type of
filmmaking at that time, the creative impulse for the film, functioning even as
director, as was arguably the case with diva Francesca Bertini. The divas' theatricality, their consummate uses of their bodies, facial expressions, and gestures, and their identification with spirituality and divinity rendered them the
priestesses of art. They were the creations of a literary and poetic sensibility derived from the nineteenth-century and modernist novel, and *fin de siècle* poetic
decadence where the image of femininity offered an aura of uniqueness, remoteness, and aesthetic inspiration and cultural value. This form of aesthetic
and affective value was to give way to a more mass-based, standardized, and
accessible automaton, the star.

Chapter 2, "The Stars Talk," explores stardom during the sound era concomitantly with the rise of mass culture and its connections to fascism.[15] Situating the star within a different milieu than that of diva, the chapter traces the
emergence of new genres and the changed treatment of the star in determining
the shape and success of narrative forms. However, given the technologically
backward, financially depleted, and perilous state of the industry, Italian cinema had to adopt measures to restore what once had been a successful international enterprise. The chapter recounts the various financial, organizational,
and technological strategies adopted to reinvigorate an Italian national cinema.
Hollywood was an important model in this moment of change, in the need to
create new images of people and their milieu and to accommodate to this
modern medium and to a faster-paced urban world.

Competing with Hollywood, the individuals who became stars during the
sound era presented different physical and character traits than the diva. The
femme fatale had not totally disappeared but was shorn of her perverse and dynamic stance. The star was now a machinic creation, inviting audiences to
gratify fantasies of romance circulated through magazines, newsreels, and fashion displays. The dominant female stars of the fascist era were Isa Miranda,
Assia Noris, Alida Valli, Elisa Cegani, and Luisa Ferida; the most popular male
stars were Vittorio De Sica, Fosco Giachetti, Amedeo Nazzari, and Gino Cervi.
Increasingly, as Italian producers learned from other European and Hollywood
directors and technicians, the industry began to regulate, to standardize aspects
of production, and to generate more capital by way of subsidies. In general, by
the late 1930s when the state had closed the country to U.S. film imports, the
Italians were achieving greater success with their own products. A factor important in the upgrading of Italian films was the return of many directors and
technicians from other European countries, their having departed at the low
ebb of cinema fortunes in the late 1920s. Their return not only ensured a higher
quality film, but it also was coincident with the greater attention paid to the

film director as preeminent in production in his ability to choose and work with important writers, cameramen, and editors, and, above all, to create stars. If not a star or "auteur" in the sense of certain postwar directors, the director was now a star maker, as evidenced in the films of Goffredo Alessandrini, Mario Camerini, and Alessandro Blasetti in such genres as comedies, musicals, biopics, historical films, and action films.

As the era advanced, there was a perceptible difference in costuming, indicating a greater correlation between advertising, the fashion industry, and images of film stars. Also, there was a concerted emphasis on highlighting the urban and agrarian landscapes as sites of cultural conflict between past and present. If, in the narratives in which she appeared, the diva was merged with the natural landscape (sea, woods, stars, and animals), the star, as exemplified by Isa Miranda in Max Ophüls's *La signora di tutti* (1934) or, obliquely, in Mario Soldati's *Malombra* (1942) emerged more distinctly as the creation of a "culture industry" tied to agents, the dictates of fashion, the words of a scriptwriter, the predilections of a director, and the technology of the camera and editing. The star became not only the *sine qua non* of the attributes of a character in a genre narrative, but a subject of fascination in the popular culture via numerous magazines that carried articles about Italian and Hollywood stars for the consumption of contemporary audiences.

Male stars assumed greater prominence in the films of the 1930s than in those of the teens and twenties. The comparison of certain Italian stars to Hollywood performers (e.g., Amedeo Nazzari to Errol Flynn, Vittorio De Sica to Cary Grant) capitalized on audience recognition and served also to depersonalize and stylize their images. The strong man underwent considerable transformation from the mythic figure of the silent era, conforming to contemporary conceptions of masculinity. If Bartolomeo Pagano's Maciste was tailored to his physical, working-class image in the cinema of *divismo*, the masculine figures in their various incarnations during the fascist era ranged from physical power to disciplined bodies of moral rectitude.

Chapter 3, "Stars amidst the Ruins: The Old and the New," addresses the phenomenon known as neorealism, connecting it more integrally not only to the cinema that preceded it, but to the cinema of the 1950s and beyond in relation to stardom.[16] By the late 1930s and 1940s a groundwork had been laid for a critical cinema utilizing stars through the calligraphic films of directors Ferdinando Maria Poggioli, Mario Soldati, and Renato Castellani, the last two of whom were to continue to make films for several decades after the war. This moment also witnessed Visconti's landmark *Ossessione* (1943) featuring Massimo Girotti and Clara Calamai, both prominent stars in the 1930s, and Blasetti's *Quattro passi tra le nuvole* (1942) starring Gino Cervi, another popular star of the Ventennio, films that, in retrospect, seem to anticipate a different relation to stars, acting, and narration in the post–World War II era.

The chapter explores the philosophic and aesthetic dimensions of neorealism to account for the divergent directions it took in both auteurist and popular cinema. While for many critics, neorealism served as a reaction against stardom and an escapist cinema that had characterized the prewar films, it functioned also to fuel new conceptions of popular cinema that involved the reworking of genre forms and, concomitantly, the remaking of old stars and the shaping of new ones.[17] In the case of the auteur cinema, stars were also not abandoned, but appropriated differently through the films of specific directors such as Luchino Visconti, Giuseppe De Santis, Roberto Rossellini, and Vittorio De Sica. In its exploration of cinematic language, neorealism altered conceptions of the male and female body to accommodate to an altered national landscape. The canonical texts of neorealism took a critical look at the glamour and artifice associated with stardom during the years of fascism, but they also served paradoxically to reinforce stardom. The persistence of stars from the fascist era was not only a reminder of the roles they had played within the preceding cinema but, simultaneously, a critical reflection on the inadequacy of preexisting cinematic models for the postwar cinema. Nonetheless, stardom remained and was even strengthened.

Anna Magnani's persona in *Roma, città aperta* was a harbinger of the resurgence of stardom. This film situated her type of maternal, working-class, and Roman-identified femininity in a world that had experienced the sufferings of fascism and war, and thus functioned to redeem cinematic images of femininity and maternity from the clichés to which they had been traditionally subjected. Magnani's portrait of Pina does not annul these cultural clichés but endows them with new properties that speak to an interface between residual and emergent elements in relation to a culture in transition. Similarly, De Santis's *Riso amaro* (1948), featuring Silvana Mangano, is a film that is exemplary of the convergence of the old and the new in postwar stardom. A beauty contest winner, Mangano would remain a star for several decades to come, and her image captures the shifting trajectory of femininity in the 1940s and 1950s. The film also introduced Vittorio Gassman and Raf Vallone, who would become major national and international film stars, functioning to introduce different forms of masculinity into Italian cinema. The conceptual character and style of neorealism played an important role in altering, not eliminating, stardom.

Chapter 4, "Popular Genres and Stars," examines the commercial success of melodramas, comedies, "peplum epics" or mythologicals, spaghetti westerns, and horror films that signaled further transformations in conceptions of stardom. In the late 1940s and 1950s, the extremely popular melodramas directed by Raffaello Matarazzo—*Catene* (1949), *I figli di nessuno* (1951), *Tormento* (1953), *L'angelo bianco* (1955), and *Malinconico autunno* (1959), often identified by the appellation "rosy" or "pink" neorealism—introduced the Italian viewing public to the star duo of Yvonne Sanson and Amedeo Nazzari. Extremely profitable at the box office, their films are an instance of wedding elements of neorealism to melodrama, fusing stardom with the cinema of genres. Their stars embodied the quest for national identity. Their suffering and redemption addressed altered perceptions of the family, masculinity and femininity, regionalism, and conflicts attendant on a changing social milieu. Despite the condescension accorded these films and their stars, they are a significant index to the cultural climate of the decade.

By the 1960s, the melodramas were supplanted by comedies that had a broader trajectory of social and political concerns—history, marriage, divorce, war, unionism, and criminality—in a cinematic style that had national appeal but also crossed national borders. Among the stars identified with these films, the most popular beyond Totò, Mastroianni, and Loren were Vittorio Gassman, Alberto Sordi, and Monica Vitti, who offered different, if not critical, images of reigning common sense and the art of surviving in a threatening and increasingly unfamiliar climate. The rise to stardom of Sophia Loren, Gina Lollobrigida, and Silvana Mangano was indebted to their well-proportioned and voluptuous bodies, often accentuated in film comedies of the late 1940s and 1950s. They married wealthy and influential men in the film industry and became associated with the sophisticated world of fashion in the 1960s on and off screen. Later, and well into the present time, the ever-popular *commedia all'italiana* shifted focus onto male stars, including Alberto Sordi, Vittorio Gassman, Marcello Mastroianni, Adriano Celentano, Paolo Villagio, and Carlo Verdone, who came to incarnate postwar, if not postmodern, conceptions of masculinity and sexuality in a cinematic world that departed even farther from traditional models of authority, competence, and power.[18] These films became popular internationally, a symptom of the growing transnational character of industries such as cinema and TV.

The changing face of stardom in Italy from the late 1960s to the present was influenced by television and the role of co-production, designed to minimize financial risks by capitalizing on the popularity of international stars, and an extremely popular film genre to emerge in the late 1950s was the peplum, the "sword and sandal" epic or mythological. The male stars of these films appealed to an assorted and growing audience composed of bodybuilders, readers of comic books, and TV viewers. The stars that reprised the image of the strong man (the Macistes, Ulysses, and Hercules of early Italian cinema) were international figures (e.g., Steve Reeves, Gordon Mitchell, Reg Park, and Jacques Cernas) who became popular stars of the moment. While such female actors as Sophia Loren and Sylvia Koscina lent their spectacular bodies to the films, the male stars were the main attraction (and the films continue to be seen in TV reruns and can be tracked via the Internet).

The spaghetti westerns that overlapped with these mythologicals were popular and influential with audiences worldwide.[19] Often made hastily, they were a hybrid form, utilizing comedy, satire, melodrama, action, and adventure. They were linked to American, European, and Asian cinema stars (e.g., Toshiro Mifune of the Japanese samurai genre and Amitabh Bachchan of Indian Idli films); they were also linked to popular television, as witnessed by the series *Rawhide*, which brought Clint Eastwood fame. The style of narrative varied with filmmakers, functioning for some as spectacle, for some as entertainment, or for others as political allegory—as in Leone's Dollars trilogy, his *C'era una volta in West* (Once upon a Time in the West, 1968), and *Giù la testa* (Duck, You Sucker, 1971), or in Carlo Lizzani's *Requiescant* (Kill and Pray, 1967).

The horror films from the 1970s to the present, identified with directors and writers such as Riccardo Freda, Mario Bava, Lucio Fulci, and Dario Argento (whom I discuss in the final chapter under the rubric of a "star" director *and* star maker), also contributed to alterations in stardom.[20] Dismissed in the past for their gratuitous violence, the films have emerged from the exclusive possession of cult audiences. Featuring international stars such as Christopher Lee, David Hemmings, Anthony Franciosa, and Barbara Steele, they introduced actors less well known to mainstream audiences who contributed to different conceptions of the human and virtual body.[21] The films introduce philosophic and psychic complexities to the lexicon of horror through grotesque images of the deformed and mutilated body whereby the star functions as a reflexive and investigative element for cinema itself. Chapter 4 concludes with a discussion of changing profiles of stardom in the last decades of the twentieth century and the first decade of the twenty-first.

Film actors are not the only candidates for star status; certain directors seem to have earned that mantle, particularly in the wake of the French New Wave, which resurrected earlier directors and created new ones. Chapter 5, "Starring Directors and Directing Stars: The Cinematic Landscape and Its Changing Bodies," examines Vittorio De Sica, Roberto Rossellini (a director canonized by *Cahiers du cinéma* and in certain of Jean-Luc Godard's films), Luchino Visconti, Federico Fellini, Pier Paolo Pasolini, Lina Wertmüller, and Roberto Benigni to identify their stellar qualities as publicized, lauded, or vilified in film reviews, publicity releases, tabloids, circulated photographs, appearances in the films of others, and documentaries of their lives and works, and through their own films (sometimes via parody). Often associated socially or through their films with established stars or with stars of their making, these directors charted new formal and political vistas for cinema.

Not only are the directors treated as stars but also national and international stars appear in, emerge from, or contribute to the films' critical encounters with film and social history. The "art" cinema has its distinctive way of using personalities and film stars. Pasolini was known for using prominent intellectuals in his films, and at times himself, along with popular and international stars such as

Anna Magnani in *Mamma Roma* (1962), Totò in *Uccellacci e Uccellini* (Hawks and Sparrows, 1966), the opera diva Maria Callas in *Medea* (1969), Silvana Mangano, Massimo Girotti, and Terence Stamp in *Teorema* (1968), and Jean-Paul Belmondo and Anne Wiazemsky in *Porcile* (Pigsty, 1969). Stars identified with these directors are Massimo Girotti, Burt Lancaster, and Claudia Cardinale in the films of Visconti, Sophia Loren in the films directed by De Sica, and Monica Vitti in the films of Antonioni (though she was also to have great success as a comedian in the popular international cinema working for other directors). The stardom of Marcello Mastroianni and of Giulietta Masina remained linked to star director Federico Fellini, who was also known for his use of international stars (e.g., Anthony Quinn and Anita Ekberg) often treated ironically, used in parodic or camp fashion, and visualized in excessive and memorable images that exaggerate or undermine commonly identified characteristics of stardom.

Dario Argento's long career from the 1960s to the present is often omitted from the canon of "auteurs" and consigned to the netherworld of popular culture, yet he is exemplary of a star auteur.[22] He makes films not only in Italy but also in the U.S., and shares the acclaim of cult audiences and now of academic scholars. Not unlike the other star directors, Argento is a filmmaker who experiments with color, sound, and special effects to investigate the psychological, physiological, and cultural implications of cinematic uses of sight and sound, introducing philosophic and psychic complexities into the lexicon of cinema through the idiom of horror. Argento's use of stars is a mixture of familiar international stars and untried ingénues. His daughter Asia has become a star in her own right, appearing not only in her father's films, but in films of other directors and as her own director.

The character and fate of stardom in the decades ahead seem today to be in doubt, given the dominant role of television and the growth of multiplexes, videos, DVDs, and the Internet, the rewriting of cinema history and theory, cult practices, technological experimentation, and unforeseen critical fashions. Stardom has now to compete with a museal culture that keeps the memories of past stars and celebrities before the public. The competition among popular figures for recognition through publicity is great, the public memory short. In the era of media moguls (e.g., Rupert Murdoch and Silvio Berlusconi), television, in its unabated production of biography, news, and tabloids, has elevated a number of personalities to star status (royals, politicians, serial killers, filmmakers).

But star status, especially of film stars, appears transitory. Roberto Benigni achieved national and international recognition in a wide variety of venues, as TV personality, political commentator, film and TV actor, director, and comedian. His winning of an Oscar for *La vita è bella* (Life Is Beautiful, 1997) might have ensured his place as a star but his fate, like that of other stars, remains uncertain. Similarly, the films of such directors as Giuseppe Tornatore, Gabriele

Salvatores, Gianni Amelio, Marco Tullio Giordana, Roberta Torre, and the Comencini sisters and such stars as Monica Bellucci, Valeria Golino, and Kim Rossi Stuart, while garnering international attention and awards, invite speculation on forms of cinema stardom in the digital age and in the global context. Can we say with any confidence that stardom continues to exist, is dead or dying, or has assumed new forms?

Stardom, Italian Style

Eloquent Bodies: The Cinema of *Divismo*

> [I]n oratory the words are not the only element: there are also gestures,
> tone of voice and so on, a musical element that communicates the
> leitmotiv of the predominant feeling, the principal passion, and the
> orchestral element: gestures in the broad sense, which scans and
> articulates the wave of feeling and passion.
>
> **Antonio Gramsci**, *Quaderni del carcere*[1]

In his writings on theater and cinema, the Marxist intellectual and political activist Antonio Gramsci was attentive to the increasing popularity of cinema over the stage. His intention was not to elevate the popular cinema as a culturally superior medium but to suggest that theater had become cinema, seeking to satisfy the need for entertainment and "pure visual distraction." His consistent mode of describing this new medium, as the opening epigram reveals, was to regard cinema (and hence the contemporary theater) as associated with an operatic view of life, emphasizing its affective and rhetorical dimensions. He singles out the novelist, dramatist, poet, and nationalist politician Gabriele D'Annunzio as being "more successful in the cinema," given that the silent film features "grimace and physical contortion."[2] According to Gramsci's critical evaluation, D'Annunzio "play-acts before himself in front of the mirror."[3] In his description of cinema as "operatic" and in his associating this form of expression with D'Annunzio, Gramsci provides insight into a significant dimension of *Divismo*: its rhetorical, stylized, affective, theatrical character and its reliance on movement and pantomime.

The Italian cinema of the first decades of the twentieth century, in conjunction with other European cinemas, and in alliance with other popular forms, novels, circus, variety, travel literature and photographs, and national legends, histories, and myths, was to develop a form of expression that enhanced the expressive power of the human face and body and that contributed to the elevation of the actor into the category of diva and divo. This version of stardom, associated with prima donnas of the theater such as Eleonora Duse and Sarah Bernhardt, was gradually taken over by the cinema through a form of acting that was largely, but not exclusively, identified with the female performer in melodramatic, historical, and to a lesser extent lyric films.

The qualities that characterize *Divismo* belong to a specific moment in the history of cinema and to a changing cultural/historical constellation not only in Italy but also worldwide. In the case of the diva, her figure was the creation of the "encounter between passion and mass production, [and] her success on the screen due to the paradox of technical reproducibility."[4] This technical and aesthetic moment of *Divismo* in the first decades of the twentieth century, with its ties to the operatic not only in its reliance on music rather than spoken dialogue, but in its existence as spectacle, is markedly different from the subsequent cinema of stars and genres characteristic of the 1930s and of the early 1940s. In contrast to stardom, *Divismo* proffers the spectacle of being unique, despite being reproduced by the camera. *Divismo* conjures up aesthetic rather then industrial values, creating the illusion of being a "one of a kind" phenomenon dedicated to a mystical engagement, as its nomenclature suggests, with the divine rather than the mundane.

The "mute cinema," in its privileging of the body, the uses of gesture, close-up, costumes, and settings, and a highly symbolic treatment derived from opera, tended to isolate its dominant figure and provide her with an aura of uniqueness and otherworldliness. The coming of sound to film altered gesture and choreography, introducing "not only a different set of poses and small gestures, but a greater emphasis on the idiolect of the performer."[5] While qualities of *Divismo* can be identified with genres such as melodrama, these are altered in acting, camera work, editing, the role of landscape, and, above all, their being situated within the different cultural and political milieu inherent to the increasing encroachments of modernity and its technologies.

Divismo was the product of an eclectic set of forces: traditions derived from nineteenth-century Italian literature and opera, conventions from itinerant forms of entertainment, and experiments with the new medium of cinema that tended to center on actors, who became distinctive performers. These distinctive performers are identified with an operatic sense of life. In Gramsci's terms, Verdean opera was "responsible for a whole range of 'artificial' poses in the life of the people, for ways of thinking, for a 'style.'"[6] Under the rubric of the operatic, Gramsci subsumes the uses of "language, oratory, and the theatricality of the law courts." While the diva (see below) is the inhabitant of "mute" cinema, her role in Italian cinema can be traced to culturally embedded forms that involve the intensity, histrionics, and lyric and romantic qualities associated with opera, stage drama, and literature. In particular, the figure of Gabriele D'Annunzio plays a critical role in the style of *Divismo*.

D'Annunzio and *Divismo*: Staging History

The theatrical and cinematic qualities of *Divismo* necessitate a backward look to the cultural contributions of Gabriele D'Annunzio, poet and dramatist, flamboyant social figure, nationalist, trendsetter, and wielder of far-reaching influence in the worlds of art and politics, and even of cinema. In her study of D'Annunzio's transformation of his villa at Cargnacco into the spectacular Il Vittoriale, Lucia Re provides a multi-layered portrait of the artist and the politician, his connections to modernity, modernism, and the milieu of emergent fascism. She describes the poet-dramatist as a "sophist, a master of rhetoric, an actor, and a master of simulation. With no 'true' self, he was free to assume a multiple series of roles, and to exercise to the full his own rhetorical (and erotic) skills as a seducer in the realms of poetic, social, and political discourse in which he operated."[7]

Aside from his eclectic and excessive poems and melodramas steeped in history and myth and *fin de siècle* decadentism, and his direct and indirect involvement in the cinema, his theatricality included his tempestuous affair with the actress Eleanora Duse, among other paramours; his participation in electoral politics; his dashing role as military figure; and his nationalist aspirations, culminating in his daring invasion of Fiume to restore the region to Italy, followed by his expulsion from the area.[8] His retirement to his villa in 1921 can be seen as signaling "the end of an era, and . . . as a symbolic moment in the history of the Italian imagination. It is the moment in which the most utopian and (also) delirious ideals of Italian nationalism, as well as the Romantic and esthetic and political ideals that had been present in Italy since the Risorgimento, all become the tools of a new political pragmatism."[9]

D'Annunzio's importance extends beyond the mere (and impossible) emulation of his life and work by Mussolini and his followers. His legacy is part of the history of early cinema, particularly its uses of the technological potential of the cinematic image for swaying the masses and for making prominent the role of *Divismo*. Aware of the power of the mass media, D'Annunzio offered to his audience an image of the hero as a divo incarnate, a fantasy to be taken as real, though at the same time paradoxically distant and difficult to emulate. Embodying a superior form of humanity, in every action he revealed his different nature and his separateness from the mediocre crowd.[10] His self-presentation and appropriation of the past "coincided with the possibility of using all the available models, scenarios, and roles of the past for 'staging' of his discourse, as if they were nothing but a vast theatrical repertoire."[11] Translated into a cinematic context in relation to *Divismo*, this "staging" involved a focus on the gendered body and on gestural language that strove to create a "total art," not dissimilar to that of Wagner, one which "replaces mundane reality."[12] *Divismo* produces an aestheticized and ecstatic world peopled by passionate and erotic masculine and feminine figures and landscapes that animate the past by means of the modern medium of cinema, drawing on theatrical acting styles, dance, poetry, painting, and architecture. For D'Annunzio, to echo Gramsci's criticism of him, the past is de-historicized and discontinuous,[13] a creation of imagination, fantasy, and ritual.

An important distinction between D'Annunzio's charismatic leader and Mussolini's embodiment of Il Duce resides in their differing relations to their audiences, the people. D'Annunzio's Caesarism, as Barbara Spackman writes, is embodied in "a charismatic hero whose very isolation is the precondition for his political theorizing about power and leadership." These qualities were associated with exceptional figures that were harbingers of a different, elite, and more nuanced sensibility beyond the mundane bourgeois world. By contrast, Mussolini's "persona in the 1920s tended to underline his common bond with the people."[14] His compelling qualities resided in his representation of himself as "the charisma of a nation, a people, a race,"[15] relying on "the people" to guarantee success. The Duce's wooing of the masses depended on offering an image of leadership that could incite affect, identification, and emulation, a portrait of the star as being both ordinary and yet exceptional.

The Making of a Political Divo: Mussolini in the 1920s

Mussolini became a film star and aided in shaping the contours of stardom. If the early "political theater" of Mussolini rejected the theatricality of the

D'Annunzian world of myth and poetry as well as its unbridled individualism, it maintained a sense of the monumental, the ritualistic, and the cultic via performance in its predilection for public spectacle. The rising stardom of Il Duce was the recipient, if not also the creator, of the mythic properties of cinematic *Divismo*. On the one hand, Mussolini appropriated the theatrical scenario of D'Annunzio in relation to the choreography of the powerful leader and his volatile masses. He "inherited the capacity to transform every political demonstration into a theatrical event, to speak with the crowd, and to incite it to the ritualistic incantation, 'Eja, eja, alalà,' central to fascist mass gatherings,"[16] but altered it to invoke consensus through "a condensation of the fantasies of the integrity of the human body and of the unity of the social body."[17]

Mussolini's creation as a divo was forged through his presentation of himself as a virile man of action, an irresistible force, a healer, and a formidable opponent. Monumental figurations of his power emerged through newsreels and posters of him as a supernatural invincible masculine being identified with daring exploits and with a studied stance and gestures that communicated solidity, infallibility, promise and threat, and an awareness of being on exhibit. His growing charisma depended on his orchestration of verbal language and visual display. His physical appearance conformed to the substance of his uses of language in his speeches, and rather than revealing his uses of language as meaningless and not to be taken as seriously, his appearance is, as Barbara Spackman has demonstrated, critical for an understanding of their character and impact, of the ways in which his use of metonymy and synecdoche invoke "the 'dressings' of the state,"[18] its clothed body exemplified as well in the body of the orator. And, as is the case with oratory, the words are successful if they coincide with an appropriate delivery and *mise-en-scène*. Mussolini's appearances in public and in film were spectacular in terms of choreography, emphasizing the positioning of his body, his bold use of gesture, his relation to his spectators, and the size of the crowds. As is the case with the movie divo, spectacle was essential in his metamorphosis from mere mortal to charismatic leader.

Along with outdoor appearances, cinema would serve to disseminate and enhance his figure, his speeches, and images of their reception by enthusiastic spectators, enveloping the political figure in the mantle of the star. LUCE (L'unione cinematografica educativa), founded in 1923, was a state-controlled organization formed to produce documentaries and newsreels[19] in order to enhance the cause of fascism through the moving image. Among the numerous films designed for instruction and education, LUCE produced many newsreels that featured Mussolini's visits to Trieste, Milan, and other cities to attend ceremonies that marked the inception or completion of architectural or military projects but were also opportunities to enhance "the volatile and magnetic image of Mussolini."[20] By means of aerial shots, the viewer can gauge Mussolini's popularity by the size of the crowds, who appear as an undifferentiated and adoring mass enthralled by his presence. Closer shots of the populace who line the streets as his car passes through the throngs capture the excitement generated by his presence, as he stands erect in his car waving to the masses on the sidelines. Later the cameras will capture him in low angle shots as he delivers an oration from a position high above, framed by buildings and by the sky. In these shots, the audiences can be likened to the frenzied devotees of Rudolph Valentino (or to the crowds in Fellini's *Amarcord* [1973]) who are hysterical and erotically charged by the presence of the divo. Thus, the highly demonstrative and affective character and reception of his persona is manifest, but, more fundamentally, so too are connections between cinema, the spectacles of fascism, and mass culture.

Newsreels also give evidence of the transformation of Mussolini from routine political figure to divo (and later in the 1930s to a star). His initial appearances in public did not reveal these choreographed and highly ritualized qualities. At first, he was not dramatically distinguished among his followers nor does his image convey a sense of exceptionality in the midst of mass adulation and hysteria. But subsequent photos of the "Man whom Providence has made us meet" disclose his changing image. Increasingly, as his star was on the rise, he was singled out by his strident gesture, his raised chin, his arm uplifted to the sky, as shown in a photo of him at a rally in 1920.[21] And a postcard from 1922, on his ascension to Prime Minister, portrays him as rakishly dressed in black silk shirt, his hands casually placed in his pants pockets.[22] His meetings with the king showed him clothed in the black tails and top hat of a dignitary in the early 1920s, though appearing less comfortable in this patrician milieu. His military garb became more ostentatious, and, when marching with his followers, he assumed a commanding position at the head of the group. As he rose to power, he was photographed in the press and filmed in a number of "masculine" activities—horseback riding, fencing, swimming, and flying on his plane. By 1924, he was indeed the man of Providence, ready to inhabit his role as Duce. As one biographer comments:

> Mussolini had become the most photographed man in history. Images of him were distributed to the Italian people through the press, or the postcard. Well before 1922 Italians had grown accustomed to collect likenesses of innumerable saints of the peninsula as mementos of a visit and as an aide to piety. Now an estimated 30 million pictures of the Duce in up to 2500 different poses began to circulate in what was a sacralisation and commercialization of political life. In 1926, a fourteen-year-old fan, Clara Petacci, daughter of the Pope's doctor, papered her room with such images, impelled by those motives that caused her successors to treasure the pictures of pop stars or football players.[23]

According to R. J. B. Bosworth, what distinguished Mussolini from other monumental figures of the era was the making public of "bodily images of his private life."[24] In this respect, these images were closer to the cinematic renderings of the masculine body inherent to the incarnation of the populist *uomo forte* (strong man), whose images appeared on the screen in such films as *Cabiria* and the later Maciste serials and spin-offs featuring classical heroes.[25] The divergence between D'Annunzio and Mussolini is most evident in the contrast between the virile, charismatic, and populist leader and the remote and aristocratic D'Annunzian hero.

The *uomo forte* as Divo: Maciste

In his *Italian National Cinema*, Pierre Sorlin compares a photo of Mussolini to one of Bartolomeo Pagano as Maciste in *Cabiria* (1914). The low angle shots of the balding figures, both Mussolini and Pagano, enhance the size of each, but most prominent are their postures, their arms embracing their torsos.[26] Acknowledging that the film precedes the prominence of Mussolini's image in public life, the question arises as to which came first—or rather, how did it so happen that this cinematic strong man resembles a political figure who is as yet not part of contemporary cinematic culture? To answer this question, one has to reach beyond Italy and to cinema history to track the strong man's appearance in myth, literature, and cinema. Thus masculine figure converged with nationalist aspirations, romantic literature, and popular lore of the nineteenth century. However, the growing power of mass culture through cinema was to bring together elite and popular myth in the service of entertainment and ideology. In the context of nationalism in Italy from the turn of the century to World War I, heroic masculine images were increasingly to feed nationalist imagination and propaganda.

Clearly, Greek and Roman mythology offered narratives of mythological strong men: Atlas, Hercules, and the Titans, among others, along with the Biblical figure of Samson. Romantic and popular literature over the centuries has kept these figures alive. Hence, it is not at all surprising that in its borrowings from literary and poetic texts (as with the popular myth of Tarzan), the cinema has often returned to these works and their images of the strong man as a source of adventure, spectacle, and modeling of desirable masculine traits. As is evident from the choice of models for the strong man, he is a fantasmatic figure identified with exceptional powers. Like his female counterpart, the diva, he is a creation of the mute cinema that emphasizes the appeal of the body in an art form that focuses on the movement-image, stressing action, affection, and an organic convergence of nature and culture. The divo is a special figure. While identified largely with physical exploits, his body is the bridge to another world where justice prevails through the saving actions of an individual who, though often verbally inarticulate, enacts an ethical transformation of the world. The divo thus is a mythical guide for the spectator, conferring power on the body and its possibilities.

Though *Divismo* has been largely identified with the female performer in melodramatic and historical films, comedy was a popular attraction in the early Italian cinema and also a source of *Divismo*. The male actors that appeared in the early comic films where slapstick and burlesque reigned did not yet qualify as divos, but, as Michele Canosa describes these figures, they are anti-bodies, "robots" or "puppet bodies" to be distinguished from *Divismo* in the ways they "disassemble" or mechanize the body.[27] However, another source for the body of the divo emerged from the serial or "film by installments," derived from "popular French novels and melodramas,"[28] featuring criminals and detectives in narratives of adventure and intrigue. Similarly, the male actors in the serialized "peplum" films that drew on history and mythology enacted the popular strong man with his large and muscular body who is able to overcome evil forces through his physical powers.[29]

The strong man was not the invention of Italian cinema but a testimonial to the international character (and the popular nature) of movies. In particular, the strong man was associated with melodramatic adventure, physical derring-do, suspense, and themes involving the overcoming of hostile social forces. He was not merely a savior figure; he could also be seen as a bully. One of the popular figures prior to Maciste was the fictional Za-la-Mort, created by Emilio Ghione and based on French models, thus reinforcing Gramsci's observations on the Francophile, if not international, character of Italian popular culture. These figures were also to be found in comic books, and their characters were also familiar from school readings in mythology as well as from popular literature and the circus. Furthermore, such narratives lent themselves to cliffhangers and to serialization in films and magazines. While the mythologicals of the strong man were not unique to Italian cinema, they did constitute a popular Italian form during the late teens and twenties and were integral to the spectacular historical films. The serial played an important role in enticing audiences to the cinema and further educating them in film viewing, and it was also central to the creation of the form of stardom identified with the operatic, magical, and supernatural known as *Divismo*.

The figure of Maciste, played by dockworker Bartolomeo Pagano and derived from *Cabiria*, launched the popularity and serialization of his star persona. There were other masculine actors who were popular on the screen as strong men, such as Luciano Albertini (Samson), Domenico Gambino (Saetta), and the actor and director Emilio Ghione. His character of Za-la-Mort was modeled on the "apache" figure identified with international serialized detective fictions. In contrast to German and French models that were largely one-dimensional and sadistic, his apache was sentimental and romantic. Ghione's character was "labile, more inclined to amnesia, and contradiction, always ready to disintegrate."[30] His highly nervous, "deliriously paranoid" persona was, according to Monica Dall'Asta, intimately tied to the persona of Ghione[31] and bore a resemblance to D'Annunzio. The character of Za-la-Mort, popular in the teens, receded during the fascist era, while Bartolomeo Pagano's Maciste became a popular cultural icon that extended beyond his own persona and contributed to the cult of the strong man. "Maciste," a positive hero, became "synonymous with power and courage."[32]

Cabiria and the Contours of the Divo

Bartolomeo Pagano as Maciste first appeared in Giovanni Pastrone's *Cabiria*, where his role contributed to the film's huge success: portraying a freed slave, Pagano created "the benevolent unselfish giant, who would be a darling of the 1920s."[33] Unlike Za-la-Mort with his meager body and skull-like face and unsettling mannerisms, Pagano with his large, muscular, and athletic body, his humorous and clever reactions to injustice, became the model of a positive cultural hero associated with nationalist values. His myth was forged largely through action/adventure narratives. But his character was also endowed with human attributes: he loved his food; he was identified with the "common man"; and he was a trickster who used humor to ensnare his enemies. Pagano's Maciste not only enjoyed a longer popularity than other strong men (until 1926), but his image spawned a host of other strong men—Saetta, Samson, Jason, Galaor, and Ajax. Central to all of these strong men was the power and supremacy of the male body, its athleticism displayed in acrobatic feats. In the case of Pagano, an ethical component is attached to his physical exploits. His role in *Cabiria* is critical for establishing the contours of *Divismo*.

Unlike later films that star Pagano, *Cabiria* (1914), produced by Itala films, creates spectacle in grand operatic style, employing a range of effects to produce an epic vision of history. *Cabiria* was not unique in the production of historical films, but the film "continued Itala's and Italian cinema's inclination toward monumental historical production, learned cultural references, and widely popular spectacular appeal."[34] The film's innovative treatment of history relies on elaborate intertitles, sculpture, architecture, Orientalist art, monumental sets, and striking and imaginative costumes to evoke the Carthaginian world, utilizing every segment of the frame to enhance and multiply actions, to create a sense of the grandeur of the set (as in the famous temple of Moloch), and to produce different levels of action. While the film employs a vast number of extras as soldiers, slaves, and servants, the protagonists of the film are Cabiria (Letizia Quaranta), Sofonisba (Italia Almirante Manzini), Fulvius Axilla (Umberto Mozzato), and Maciste (Bartolomeo Pagano). The framing and choreography of the scenes connect individual characters to the crowds in a film that valorizes heroic action, physical power, and passion, providing a visual milieu appropriate for the divo.

Set during the time of the Punic Wars, *Cabiria* features two male heroes, the patrician Fulvius and his former slave Maciste. The film, testimonial to early Italian cinema's mastery of historical spectacle, is a highly eclectic production. It combines adventure, historical episodes in relation to the eruption of Mt. Etna that set the narrative in motion, the Punic Wars, the Roman slave market, the ritual sacrifices to pagan deities, magic, romance, and melodrama. According to Angela Dalle Vacche, "*Cabiria* is a survey of conflicting traditions. This hybrid constellation of cultural sources documents a changing taste. Pastrone's eclectic use of cultural sources reveals how the Italian as well as international cinema reconfigured the artistic landscape. Cinema broke the division between elitist and popular culture."[35] The film revels in statuary, architectural monuments, lavish interiors, and instruments of war.

The film is a dizzying array of moving images that elicit actions and reactions, but on a plane that is sensory and affective and that contributes to the spectacular character of the divo and his actions. This movement is anterior, if not resistant, to signification, thus validating Gilles Deleuze's analysis in his cinema books of how the early cinema (from the teens through the 1930s) can be identified with what he terms the movement-image in its invoking an affective response to visual and auditory cues. These images do not yet signify but provide the necessary elements for perceiving the relation of parts to a whole, translating perception and affection into forms of action, enabling differentiation of the parts and of their relations to the whole. This is not given in advance, but rather recognition arises from preliminary perceptions that develop as the narrative proceeds. In *Cabiria* the power of the divo relies on a dual register: shots capturing physical size, posture, and gesture; and shots linking this figure to a spectacular landscape over which he reigns.

The film's protagonists are integral to how the image is made to serve a "truthful narration" involving those who seek certainty through actions that will finally guarantee the triumph of a healthy over a decadent civilization. Fulvius, the master, and Maciste, the slave, are the agents of what finally results in a reconstituted order. Fulvius's characterization relies on a familiar disciplined stoic model. Maciste, by contrast, is identifiable by his closeness to natural phenomena. His gigantic body is nude to the waist and adorned only with a loincloth initially of leopard skin, later of patterned fabric. If Fulvius evokes an image of the Virgil-ian hero in popularized form, Maciste's image is more permeable. Not merely a savior, Maciste also becomes a victim and undergoes his own suffering similar to that of the biblical Samson, chained by his captors to a grindstone until saved by his master. He is also an incarnation of Hermes, carrying life-and-death messages from the Romans to the Carthaginians. He is twice the savior of Cabiria, and also the bearer of death, bringing Sofonisba the poison sent by Massinissa that will end her life. His strong man image does not preclude "feminine" elements, as made evident in his maternal care of Cabiria as a child and particularly in his nurturing role in relation to the exhausted Fulvius.

As the film's strong man, he is not acrobatic like Fulvius, who can dive from rugged heights into the sea. In this film, Maciste's character is closer to Ursus and to the gladiators in *Quo Vadis* (1913) than to his role in *Maciste alpino* (1916), where he is a combination of the common man and the superhuman. In *Cabiria*, though freed, he remains obedient and subservient to his former owner. Another element of his incipient *Divismo* in *Cabiria* that will subsist and be augmented is the element of comedy. The scene in which he and Fulvius hide in the lower depths of the palace among huge casks of wine and regale themselves by drinking and jesting with each other serves to momentarily narrow the social distance between the two, reinforcing their mutual dependency and "humanizing" their superhuman status. Unlike in later Pagano films, in *Cabiria* Pagano's great physical powers as Maciste are limited by his inferior social position. While presumably he should be able to free himself by ripping his chains from the millstone, he remains imprisoned and only recovers his strength after the arrival of Fulvius "ten years later." His phenomenal strength is evident in his bending the metal bars of the prison where he and Fulvius are later held captive so that he is free to rescue Cabiria, and to enable Fulvius and Cabiria to return to Rome. Maciste serves the nation, as the ending allegorically visualizes. However, Maciste is also united to the patrician Scipio, revealing the two men as complementary aspects of the Roman ideal involving the union of body and mind. Maciste "serves" Scipio, but both figures are placed in the service of a higher power, the nation, as the ending allegorically visualizes. According to Angela Dalle Vacche, the depiction of Maciste "tends toward the athletic, emphasizes movement, and suggests spontaneity," whereas Scipio "leans toward the statuesque, privileges stillness, and underlines self-control. As allegorical embodiments of the national self, Maciste and Scipio are terms of identification."[36] Significantly, the underscoring of the physical and the statuesque inhere in the iconography of Il Duce.

Two years later, Pagano reprised the role of Maciste in a film set in wartime, *Maciste alpino* (1916), and while not clothed in the garb of a slave but properly attired in contemporary fashion, he is instrumental in extending the characteristics of the Maciste persona. Not a spectacular historical film but situated in the contemporary milieu of World War I, the film features Pagano as the driving force of the war effort against the Austrians. In this film, Pagano displays a penchant for comedy as well as physical feats of bravery. There is little magic entailed in his overcoming of hostile forces: his physical force and his cleverness ensure his success against the enemy and on behalf of the Italian people. Among the elements that distinguish Pagano's persona in this film is his indifference to the Austrian military even before he becomes a bona fide member of the Alpine regiment. In the opening moments of the film, he refuses to follow an Austrian soldier's orders to leave the restaurant, but stubbornly insists on finishing his meal, a testimonial to his gargantuan size, strength, and appetites. Arrested with other guests from the restaurant, from his place of temporary detention he defiantly throws his shoe at his captors, who are practicing drills on the street.

His large appetite for food continues to play a role as he steals food from a huge cooking pot, after revealing to other detainees how he has been forced to tighten his belt. His acts of subordination include his tying up two Austrian soldiers and hanging them up on nails. He becomes the leader of the dispossessed persons, guiding them through the countryside until they reach the "ancient castle of Pratolungo," where Count Lanfranco lives with his daughter Giulietta, a patriot, who is sewing a tricolor flag. The Count invites Maciste and his retinue and feeds them. Unfortunately, Austrian soldiers in pursuit of the group arrive and the people with the Count at their head escape, finding themselves on the road again, seeking refuge. Chased by the soldiers, Maciste, on horseback, attempts to cross a river but is assaulted by Austrians. His movements are agile and acrobatic. In his carefully choreographed gestures and movements, he conveys his physical superiority, and the camera, in the timing of and greater focus on his actions, conveys his dexterity and skill. He leaps, he ducks, and he slips out of the hands of the enemy, but though he is portrayed as agile, he is finally captured, led off by a rope, and tied to a tree. As conveyed via several close-ups of his bound hands, he is able to extricate himself from his captors, and jump on a horse and ride away. Again pursued, he overleaps the wall of a bridge and once again a chase ensues until he is forced to confront the Austrians and fight them off. Dismounting and climbing a tree, he disperses the enemy, but not until he has physically overcome and routed them by raining sufficient blows upon their bodies.

Increasingly, in his encounters with the enemy, he emerges as one man against the multitude. Even when he finally becomes a member of the Alpine regiment, it is clear that he is a leader of men, not merely one of the mass, and he ultimately prevails by dint of his agility and bodily force. A large segment of the film situates him in threatening physical terrain, especially the high, craggy, and snow-covered mountains that he scales to elude the Austrians. Maciste's persona incarnates the movement-image where an antagonistic natural land-

1.1. Maciste against many. *Maciste Alpino* with divo Bartolomeo Pagano. *British Film Institute.*

scape is central to an organic form of narration. The protagonist is placed in a situation where he must act to overcome a threatening milieu and restore moral order. By intercutting scenes of conflict with scenes showing the dispossessed people led by the Count, the film establishes the moral imperatives that guide Maciste's (with the aid of the Italian army's) actions as savior of the imperiled nation. The actions of the Count and his daughter, especially the Count's altruistic caring for the displaced persons, are contrasted to the inhumane treatment of these people by the Austrians. Once again, Maciste embodies the virtues of patriotism in the name of the Italian nation. And once again his figure establishes the appeal of the *uomo forte*.

In addition, the film displays Pagano's comedic penchant as critical to his image as strongman, since rather than diminishing his powerful persona, the comic scenes underscore qualities that reinforce his uniqueness. His conflicts with the pretentious Corporal Fritz Puffer not only establish the superior qualities of Maciste's character but also serve affectively to diminish his opponents by dramatizing the ineptness and the devious character of the enemy. For example, when Maciste confronts Puffer, who is clinging to the top of a tree, he shakes the Corporal loose, tears the tree up by its roots and chases the now-unfortunate victim. At another moment, when Puffer signals a patrol to aide him in capturing Maciste, the tables are turned and Maciste overwhelms him (and a couple of other soldiers), sitting on one of the men as he struggles with the others, tying them all up, and dragging them down the mountain ignominiously. Another comedic moment involves Maciste's initiation into the Alpine regiment. He is fitted for a uniform but none of the sizes is suitable for his massive frame. He splits the seams, and has to be measured for a uniform that is unique to his size. Still another scene that foregrounds Pagano's powerful body takes place in the snow-covered mountains where, filmed stripped to the waste like a bodybuilder, he exercises, washes himself with snow, and lifts an enormous weight. The final moments, after Maciste has saved Giulietta from the crass and vulgar officer Fischer, portray him lifting her and her lover on his shoulders and then show him in close-up with a broad, self-satisfied smile on his face. *Maciste alpino* reveals the multi-faceted character of the film divo: as *uomo forte*, appearing as moral and physical giant; as the consummate image of the strong man as leader; as benevolent, humorous, virile, and athletic; as a common man with exceptional qualities; and as morally superior, though not without minor shortcomings.

What accounts for Pagano's *Divismo*? He was fortunate in the film directors with whom he worked—Pastrone, Campogalliani, and Brignone. His reviewers seem to be agreed that he "was the personification of a mythic hero."[37] His reign as divo owed something to his powerful physical body, his command of gesture and movement, his athleticism, his connection to popular myths of the superman, and the wartime propaganda of World War I, which highlighted the importance of masculine discipline and prowess as incarnating the virtues of service and patriotism. If there are connections to be made with Mussolini and Maciste's *Divismo*, they are obviously situated beyond the immediate and individual character of the two figures, residing rather in a fantasmatic cultural and political matrix that was congenial to the cinema of the silent years, with its emphasis on the body, and, beyond that, to the power of the media to materialize mythology.

Pagano's other roles as Maciste offer a visual lexicon of the various attributes that compose the images of the divo, involving physical strength, an intact, sensuous, and powerful body, and a commitment to adventure and action, all qualities further embellished to guarantee the divo's popularity into the 1920s (and his resurrection in the "epics" of the 1960s). The indebtedness of his persona to theater, opera, comic books, and classical myth also render his figure familiar and captivating, if enigmatic. His *Divismo*, however, is subject to the same mystique as that of the diva, a mystique that renders it more iconic than symbolic. According to Michele Canosa, the divo "is what he is. . . . There is very little to 'interpret.'"[38] In this elusiveness and resistance to interpretation resides, I believe, a significant difference between the impact of the divo and the star. The divo, for all of his apparent human physical attributes, belongs to a rarified mythic world to which only exceptional figures have access. The star, on the other hand, is both similar to yet different from the mass, common and yet extraordinary. This resistance to interpretation renders the divo immortal, invulnerable, and invincible. This distinction can perhaps shed light on the connection between the charisma of the strong man image and the figure of Il Duce in life and in death.

Incarnations of the Diva

As a creation of the silent cinema, the strong man as divo was a counterpart to the image of the diva[39] evident in *Cabiria* through the contrasting characters of Cabiria and the Carthaginian queen, Sofonisba. Played by Italia Almirante Manzini, Sofonisba is the *femme fatale* who loves passionately but not well. She is one in a line of divas in literature, theater, and opera who inherit the consuming passion of Dido for Aeneas and are tied to a threatening and decadent, if fascinating, image of the fatal woman who stands in contrast to the pious and wholesome image of Cabiria. Sofonisba's character is developed through her identification with an Orientalist setting, an "African" milieu that underscores her temperament as alien to the Roman imperial ideals. Her gestures are carefully choreographed to convey her regal character, her imperiousness, her eroticism, and her rebelliousness culminating in suicide. Her lineage can be traced through Virgil's Dido, Cleopatra, and Verdian grand opera, or Bellini's high priestess Norma. Associated with fire, primitivism in her connection to wild animals (e.g., her leopard), flowers, flowing robes, and jewels, she also provides an index to the clothing, hairstyles, styles of architecture, and interior decoration of the teens and twenties.

These feminine images of the silent screen were the creation of light and shadow, silhouetted images of the body, close-ups of the face, choreographed movements akin to dance and lyric opera, acting styles expressive of the world of dreams, and exotic and dreamlike landscapes indebted to the Symbolist poets and to the Surrealists. These elements were then transformed into cinematic spectacles of transgressive passion. While Gabriele D'Annunzio's actual work on *Cabiria* has been overrated and was restricted to intertitles and suggestions, nonetheless his influence was powerful. His reputation played a role in publicity surrounding the film and, more extensively, in the development of the pre–World War I cinema, in its narratives, its female iconography, and its theatricality and use of dialogue via intertitles, gesture, costuming, and makeup; in short, in its production of the diva.

In discussions of Italian national cinema, the diva has largely been examined in the context of the D'Annunzian world and connections to the character and popularity of historical spectacles; however, in the case of *Divismo*, the system is characteristic of international cinema, of Hollywood, Europe and India, indebted to a particular moment in the development of the language of silent cinema and also to the cinema's dependence on both international and national cultural models. The period prior to World War I and during the interwar years was a striking blend of experimentalism associated with painting, architecture, and the new medium of cinema and also *fin de siècle* decadence associated with romanticism, a fascination with death and sensuality, and explorations of the psyche, particularly of hysteria (via Freud) and other attributes identified with femininity. The films of Rudolph Valentino (1895–1926) are comprehensible within this culture of *Divismo*, affording an Italian and Orientalist image of masculinity that appealed largely to female audiences. Italian audiences knew Valentino, though there were few Italian films in the 1920s that were created on the models of Valentino, Ramon Novarro, or Douglas Fairbanks, and responses in Italy to the emigration of "the great lover" were mixed. For example, Mussolini, incensed that Valentino had become an American citizen, only acknowledged the impact of Valentino after the divo's death by sending a wreath to the star's funeral.

In Italy, the figure of the diva, identified with the middle and upper classes, dominated the arts and high fashion. In addition to its literary and theatrical origin, the cult of the cinematic diva can be linked to the publicity surrounding the rich and famous. As Vittorio Martinelli has written, "the first public figures capable of igniting cinematic interest were instead royal families, protagonists of the political and religious scene, aristocrats."[40] As Martinelli explains, it was not merely the rituals—marriages and funerals, processions—that were of the greatest interest to viewers but the possibility "of seeing at close hand, of feeling part of this elite world, of touching the hands of personages formerly unapproachable."[41] While this phenomenon was disseminated by means of actualities, newsreels, and photographs, it was transmuted into the cinematic fictions that were to follow in the teens and twenties.

Early manifestations of cinematic *Divismo* can be seen in Danish films exemplified by the work of Asta Nielsen in Urban Gad's *The Abyss* (1910), which "achieved its reputation as an erotic film with a touch of dark fatalism."[42] Nielsen's films seized the imagination of such modernist poets as Apollinaire. While the output of Danish films was slim in comparison with the films Nielsen made in Germany, her reputation grew with such titles as *Sins of the Father* (1911), *Gypsy Blood* (1912), *Eternal Night* (1914), *Death in Seville* (1913), and *Fire* (1914), and, in the 1920s, *Pandora's Box* (1922) and *Joyless Street* (1922). Of her screen image and acting in relation to the mythical dimensions of *Divismo*, Lotte Eisner has underscored Nielsen's "Nordic qualities, issuing from the savage legends of the Edda." Characteristic of the operatic diva, Nielson made audiences "feel the fire which was to destroy not only men but also herself."[43] Greta Garbo's reign as a diva was to come with *Gösta Berling's Saga* (1924). In Poland, Germany, and later in U.S. cinema, Pola Negri enjoyed great popularity, and in France, the divine Sarah Bernhardt was supreme in the theater and important for influencing the qualities of the diva. In general it is fair to say that the diva crossed national boundaries. It is tempting to think of *Divismo* solely in relation to lyric opera, but the lyric opera was a European phenomenon of the nineteenth century that capitalized on the romantic and historical novel, music, and, to a lesser extent, the visual arts. Opera's characters were archetypes of passion and perversity that reached deep into European mythology. However, the national dimension was also apparent in how the operas (and later films) drew on sagas and historical dramas. Music, so integral to conveying the affective character of the heroines, was translated to film via their physiognomies, the choreography of their body movements, their costuming and makeup, their highly affective acting, and a landscape remote from a quotidian world.

While divas were identified with particular national cinemas, their properties were often a fusion of "Orient and Occident," primitivism and modernism, and myth and dream. The brief sovereignty of the diva was a further instantiation of the international character of the silent cinema and of the widespread emphasis on corporeality that the divas displayed through their specialization in choreographed bodies of movement and gesture. Moreover, the divas belonged to what Tom Gunning has identified as a cinema of attractions. They were less narrative agents and more creations of spectacle, drawing on the properties of the camera, lighting, framing, choreography, and editing to produce strong affective responses of curiosity, wonder, and even fear. The world of the diva was intimately tied to reigning cultural conceptions of female sexuality that "speak in an 'ancient tongue, pictographic language,'" a form of "mystical hysteria."[44] And it was cinema that was to produce fascination with these feminine avatars of pleasure and pain.

In Italy during the teens and early twenties the celebrated divas were Pina Menichelli, Lyda Borelli, Francesca Bertini, Italia Almirante Manzini, Leda Gys, Soava Gallone, Carmen Boni, Hesperia, and Maria Jacobini. In fact, their names were linked to their acting styles, and to the world their images embodied that which came to be described as *Borellismo* and *Menichellismo*. The heyday of these divas lasted less than two decades, and many of these women retired from the screen and, not unlike Hollywood star Gloria Swanson, married aristocrats, tycoons, or film directors. The regime of the diva in Italy coincided with turbulent political events: the war in Libya, the cataclysm of World War I, large-scale poverty, attempts at economic modernization that benefited the middle classes, and mass emigration. However, the films that featured these divas were far removed from catastrophic political occurrences, "symbol[s] of everything that the country was not."[45]

The films of Pina Menichelli are a consummate expression of the dreamlike world of the diva, freighted with the suffering, passion, and aggression exemplified by *Tigre reale* (Regal Tiger, 1916) and Pastrone's *Il fuoco* (Fire, 1915), a work that borrows its title from a D'Annunzio novel. Thanks to its D'Annunzian aura and plot, which contributed to the emotional intensity of the film, scriptwriter Febo Mari (who also acted in the film), director Pastrone, and Menichelli's acting, the film catapulted Menichelli to the pinnacle of fame as a prima donna. Beyond his acting, Mari may have also played an important part, under the pseudonym Piero Fosco, in directing this film attributed to Giovanni Pastrone.[46] In addition to enlarging the conception of the director at the time, Mari's shadowy identity in the filmmaking of the teens may shed light on the construction and design of the film, its characters, and their establishment of the character and limits of the diva and divo.

Mari's contributions to the filmmaking of the time are ambiguous: "Like a craftsman he hides his name," and like a hero from D'Annunzio, "Mari is cloaked in mystery, attracting unworldliness, feeding the legend of an identity, playing hide-and-seek with journalism."[47] The mystery surrounding his identity can be extended to his role in *Il fuoco* as "'an artist of genius' in a base and commercial world."[48] The film is exemplary for expressing the "unworldly" qualities associated with the melodramatic and operatic dimensions of *Divismo*, shared in this film between the two central characters, who live in a mystical realm that transcends mundane necessities of ordinary existence. The sensitive, often tormented, character of the male enhances the powerful figure of the diva, her actions determined by his masochistic attraction to her arbitrary whims. While the diva elicits critical attention, the male figure often recedes into the background, thus obscuring the complex relations between masculinity and femininity that are central to these films.

Il fuoco features a tempestuous love affair between two artists, a poet and a painter, played by Menichelli and Mari.[49] The two meet by a lake and consummate their love in an ancient castle that situates their relationship in a primordial and legendary landscape. The ancient castle is the entry into the past and into an all-consuming world of ungovernable and overwhelming affect, the *femme fatale* the entry into this sexually promising and threatening space. He paints her portrait, and their relationship then involves them in an affair that fuses them in passion and creativity but is also based on the inevitable expectation of separation, loss, and suffering engendered by a capricious and fatal woman who, in Angela Dalle Vacche's description, is "a goddess of pain,"[50] but is not merely the recipient but also the giver.

The affair ends with the husband's homecoming. The poet leaves her artist lover (after drugging him) to return to her husband. When she by chance sees the painter again, she refuses to recognize him. She had left him a substantial check to compensate for his labor on the painting, but she purchases the portrait that is revealing of her narcissism and proleptic of their reunion. Her rejection causes him to become mad with grief. The diva is the *femme fatale* who embodies the dominating power and destructive character of consuming erotic passion. *Divismo* is linked to a romantic conception of art that elevates suffering, and celebrates renunciation as the source of vitality. In this scenario, the male figure regards femininity as a cruel and necessary instrument for confronting and transcending nature to realize artistic creativity.

The visual clues to this world of "spirit" and desire are evident in images of nature, the identification of the eternal feminine with the water, the birds, and, above all, the corporeal body. Menichelli becomes a force of nature, contradictory, consuming herself and others. Her intense and erotically inviting facial expressions, her wild and tangled hair, the uses of light and shadow, her languid and also imperious postures, and her mocking smile distinguish her performance. In Brunetta's description of the diva, as can be seen in Menichelli's performance, her power is "not only constituted by a body, a particular look, and a compendium of characteristic gestures, she was at the same time the most emblematic embodiment of the world she inhabited and over which she exercised absolute dominion."[51] The familiar pattern of femininity as creative inspiration and as destroyer is critical to her diva image. The film highlights the impossibility of love at the same time as it invokes and celebrates the "power of the senses, of sex, and the laws of nature."[52] Art plays a critical role, underscoring the triumph of a visionary world that existed in imagination and fantasy via poetry, painting, and theater.

In *Tigre reale*, attributed to Pastrone (and the elusive Febo Mari), Menichelli as the Russian Countess Natka is the object of men's attentions but affects the pose of a bored and capricious aristocrat until it becomes evident that her past history has inclined her to this behavior. She is clothed in fashionable gowns of the era that are dark and slightly décolleté, loosely clinging to the body. At one point she wears a sumptuous floor-length fur cape that she wraps around her. These outfits, characteristic of the international, particularly French, fashion of the time, contributed to the diva's elegance and to her remoteness from the quotidian world but also situated her in the past. One of the first dramatic events in the film is a duel fought between an admirer, Giorgio, played by Febo Mari, and

Major Giudoni, a swordsman whom Giorgio offends by striking out the man's name on Natka's dance card and substituting his own. Capriciously, she leaves before the dance ends, and he is left to fight the duel and be wounded in vain. After several attempts to visit her, Giorgio finally gets to see her alone and witnesses the agonies that account for her unpredictable behavior. Another familiar (literary and operatic) symptom of the diva's world is articulated through Menichelli's Natka. Her suffering is expressed in her physical symptoms. She complains of a migraine, of being exhausted from having to indulge in the humdrum world of social rituals and their hypocrisy. Frantic, she runs outdoors and seeks to end her life, and Giorgio castigates her for trying to kill herself. Her writhing body movements, her hands clutching her head, her body contorted and convulsed with coughing all convey the excesses of her agonized suffering. Her physical and mental health is an index to the tumultuous responses she displays and a critical dimension of the diva's precarious connections to the external world.

Giorgio calms her, and in several interrupted flashbacks to the past, she recounts to him her earlier life in Russia and her ill-fated love affair that ends in the death of Dolski, her lover, played by Mari, who betrayed her with other women. The scenes that lead to his death allow Menichelli to display her rage through magnificent use of facial expression and hand movement, pointing ominously toward the door while he remains shut out from the room. Several times she rears herself from her fur-covered pallet in a peasant's hut and then falls backward, looking like a vampire, her kohl-lined eyes opened wide. Rising and falling on the pallet, laughing hysterically, she refuses to see him, sending an old peasant out with money to pay him. Dolski then shoots himself. The intertitles describe her consumption and her feeling of psychic death, ending with the statement, "So this is love." Returning to the present, she rejects Giorgio's declarations of love despite the fact that she has admitted to reciprocal feelings.

A following scene takes place in the theater as she and Giorgio go to see a performance of *Ruy Blas* (1869), a romantic revenge drama by Filippo Marchetti, based on Victor Hugo's play (1838), of an affair between an aristocrat and a plebian. Act 3 contains a love duet, "oh, dolce voluttà / Desio d'amor gentil." The scene in *Tigre reale* intercuts between the stage and the intense struggles between Natka and Giorgio in which she, overwhelmed by the passionate duet, struggles between her desires to succumb to and to resist him. In the choreography of her bodily movement and changing moods, she leans her head against the wall of the loge, and then, hiding from him in a corner, she suddenly turns and falls into his arms. In a climactic moment, she sends him away disdainfully, ensconced in her automobile and clutching a bouquet of roses, thus reinforcing the identification of the diva with flowers.

The second theatrical moment occurs after Giorgio, at first willing to marry a wealthy grocer's daughter, runs off when he receives a love note from

Natka, now spending what she believes will be her last day of life in a room at the Grand Hotel by the Odeon Theater. She takes medication prescribed by her physician and revives. Looking into the mirror, she stretches her body like a dancer and caresses her face. She is dressed in a flowing satin floor-length gown with a cape attached that looks like wings when she raises her arms. He comes to her and they fervidly embrace, but then, in a scene reminiscent of *La traviata*, she staggers, and falls. He carries her to the bed, and revives her with the medication. This tempestuous drama is now intercut with scenes from the theater, where a dancer performs a "fire dance" and collapses, now surrounded by other dancers. The hotel breaks out in fire and the couple, having been confronted by Count Natka, are locked into their room, where it seems likely they will have the Romeo and Juliet death alluded to earlier in the film. However, rescued by fire fighters, they jump from the window of the room onto a net below. Thus, the expectation of a fiery and catastrophic ending is overturned as the two lovers, now on a boat, sit side by side and the intertitle announces that Natka feels herself restored to youth and to life.

Menichelli's performance captures familiar dimensions of *amour fou* in cinematic language that evokes theatrical and operatic moments through the diva's gestures and facial expression, as well as through affective states ranging from disdain, anguish, despair, rage, physical pain, and vengefulness to ecstasy. Her costumes further situate her in an upper-class and fashionable world and also recall other passionate Italian and European divas from literature, drama, and opera. The linking of her states of mind to that of the dancer (as in the fire dance) is central to *Divismo* and its lyrical, operatic dimension. This operatic moment underscores how the diva, as a melodramatic figure of sensual excess, defiance, and morbidity, was removed from everyday life. The diva's power was not primarily her physical beauty, though she was attractive: it arose from her mysterious and arbitrary character. She did not, like later stars, conform to codified measurements of body size, or physiognomy. She was the consummate interpreter of affect through gesture, a key to the dynamic character of early cinema, which expressed psychic force and physical energy by way of a technology that relied on remoteness and in which seeing was not confirmed by hearing, though sound might be implied. The diva was a creation of light and shadow, movement, and memory, and the viewer had to summon new modes of sensory perception that entailed synesthesia. Her affective power resided in the subtlety of her bodily movements and in her penetrating, varied, and theatrical poses, rendering her a figure of transgression remote from the life of the spectator.

In contrast to the later stardom of the sound film, *Divismo* was not an organized phenomenon and divas were not pursued on the streets.[53] Until the 1920s, and the rise of fascism, little was written about Italian divas and Hollywood stars except in magazines, rotogravures, newspapers, and articles on film limited largely to urban centers such as Rome, Milan, and Turin;[54] contact with audiences was largely through the films themselves. The diva's inaccessibility also contributed to her exotic character. Her presence on screen was epitomized by her "languid poses, slow gestures, affected speech, dress of a classicizing and Orientalist taste,"[55] suggesting that the theatricality of the diva's performances relied heavily on the expressiveness of body as much as on the face to convey a range of "emotional resonances."[56] The diva was the site of "overlapping and conflicting class interests. In fact, the fantasy world in which the diva lived—grand hotels, mansions, holiday resorts, enchanted gardens, and tabarins—congealed into an escapist universe where petit-bourgeois audiences could forget about their economic disappoint-ments."[57] She was identified with the world of passion, with strong affect, and with power even if this power was destructive to her person. As an aristocrat, she was often associated with transnational characters and narratives—in the case of Me-nichelli as Natka, with Russian literature—to enhance her exceptional persona.

By later standards of femininity, Lyda Borelli's physical appearance was unexceptional. Somewhat stocky, not willowy or heavily made-up, she consti-tuted a stage in the evolution of the silent Italian cinema: "In the style of acting, recitation, in the repetition of her gestures, she gave birth to a typology of the gesture destined to be reproduced, repeated, multiplied in the long arc of the cinematic system,"[58] albeit with significant variation and effect. The diva be-longed to the world of the Symbolists and Decadents and in her persona "dis-tilled all of the characteristics of the European culture that preceded the world war."[59] *Divismo*, possessing an affinity with the upper classes and adopting an operatic and theatrical mode of presentation in its fascination with the femi-nine body and with the gestural, is a force of nature that threatens masculinity. Not merely an expression of escapism that in retrospect can be ridiculed and dismissed for its excesses and its "unrealistic" properties, its religious and cultic aura, its "heroic" rhetoric, and its fascination with death and violence, feminine *Divismo* is marked by its disdain for a banal and mundane world identified with middle-class values of love, marriage, and family.

The femininity that emerges from *Divismo* is opposed to traditional feminin-ity as well as to those dimensions of fascism that elevate maternity, reproduction, and service to the family and the nation. On the one hand, the diva's transgres-siveness challenges complacent and submissive femininity; on the other, her sev-erance from traditional femininity and its affirmative identification with nature serves also as a prefiguration of her annihilation as a transgressive force. This form of cinema contributed not only to destabilizing taken-for-granted assumptions about women but also to dematerializing and de-historicizing femininity, making it serviceable for the cult of the new fascist man that gained ascendance in the 1920s and 1930s. The divas disappeared or were transformed in the post–World

War I era, giving rise to a populist version of stardom that could be translated to the masses and emulated (see chapter 2).

A work that dramatizes embattled and battling femininity is Nino Oxilia's *Rapsodia satanica* (Satanic Rhapsody, Cines, 1915), starring Lyda Borelli. While this film bears similarities to narratives acted in by other divas, what constitutes its distinctiveness is its particular emphasis on metamorphosis, on the transformation of the woman into a butterfly, returning her to nature. Her distinctiveness resides in the ways she is choreographed through her gestures, in the orchestration of her hand movements, her rich and abundant hair, her intense and variable facial expressions, her mesmerizing gaze, and the often contorted and tortured movements of her body. In this film, she undergoes several metamorphoses. She appears in a dual role, as an aging woman and as an eternally young seductress, and finally as a butterfly. The film's self-reflexive quality draws on the body of the diva both as character in a narrative and as a reflection on the erotic power of the cinematic body in the silent cinema.

The Faustian myth of the human compact with the devil is altered in that it features a woman, an upper-class woman who desires youth and beauty, rather than a male scientist magician who seeks total knowledge. In this film, the pact is based on the attainment of eternal youth but at the price of the woman's renunciation of love. Of course, the woman, Alba d'Oltravita, played by Borelli, defies her contract with the devil, falls in love, and, as with the opening of Pandora's box, produces chaos that leads to her lovers' deaths. However, the woman does not die but is metamorphosed into an ethereal human-like butterfly. The butterfly image is one that frequently recurs in myth, opera, and melodrama and is associated with femininity in being fragile, light, decorative, and changeable. Defiant femininity struggles against aging and death in a paradoxical attempt to transgress the forces of nature.

Gramsci's oft-quoted comment on Borelli's appearance and acting style captures a quintessential aspect of her cinematic persona. Gramsci writes, "In the beginning was sex. . . . In the beginning was the word. . . . No, in the beginning was sex,"[60] and Borelli represents for him a creature "who is a part of prehistoric and primordial humanity. To say that one admires her for her art is not true. No one can explain what is Borelli's art, because it doesn't exist. Borelli does not know how to interpret any diverse creature other than herself."[61] What is intriguing about these comments is not only the identification of Borelli with primordial sensuality but also the idea that *Borellismo* designates an isomorphism of the actress and the parts she assumes. Borelli *is* the film; she and its theatricality are fused, and her role both captures and transgresses social (and aesthetic) forms and conventions.

Despite its negative assessment of Borelli's cinematic performance, Gramsci's description of the diva as pre-historical contributes to an understanding of *Divismo* and its appeal and power. Borelli's roles are resistant to interpretation, as are the other roles assumed by divas. However, her narratives and acting are amenable to investigation, as symptomatic of particular forms of femininity—the *femme fatale*, the cruel maternal figure, the vamp, the priestess, and the madwoman—that confound the constraints of conventional social roles assigned to women.

One of the most reiterated narratives of divided femininity and its relation to madness is Antonio Fogazzaro's novel *Malombra* (1881), which presents yet another aspect of the diva's tenuous connection to mundane reality. In this work, the obsessed heroine asks, "se credete possible che un anima umana abbia due o piú esisteze terrestri?" (Do you believe it possible that a human soul can have two or more earthly lives?).[62] This same question dominates two Italian films adapted from the novel, the silent *Malombra* (1917), directed by Carmine Gallone and featuring Lyda Borelli, and the sound version of *Malombra* (1942), directed by Mario Soldati and starring Isa Miranda, a major star of the era (see chapter 2). Each of these texts involves writing—letters and books—as an incitement to reflection on the question of whether history repeats itself. In particular, Gallone's film explores the uses of the past in relation to beliefs in reincarnation and supernaturalism. The novel and the silent film version investigate the question of whether repetition is inevitable or whether it is possible to alter the course of events. The film is an ideal vehicle for the operatic diva where the dilemma of embattled femininity is at stake.

Fogazzaro's novel is a Gothic melodrama, a form largely identified with female protagonists and one that lends itself to visualization. The specifically Gothic elements involve a house haunted by mementos and spirits from the past, the presence of a dependent orphaned and impressionable young woman, and imperious and/or malevolent male authority figures. The treatment of supernaturalism in the novel expands beyond these familiar generic characteristics to produce reflections on time, memory, mortality, and especially the consequences of entrapment in the past, all of which belong to the psychic landscape of the operatic and cinematic diva. In dramatizing these issues, the novel relies on literature and music as a means of entry into the metaphysical issues posed. The question of whether a person can live twice is critical to the novel's reflexive concern with historicizing that captures in melodramatic terms conflicts between modernity and tradition, religion, science, and art, logic and fantasy.

Carmine Gallone (1896–1973), a prominent director during the silent and sound era, was identified with highly melodramatic and operatic films, which, early in his career, often starred Lyda Borelli. His silent film credits include *La donna nuda* (1914) and *La falena* (The Streetwalker, 1915) as well as *Malombra*. His films are characteristic of the phenomenon of *Divismo*, and his version of *Malombra*, similarly to his other films, highlights the character and power of the diva in the Italian silent cinema. Characteristic of many of the films that focus on the *Divismo*, the culturally intriguing dimensions of the style are centered on the figure of a woman driven mad by fantasy and desire.

The idea of a second life is carried over in the cinematic adaptation. The dominant female character from the novel is transformed on the screen and projected onto the persona of the diva. The literary work and the film are both studies of femininity and particularly of madness via obsession. However, the film more than the novel, especially through Borelli's portrayal, favors the figure of the protagonist and her states of mind. The novel is a study of the aristocratic world that the diva inhabits but the film relegates this world to the background, allowing her center stage in the narrative involving physical and psychic struggle. Gallone's *Malombra* largely epitomizes this tradition, focusing on the heroine's actions in and reactions to events drawn from the novel—her arrival at the D'Ormengo home, her discovery of objects belonging to the dead Cecilia, her growing opposition to her guardian the Count, and her revenge in the name of Cecilia—altered to suit the cinematic medium and the persona of the actress, Borelli. From the initial scenes, "through her body, Lyda Borelli has the ability to make you *feel* what is happening *with* her, *to* her, *in* her."[63] Unlike the novel, which opens with the arrival of Silla to the palazzo, the film begins with Marina di Malombra's advent and from that point on her presence guides the film. Her struggle over control is immediately introduced in her peremptory rejection of a room without a view of the lake, and her preference for one that is described by the servants as the abode of the devil.

In a scene exemplifying Borelli's ability to convey affect through gesture and pose, the maid removes Marina's long gauzy black veil. Marina moves to the window to gaze at the lake in a scene that captures her restlessness through her bodily contortions, her facial expressions, and her hand movements. She glides like a dancer from one place to another, touching various objects in ways suggesting curiosity, attraction, and repulsion. In her close-ups, through the opening and closing of her eyes, and the tilt of her head, she evokes the various states through which she passes—arrogance, confusion, and internal conflict and control. Her frequent caresses of her body suggest her narcissism, her separateness from others, her struggle with intruding and threatening thoughts. Many shots of her wrapping her arms about herself function as tactile signs of her isolation and self-absorption.

Borelli's costumes are characteristic of the pre–Word War I era, featuring draped and non-restrictive "flowing garments based on historical costumes from various sources and periods, creating a column from the shoulders to the ground" that facilitated movement and gesture.[64] Her dresses are, for the most part, unobtrusive, classic, loose-fitting, and flowing, the fabrics gauzy and delicate, allowing her to move freely, sinuously, and quickly. They are generally décolleté, revealing of her shoulders and neck. The film's selections of clothing

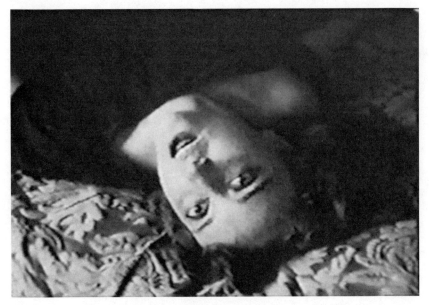

1.2. "Goddess of Pain." Lyda Borelli in *Malombra. Author's Collection.*

and objects not only suggest her psychic state but also reflexively call attention to the paraphernalia identified with the world of the diva. Borelli's Marina is identified with nature—with flowers, trees, and water. As she wanders through her room, she carries flowers. As she walks on the grounds of the villa, and particularly as she strolls in the garden, a young and admiring gardener gives her flowers. On a boat ride, conducted by the young male servant, she stretches out languidly on the boat, raising one arm slowly behind her head, moving her head slightly from side to side. As their boat passes the boats of others, the passengers drop flowers on her: she smiles but does not unduly rouse herself and indolently acknowledges their admiration. The scene thus suggests a link between the character and that of the cinematic diva.

Marina's response to her discovery of Cecilia's book, glove, mirror, and lock of hair, hidden in a desk, is similarly conveyed through movement and gesture. Borelli picks up each object slowly and deliberately and lays it down gently. Shots alternate between close-ups of her face or torso and shots of her hand with the glove, the mirror, or the letter as if she seeks to draw from these objects a meaning beyond their materiality. Her body postures, her standing, bending, crouching, and sitting, are indices of her restlessness and her straining for the hidden meaning of these objects. After examining the lock of hair, she unwinds her own hair, matching the colors with her own tresses. Slowly, and to erotic effect, she wraps her long hair around her body as if momentarily wrapping herself in Cecilia's identity.

In keeping with the theatricality of the diva, a range of poses characterizes the diva's disdainful interactions with others: leaning against a lectern, a wall, or a pillar on the loggia, or assuming the position of a detached observer. At a lunch with her guardian the Count and Silla, a young man that she believes is the man selected by the Count for her to marry, she displays an arrogant manner evident through her upright posture, her twisting a napkin in her lap to convey her disdain, and direct and imperious glances at her assumed adversary. In a scene entitled "A Game of Chess," she approaches Silla, swaggering, hands placed on her hips, and the intertitle communicates her challenge to him: "Are you afraid of me?" When they sit, the camera glides from her to him, similar to movements in the chess game they are playing. Her glacial and controlled facial expressions, the sideways tilt of her head, and the sinuous movement of her hands convey mastery as she fingers a chess piece, drops it indifferently, folds her hands, and leans her face forward to gaze at him, thus reinforcing her antagonism toward him.

Marina's remoteness, her isolation from others, is reinforced by her preference for solitude, visualized through her frequent visits to an isolated spot among trees on the shore of the lake. Filmed in middle distance and seen in silhouette from Silla's point of view, her movements suggest a communing with otherworldly powers. After Silla and she embrace, she runs her hands through her hair and then raises her arms as if in supplication to some unseen power. This gesture also evokes the diva's exceptional and celestial character: her communing with the muses, if not with demonic forces. Her conflict over human contact and the desire for solitude are also evident in her reactions to the advances of Count Nepo, the man selected by the Count to be her husband. It is not merely her look of contempt but her nuanced hand movements that convey her distaste for him. She tilts her head upward and away from him, slowly withdraws her hand from his grasp and places it against her chest in a gesture of pain. When he seeks to embrace her, she lifts her hand palm outward to keep him at a distance, and then aggressively pokes her parasol at him.

In executing Cecilia's revenge, Borelli is first filmed in a contemplative posture in middle distance and close-up. She is dressed in a loosely flowing gown trimmed with fur, another nod to the style of the time. Having obtained permission to postpone the marriage ceremony for a day despite the preparations and the arrival of guests, she shakes off her calculated and controlled responses to the impending event, allowing her passion to emerge. With rolling eyes and shuddering figure, hair loosened, like a distraught operatic heroine, she picks up a candelabrum and slowly glides along the balcony to Count Cesare's room. Her descent into madness, one of the hallmarks of the operatic and cinematic diva, becomes more pronounced with Silla's return from Milan in time to witness it. After a passionate embrace, she becomes aloof, and withdraws from him. The intertitle describes her as "under the compulsion of her madness." Borelli is now dressed in a flowing dark gown and a veil that hides her face, an outfit similar to the one she wore upon her arrival to the house. She now calls Silla by the name of Cecilia's lover, "Renato," showing him Cecilia's memorabilia and revealing to him her perpetration of revenge on the Count. Her hair is loose, her mouth contorted, and her gestures more disjointed and frenetic than during her visit to Count Cesare's chamber. The scene is intercut with a flashback to Marina's nocturnal and deadly encounter with him. Her maid Fanny abruptly interrupts her recounting of events with a request to come immediately to the dying Count's chamber. When Marina enters, she rolls her eyes, waving her arms and wildly twisting her body, and the title cuts in, "Cecilia is here!" Marina collapses, and Silla carries her, prostrate, from the room.

Borelli presents the final permutations of Marina's madness largely through close-up and gesture. She awakens in her room, draped on her bed, and is shot in close-up. Her wide-open eyes slowly close. She rises from the bed and paces, moving like one possessed, like a somnambulist. Silla comes to tell her that he is leaving, and she receives the news coldly. She joins the doctor and another guest at the table for the Count's funeral feast, holding a few flowers that she slowly rubs on her throat. She rises and goes to Silla's room, observes him as he writes at a desk, and then returns to the table where she sits, takes food from the servant, picks up the knife, and pounds it on the table before rising again. She leans against a pillar, drapes herself on the railing of the loggia, seizes and then drops a pillow. Finally, determined, she goes to Silla's room, shoots him, and runs to her boat, hair flying, presumably but not definitively to complete the reenactment of Cecilia's suicide. The final shot is of the doctor and servants bent over the dead Silla.

Thus, the melodramatic and operatic in Fogazzaro's novel are adapted in a way that is congenial to the Italian silent cinema with its penchant for theatricality and its focus on sexuality through the highly expressive body of the diva. In this film, the other characters and the philosophical investigations of the novel are subordinated to Borelli's portrait of Marina. In her acting, her expressive face and body, she succeeds in incarnating a portrait of transgressive femininity. True to its Gothic antecedents, the film dramatizes her struggle between a forbidding and confining domestic space and a natural setting identified with freer movement, highlighting the diva's uneasiness and imprisonment in a body from which the only release is madness or death. A brooding and defiant female burdened by the past, she is doomed to exist only in her fantasies, in a realm removed from religion, marriage, and the familial responsibility identified with more conventional social conceptions of femininity. Consistent with the cinema of *Divismo*, the Gallone film elevates the role of the enigmatic diva, rendering it operatic. Her particular physical attributes and style of acting are expressed through the choreography of her movement, the framing of her as separate from the other characters, and the use of close-up, all of which subordinate the narrative and transform the narrative into a study of the diva's primordial affective states.

Among the dominant divas, particular attention has been paid in the critical literature to the career of Francesca Bertini, due in part to her long career, to Gianfranco Mingozzi's film *L'ultima diva* (The Last Diva, 1982) and his volume on the actress, and to the associations that have been made between *Assunta Spina* (1915) and reassessments of realism prior to the 1940s in Italian cinema. However, La Bertini, as she was called, made over one hundred films from 1910 to 1976, interrupted only by her marriage to Count Cartier, after which she abandoned making films from 1921 to 1924. Many of her films, like those of Pina Menichelli, Lyda Borelli, and Leda Gys, have been victims of indifference to preservation from loss, fire, and the disasters of war.[65] Those that remain in entirety or in part as well as reviews and descriptions of them reveal the character and quality of her acting, evident in her contributions to the Film d'Arte Italiana, the films she made for the Cines, Celio, and Caesar studios, and her performances in German, Italian, and Spanish productions.

The titles of Bertini's films are indicative of the types of narratives—historical, Shakespearean, operatic, allegorical, and melodramatic: *Francesca da Rimini* (1910), *Il Mercante di Venezia* (The Merchant of Venice, 1910), *Ernani* (1911), *La bufera* (The Blizzard, 1913), *L'histoire d'un Pierrot* (1914), *Assunta Spina* (1915), *La signora delle camelie* (1915), *Tosca* (1918), *La contessa Sara* (1919). While she appeared in a number of popular films, it is her performance in *Assunta Spina* that has remained as a landmark in the early cinema of *Divismo*. Her much-vaunted beauty, statuesque poses, aura of remoteness and secrecy, and elegance of dress were celebrated not only by film critics but also in the popular press. While she could play such legendary roles as Camille and Tosca, she could also cross-dress and play a Pierrot in the charming *L'histoire d'un Pierrot*. She was for many critics the incarnation of feminine mystery. What distinguishes the performances of Bertini from those of other divas is her subtle, understated, but expressive acting. Her incarnation of femininity was dependent on her attractive physical appearance, her more naturalistic style of acting, and her elegant fashionable attire, and on lavish and luxurious upper-class settings.

Yet even in the humble working-class world of Naples in *Assunta Spina*, she also dominates. Her acting in this film is reliant less on excessive and broad gesture and more on an understated modern acting style. Her performance is consonant with the quotidian aspects of her character's lower-class existence— tearing a piece of bread, wiping her hands on her apron, performing domestic activities. Yet her actions are representative of how the diva, even in the quotidian and naturalistic milieu, transforms commonplace events into an exceptional event. *Assunta Spina* has in histories of Italian cinema been singled out, along with the lost text of *Sperduti nel buio*, as a predecessor of neorealism.[66] In this recounting, *Assunta Spina* is distinguished for its "realism" and its ties to regional cinema. Like the films of Elvira Notari, *Assunta Spina*, directed by her but attributed in the credits to Gustavo Serena,[67] was filmed in Naples and relies on the ambience of the city and of Neapolitan culture. This film, too, is an instance of the existence of a regional cinema before the consolidation of filmmaking in Rome and of the city's significant role in the silent as well as sound cinema. Also distinctive about *Assunta Spina* is the transposition of the aristocratic diva into a working-class milieu.

Bertini's acting is an instance of how acting styles were altered by the personalities of the various actresses and the characters they assumed. The parts undertaken by Bertini were more varied than those of Menichelli or Borelli, ranging from melodramas to comedies, fantasy, and musical pantomimes.[68] In *Assunta Spina*, a film dependent as much on the film's uses of the Neapolitan landscape as on her acting style, Bertini plays a working-class *femme fatale*. Her character, her costuming, and her makeup eschew the supernatural and exotic, muting the spiritual aspects of the diva; however, the close-ups, the choreography of her movement in the context of the street, and her behavior in the antechamber and the courtroom, on the boat, and in the basso are consummate opportunities for the expression of the diva's enigmatic character. Her free spirit is conveyed in the scenes of her movement through the streets where much of the action takes place. Her contacts with the three men in her life are outdoors, for the most part: on the street, in her strolling with Raffaele, during the engagement party on the boat, in her leaving the courtroom after trial, and in her seeking Don Federico out after he has abandoned her.

In many of the scenes, the spectator is treated to views of the Neapolitan landscape, a landscape that is critical to the development of Italian cinema. While in other films, the diva seems to inhabit an imaginary and ahistorical landscape, in this film the city is linked to the character of the diva. Most prominently featured is the Bay of Naples, against which Bertini as Assunta and her lover Michele (played by Gustavo Serena) are filmed. In one of the romantic scenes, Assunta and Michele are filmed on a boat with the Bay as background as they exchange embraces. Also in prominence are the streets—not the major metropolitan centers, but the narrow byways, the shops where the protagonists work, and the backstreets where Raffaele (Alberto Albertini) stalks them, planning his revenge on them for Assunta's transfer of her affection from him to Michele. The buildings are shabby, with graffiti on display; the passageways narrow and serpentine. The film is shot largely from stationary and middle-distance positions, eschewing excessive close-ups and camera movement. The action occurs within the frame, and characters enter from off-screen as onto a stage. The intensity of affect among the characters is largely conveyed by the choreography of movement through the landscape, by the subtlety of bodily movement, and by narrative evocation of the viewer's prior knowledge of the diva's melodramatic scenario of transgression and violence.

A look at exemplary moments in *Assunta Spina* further reveals Bertini's style of acting. Her role as *femme fatale* is conveyed delicately. She is not obsessed or mad, vindictive, distraught, or teetering on the brink of madness even after the deaths of Don Federico and of Michele. Her rendition of the fatal woman seems to spring from other sources. She moves through the landscape in light-hearted indifference to her impact on the men who desire her, focused on her own pleasure. Her modest clothing, befitting her social station, differs dramatically from the elegant, Orientalist, classical gowns and haute couture associated with the upper-class diva, and yet her simple outfits enhance her character as diva. In particular, the large shawl she wears at the festivities celebrating her engagement to Michele becomes an index to her changing responses to the company. She sinuously wraps it about her as she enters the boat that will take her to the outing to celebrate her engagement, drapes it loosely over her body as she sits at a table enjoying the occasion, and seductively twists it around her body to flirt with Rafaelle as retaliation for Michele's jealousy. She wears it again during Michele's trial, where she stands before the judges and fingers it, draping it over arm, as she attempts to defend Michele. Her posture is defiant but entreating. Similarly, still wearing the shawl, she allows it to hang loosely over her arms, enabling her to use her hands during Don Federico's attempt to seduce her. She then winds it around her, signaling her initial refusal of Don Federico's proposal to "help" her by seeing to it that Michele remains in Naples, but wraps it tightly around her as she succumbs to him after learning that Michele is to be moved to the prison at Avellino. During the sequence of the engagement party, her disfigurement by Michele, and the scenes in the courtroom, she uses the shawl to express changing emotions without recourse to facial grimaces, contortions, and theatrical conventions.

In subsequent scenes, she no longer wears the shawl but is dressed in simple black, foreshadowing her demise, her remorse, and her acceptance of circumstance. Her restrained acting throughout serves to accentuate the moments of crisis where she is called upon to express sorrow, disdain, and finally submission to her fate as foreshadowed by the old gypsy's prophecy, "I see blood in the future." At film's end, her assumption of blame for the death of Michele is again a model of the diva's ability to convey affect through her body. Her final gestures are elegant, ever understated, as she acquiesces to the crime she did not directly commit, submitting herself to the law. But, consistent with *Divismo*, hers is the fate of women who transgress against social conventions, and she confronts her situation

1.3. Francesca Bertini as working-class diva in *Assunta Spina. Photofest.*

---

with composure and dignity. Her long hair is loose but not wild as she lifts herself from her cowering position, rises to her full height, looks down at the dead man, and slowly exits with the police.

Assunta Spina poses a number of questions about the nature of realism, its relations to melodrama, and its compatibility with *Divismo* in a working-class milieu. In several ways, *Assunta Spina* follows many of the thematic and stylistic aspects of Elvira Notari's films in its focus on street life, on the lower-class characters portrayed by Neapolitan extras, on the linking of their bodies to the city's geography and architecture, on the interpenetration of public into private space, and also on the reliance on melodrama. Beginning with the views of the Bay of Naples and of the urban landscape in the distance, focusing on the images of the water and of the boats in the bay, and moving to the streets as the site of movement through the images of pedestrians, crowds, and traffic, the film increasingly narrows its landscape to the legal, then domestic, realms. In using the ambiance of Naples, *Assunta Spina* also reveals how the Italian cinema has utilized geography to locate the spectator in a regional landscape that entails a sense of everyday life, work, family, and social institutions such as the law courts, though the presence of the diva qualifies the "objective" character of this world. Giuliana Bruno connects this type of *vedutismo* to a sense of the city's "prominent scenic quality and its street energy."[69] These shots serve more than others to convey a sense of a panoramic gaze, exhibited also in paintings and photography of the city: the shots are also intimately wedded to melodrama and to theatricality, revealing the city as an integral feature of Italian life in regard to negotiating the various aspects of the conflicts attendant on daily existence. Yet the presence of the diva alters quotidian "reality," bestowing subjective and emotional resonance on the exterior landscape.

The film's uses of landscape reinforce the character of Assunta as a working-class diva. For example, Assunta's dwelling (with its portrait of the Madonna) is a *basso*, a small, cramped basement room that, having been originally intended for a shop, opens directly onto the street. Thus the spectator is aware of the movement between the street and the *basso* that links interior to exterior, the public to the domestic spheres. The struggle between Michele and Federico (and Michele's escape) takes place on the street, whereas the death of Federico and Assunta's arrest take place inside the *basso*, invaded by the law. In the finale, the world has shrunk to the narrow dwelling that, in its use of closed space and noir lighting, appears like a prison that ultimately entraps Assunta and leads her to resist offering any explanation to the police of the death of Don Federico.

While *Assunta Spina* focuses on the transgressiveness and disruptive nature of the femininity that constitutes the regime of the diva, the film does not present a sentimental portrait of a virtuous woman gone astray. Far more interestingly, and befitting *Divismo*, Assunta's past is portrayed as less conventional than the melodramatic scenario of virginal and innocent victimhood. She assumes a transgressive role in her demise, but her transgressions are not those of a vindictive character. They seem to emerge from her supreme indifference. Her history involves relationships with other men even before her engagement to Michele, and it is this past that creates difficulties for Assunta in the unraveling of the narrative. Though men initiate the violence in the film, violence is ultimately traced to the woman and to her departure from accepted standards of fidelity and monogamy—a pattern repeated more than once.

When Michele goes to prison, Assunta is seduced by Don Federico's offer of arranging for the transfer of Michele to a Neapolitan prison in exchange for sexual favors. Initially Assunta agrees in order to aid Michele, but inevitably she becomes more involved with Don Federico. In predictable melodramatic fashion, she becomes more dependent on him as he tires of her, and, also predictably, she becomes more distressed by his withdrawal from her, which ultimately places her in the familiar role of feminine abjection. In the final moments of the film, Michele, having been released from prison two months early, is now eager to resume his relationship with her. He enters her home, sees the table set for company, becomes suspicious, and questions her about the identity of the guest. After his persistent, increasingly angry, and failing attempts to regain her affection, she confesses her relationship to Don Federico. From the window, Michele sees Don Federico, grabs a knife from the table, and runs out, unable to be restrained by Assunta. He struggles with Federico on the street and stabs him. Mortally wounded, Federico staggers into the room and dies. Assunta crouches on the floor as the police enter and neighbors gather on the street, observing the drama. Assuming responsibility for Don Federico's death, she is led away by a policeman.

The socially transgressive character in the film is finally revealed to be Assunta. Not content to be a submissive partner to any of the men in her life, she, like a *femme fatale*, like Bizet's Carmen, is unable to remain faithful and brings misfortune to the men in her life. As a fatal woman, she incarnates all of the desirable attributes associated with the diva as object to be viewed and possessed, but she is also a danger, since she is the incarnation of a threatening cultural fantasy involving rebelliousness, a threatening yet fascinating figuration of a femininity that must be contained and restrained juridically or through her death. By confessing to a crime she does not directly commit, Assunta indirectly admits to a different infraction—namely, her violation of codes of feminine behavior, already enumerated by Michele's mother and foreseen by a fortune-teller.

In its focus on femininity, on the woman's body, and on the problem of who lays claim to that body—the father, the men in her life, and the law—the film does not present her transgression as unattractive. In fact, the appealing dimension of Bertini's Assunta resides in her beauty, her indifference to others, her self-absorption, and her resistance to conventional expectations. She glides through the film like a somnambulist, the camera and her actions stressing her isolation and distinction from others. If she embodies the essence of the diva, it is less in her fiery passion and more in her seeming lack of awareness of her overwhelming effect on others until too late. The film focuses predominantly on her. All events are satellite to her actions. Her gestures are carefully choreographed to convey her ambivalence toward the men in her life. The men, on the other hand, are involved in scrutinizing her, dogging her footsteps, possessing her, and punishing her. In her initial meeting with Michele at the train station, she seems reluctant to participate wholly in the joy of union with him. In the following scene in her home with her father, her distance is revealed in understated but nonetheless obvious ways, as when she takes her food even before serving him, seeming more interested in it than in him. Even at the engagement party, she appears indifferent to the consequences of Raffaele's toying with her to create conflict with Michele.

The film plays with alternating scenes between the home and the outside world. In her discussion of the melodramas of Notari, Bruno comments on the importance of alternating shots of the home and the street, on the dual role of landscape, in terms that are applicable to *Assunta Spina:* "More than just a background or tableau, the architecture of the city blends into the architecture of the melodrama. Notari's melodrama is intricate, obscure, dark, tortuous, and at times suffocating, like the space of the old district of town used to be."[70] In *Assunta Spina* the landscape dramatizes the tension as well as the relationship between the domestic and the public. The film also preserves links with the cinema of attractions insofar as it highlights the urban landscape, calling attention to the tendency of early film to focus on the visual sights of the city, to capitalize on the fascination with the metropolis, and to create vignettes of a familiar urban world. Thus Bertini, consistent with the world of the diva, provides a bridge between the domestic and the public which is central to the drama of a beleaguered femininity that stands in the intersection between the public and the private, the home and the world, transgression and, finally, subjection to the law.

Assunta Spina does not use many close-ups of the key characters; during moments of tension the camera remains stationary, confined to the space of the action and the gestures and actions of the characters that convey their emotional dilemma as on stage. The film's theatricality transcends this form of staging, however, implicating the external audience in the narrative as observers to the events along with the internal audiences. Significantly, the conflicts between Assunta and others are underscored by the frequent inclusion of an audience within the frame. There is much about the film that calls attention to spectatorship, involving interactions of the protagonist with the various crowds that observe her in critical moments of the action—at the engagement party, during her disfigurement by Michele and his arrest on the street, in the courtroom scenes, and during the final, public act of violence observed by a passerby: the presence of groups of people creates a sense of the vitality of Neapolitan life but also reinforces the sense of melodrama as theatrical—and juridical. The diegetic and extra-diegetic spectators are necessary as witnesses, playing a role as jury in the unfolding of the drama of justice that involves the relations between women and the law, and lending greater prominence to the diva as a figure of transgression.

In contrast to *Cabiria* and *Quo Vadis? Assunta Spina* (1915) has been singled out in histories of Italian cinema, along with the lost text of *Sperduti nel buio*, "as cinematic paradigms of the naturalist literary tradition of *verismo* and examples of the great national realistic tradition [and] as singular predecessors of neorealism."[71] Another film that is not often, but deserves to be, considered along with *Assunta Spina* is Febo Mari's *Cenere* (1917), a film credited to Mari that features a diva of the European stage, Eleanora Duse (1858–1924), in a work that also incorporates "realism" and theatricality. In her limited film roles, Duse vied with the other divas in prominence. Her acting was linked to theater rather than cinema, though she left a legacy on film in the underrated *Cenere*, where her nuanced acting style is transferred effectively to the cinema.

Duse's affair with D'Annunzio belongs to the lore of *Divismo* as the union of two celebrated and eccentric artists. Though Duse was known for affairs with other artists, most notably Arrigo Boito, poet, composer, and Verdi's librettist, her relationship with D'Annunzio was notorious. She specialized at first in classical theater, then later in contemporary drama (e.g., the plays of Alexander Dumas the younger, Verga, and Ibsen). Her 1894 meeting with Gabriele D'Annunzio was fateful. As an inspiration for his *Il fuoco*, the internationally prominent actress rose to the heights of *Divismo* as "the promised woman; tragic muse; the Dionysian woman; a night creature shaped by dreams and passions; a wandering temptress; a bird of prey; a thing he could hold in his fist; a dangerous threatening thing; his carnal mistress."[72] Though her relationships outside of the theater were highly tempestuous, in contrast to those of French diva Sarah Bernhardt, Duse's acting style was restrained, resistant to codified postures, reliant on subtle and more spontaneous movements of the body and on the expressive treatment of objects. Her acting style was, in contrast to Bernhardt's, known for its "decorative, romantic . . . sculptured movement."[73]

Cenere's realism is the result of Duse's affective though understated performance and of the film's focus on a regional landscape. The film is set in Sardinia and located largely in a small village where a woman, Rosalia, played by Duse, is compelled to give up her natural son, and turn him over to his father and his wife. In a moving scene of separation, she relinquishes him, giving him an amulet to wear always. Dressed like the peasant women of the region, her head covered by a long shawl, while standing outdoors and peering into a window she observes his reception by his rough and unenthusiastic father. Unlike such films as *Malombra* and *Tigre reale*, *Cenere* focuses on the rocky countryside with its flora, animals, and scenes of workers in the mill and in the fields. The lingering bond between mother and son is conveyed through a dream sequence where the mother stands outside as the boy moves from his bed to the window, but all that is visible of her to the boy is a shadow on the wall. When he looks out to the road, no one can be seen. In a later scene, again, she appears to the left of the screen as the son, Anania, now grown, working at his desk suddenly rises and moves to the window and closes it as if shutting out his mother's image.

Having developed a relationship with a young girl, Margherita, from his early school days, he writes letters to her in which he expresses his desire to save his mother. He returns to the village to see Rosalia. In a crude stone cottage, he finds her again, but she is reluctant to see him. The peasant woman bows her head and backs away to the wall, dropping the bundle she has been carrying. Her movements signal more than rejection of the young man; they convey her hesitancy, her conflict over his presence, and her recognition that they must part. She tells him to let her go. As she crouches on the floor, he caresses her head, but she covers her face with her hands, withdraws, and then falls back on him. Her refusal sparks

1.4. Eleanora Duse's eloquent gesture in *Cenere*. *Photofest.*

his anger and he rejects her, but, imperious now, she retreats from him. However, he promises to write, and since she cannot read, she asks him to send her a sign of his coming. Once again home, he struggles about his promise and tears off the amulet that he has worn all along, and sends it as the sign. Rosalia wanders in the countryside and then returns to the cottage, where she lies down on the floor and expires. The villagers enter and cover her body, and Anania comes to her body, kneels, and kisses her hand, where he finds the amulet. Her body is carried out as he calls "Mamma" and kisses her forehead, and the intertitle, "Cenere" (Ashes), is repeated several times and is the last image on the screen.

While Brunetta regards Duse's performance as the antithesis of the diva, it could be said that she offers another portrait of *Divismo*, that of a passionate woman who conveys the fierce independence and the exquisite passion and suffering of maternal femininity. Her use of gesture communicates the internal agonies of loss and of enforced isolation. She choreographs her movement so as to withhold facial expression, almost as if her gaze would be too revealing, yet her cowering, her rocking to and fro, and her bowed head speak to her anguish and grief. Unlike the frenetic movements of the operatic diva, her gestures speak eloquently to what

Giorgio Agamben has described as "pure mediality," revealing how the gesture is expressive "of not being able to figure out something in language."[74]

Duse's acting is a study in movement and stillness. As in her acting on the stage, she eschews makeup, relying on expressive and eloquent gestures to render disappointment and loss. Her *Divismo* springs from sources other than those of Menichelli and Borelli and other than a theatrical tradition that derived from nineteenth-century manuals on acting. She is a diva in the sense that she conveys suffering, loss, and passion without resorting to stylized movements and facial expressions. In a film that utilizes natural landscape, ethnographic moments in the portrayal of the villagers, and dreamlike episodes, Duse's presence, her physical appearance, and her gestures attest to a form of *Divismo* that is made possible by her mode of acting in concert with the camera to penetrate an interior world. Her performance in *Cenere*, like that of Bertini in *Assunta Spina*, is evidence of the existence of a different, more rare, expression of *Divismo*. Bertini's performance as a *femme fatale* is distinguished by how she "dominates the screen," portraying a character who is "humble, but proud, ill-educated but full of passion."[75] Similarly, Duse's performance captures the intensity, passion, and also defiance, rather than submissiveness, of maternal femininity. These two divas, while not adopting a hyperbolic form of expression, were able to communicate through their personally inflected styles conflicts and emotions that were reminiscent of opera.

Divismo and the Movement-Image

Divismo has elicited and continues to elicit a wide range of critical studies that link it to the cultural milieu of the developing and innovative cinema of the teens and twenties, offering important insights into its various connections to the literary, theatrical, historical, and commercial world of that era. *Divismo* is an incarnation of the power of the cinematic apparatus to make visible to mass audiences a world of desire, dreams, and passion.

In its fascination with the human body and with movement, the early cinema drew on a number of forms of entertainment: the theatre, the circus and acrobatics, the novel, the lyric opera, painting, magazines, rotogravures, and *fumetti* (cartoons). Equally important to the phenomenon known as *Divismo* is the character of the cinematic image in the period prior to sound and in the early sound cinema. Unlike theater, the cinematic image is able, as Benjamin indicated, to penetrate the minutiae of the world as seen directly through the lens of the camera. Invoking an analogy between the camera and the surgeon, Benjamin claims that the camera "greatly diminishes the distance between himself and the patient by penetrating into the patient's body, and increases it but little by the caution with which his hand moves among the organs."[76] In the case of *Divismo* the close-up is only one instance of how the camera penetrates private space. The camera's penetration of the diva's world pays attention to aspects of interior life that are not easily accessible to the naked eye. The diva is not merely a sociological phenomenon; she is an avatar of a modern regime of vision despite the religious and ritualistic qualities she incarnates.

This regime of vision, termed by Gilles Deleuze the "movement-image," belongs largely to the pre–World War II cinema and is helpful for articulating the philosophical character of the silent cinema and the early years of the sound cinema and, by extension, of *Divismo*. His writing on cinema is a daring attempt to conceptualize how modernity is exemplified in the cinematic image. By focusing in molecular fashion on the movement-image, Deleuze's writings in *Cinema 1* extend the early critical writings on the "arte muta" by shifting focus from a comparison of cinema to the other arts (e.g., music, theater, literature)[77] and from paeans to the extraordinary character of the diva to a consideration of how subject and object relations are generated and perceived through visual technology. What Deleuze termed the movement-image accounts for different perceptions of subjectivity and objectivity. He asks, "Is it not the cinema's perceptual destiny to make us move from one of its poles to another?"[78] In the strange, surreal world of *Rapsodia satanica*, *Tigre reale*, and *Malombra* a constant oscillation occurs between these poles, and the diva becomes the bridge between these poles by virtue of the affective properties she conveys. The movement-image is different from a photographed image and from simple reproduction of "reality." Brushing aside the notion that consciousness consists of perceiving an image, Deleuze writes, "In the movement-image, there are not yet bodies or rigid lines but only lines of figures of light. Blocs of space-time are such figures. They are images in themselves. . . . In other words, the eye is in things, in luminous images."[79]

In the case of the silent cinema and its expression through *Divismo*, what the viewer takes for the projection of the female figure and experiences as its affect is complicated in that the images that she perceives are not merely coherent shapes; they are indeterminate, molecular, and in constant movement and variation: "we go from total, objective perception which is indistinguishable from the thing, to a subjective perception which is distinguished from it by simple elimination or subtraction."[80] There is more to the movement-image than the process of subtracting what does not interest the viewer. Also involved are connections between perception and action whereby the viewer responds by means of "organizing an unexpected response—because it perceived and has received the excitation on a privileged facet, eliminating the remainder. All this amounts to recalling that all perception is sensory-motor."[81] Further, the element that connects the perception-image to the action-image is the affection image that translates how the subject perceives it, or rather experiences itself "from the inside," and it is precisely "in affection that the movement ceases to be that of translation in order to become that of expression."[82]

The affection-image serves to "tear the image away from spatio-temporal coordinates in order to call forth the pure affect as the expressed." In the case of this image, the face (or faciality—that is, other objects in close-up) constitutes a sensory-motor relation to the image and conveys emotional states. However, as David N. Rodowick is quick to point out, Deleuze is not talking about "literal faces" but rather changing emotional states that pass "from one quality to another."[83] The close-up can be a face but it can also be an object or a landscape. What is important is that "What cannot be fully expressed by an action or conflict is experienced as a visceral response, according to the dynamics of action and reaction in the sensory-motor whole. In the latter the affect is abject in the sense of an objectless emotion or feeling. In both cases affect produces a movement whose trajectory cannot be precisely plotted."[84] In this configuration, the diva transports the spectator into the realm of any-space-whatever, producing desire and astonishment.

These early melodramas and their divas are instructive as well for what they have to say about cinema spectators of the time—who they were, what the films assumed about their knowledge and what they liked, and also what they could tolerate. Sorlin reminds us that Italian audiences, like other early national audiences, were "educated" into becoming spectators. The process of film-going was a gradual coming to terms with the magic of cinema, from the early encounters with the mixed media of cinema and the theater, the circus, and magic shows to the longer melodramatic and spectacular historical narratives that assumed prominence in the teens with such films as *Cabiria, Assunta Spina, La caduta di Troia,* and Caserini's *Gli ultimi giorni di Pompeii,* among others.

In relation to the reception of these films, Sorlin cautions us that "We must accept the fact, even if it does not square with our habits, that spectators liked narratives based on major events easily comprehended and remembered, gaps or elisions of minor incidents or even of explanations did not perturb them, and they thoroughly enjoyed the magnificence of the outdoor pictures, the skill in staging massive scenes and the art of the actors."[85] In short, audiences were receptive to and familiar with the "theatricality," the grandiose narratives and style of the films: "Enjoying tear-jerkers was a cultural attitude."[86] This "cultural attitude" depended on what Antonio Gramsci has termed the "common sense of folklore." This folklore is composed of "various strata, the fossilized ones which reflect conditions of past life and are therefore conservative and reactionary, and those which consist of a series of innovations, often creative and progressive, determined spontaneously by forms and conditions of life which are in the process of developing and which are in contradiction to or simply different from the morality of the governing strata."[87]

Popular culture drew unashamedly on residues of the past but shaped these according to the tastes of the new media and exigencies of modern life, much as television would do in the 1960s. The melodramas that elevated *Divismo*, rather than subjugating their audiences to a monolithic sense of the ideology of nationalism, were more complex: they were educating audiences to the dramatic changes being wrought by the growth of a mass visual culture that could plunder all aspects of history, art, and politics, and the diva was the emblematic figure in this transformation. Thus, it seems counter-productive to argue either for or against the idea that Italian cinema was already inherently a nationalist medium, or, conversely, merely an escapist opiate of the masses. Indeed, the cinema was intimately tied to a new politics of style and vision that eclectically incorporated nationalist images, conceptions of power identified with images of masculine leadership, virility, and power, and the figure of the diva as a disturbing site for conflicting values about modernity.[88] *Divismo*, with its highly theatrical acting, could not help but suffer from dramatic changes effected by the institutionalization of the fascist regime, the impact of Hollywood on popular taste, shrinking box office receipts, and the technological and social effects of sound on film, as well as other modernizing trends in the culture. The world of the diva gave way to the more familiar world of stardom in which stars fell out of the heavens and became automata, reproducible and substitutable, giving rise to a new politics of style in the 1930s and early 1940s.

The Stars Talk

Telephone. His voice makes him visible.

Bresson, *Notes on Cinematography*

Off-screen: From *Divismo* to Stardom

If the Italian cinema in the early years of the twentieth century had been influential at home and abroad, by the end of the second decade it had gone into eclipse and with it the world of the earlier divas.[1] The types of successful film produced during the early teens—the historical dramas, melodramas, and comedies—had become formulaic and did not address the changing tastes of audiences. Not only had the heyday of *Divismo*, with its emotionally charged narratives, been devastatingly expensive thanks to the excessive salaries demanded by the divas, but films of this type were no longer successful at the box office. The 1930s witnessed transformations from *Divismo* to stardom coinciding with cultural and political events, not the least of which was the increasing growth of fascism as a regime that was to affect the production and reception of cinema. Technical facilities were in need of upgrading.[2] More urgently, the industry was in need of reorganization. The coming of sound on film produced a gradual reorganization of the industry. The first complete talking films did not appear until late 1930, though some films in the late 1920s had limited sound tracks restricted to music and descriptive sounds.[3] Hollywood had begun its "long march" into Italy,[4] which was to have a profound effect on the types of films produced, and hence on the kinds of stars that emerged during the 1930s and 1940s. The threats of Hollywood, of modernized technical resources, or of shrinking exports were not, as has been assumed, the major source of crisis in the industry, but, as Pierre Sorlin indicates, the crisis was generated by unwise economic practices: "One of the structural weaknesses of the peninsula . . . was its deficiency of short-term capital."[5]

Attempts were made in the late 1920s to recover the industry through the formation of the *Unione Cinematografica Italiana* (UCI), which was to serve as a means of floating loans, regularizing investment in production through the purchase of smaller failing companies, and acquiring certain artists. Unfortunately, this attempt failed. Directors deserted to other countries, as did technicians. The UCI continued to turn out "the same old rubbish."[6] Remakes and lavish spectacles were the order of the day. To counter the retrograde policies of the UCI, Stefano Pittaluga (1887–1931), a producer and distributor, founded an organization to act as a controlling body for the film industry: the *Ente nazionale per la cinematografia*, under the auspices of the fascist regime. Pittaluga was also charged with distributing the films of LUCE (*L'unione cinematocrafica educativa*), a state-sponsored organization that produced documentaries, newsreels, and scientific, historical, and patriotic films. Overall, the precarious situation of Italian cinema did not substantially improve financially until the mid-1930s.

Among the changes witnessed in the role of media in the 1930s, radio was to play a significant role. While radio broadcasting was introduced in 1924, it was not until the 1930s that the medium gradually became more influential, though still "by 1930 there were only 100,000 radio sets among the forty million Italians."[7] By the mid-1930s, radio technology was an increasingly dominant force serving the regime and also playing a role in gradually altering the social structure of everyday life within and beyond the ideological pressures of fascism. While the regime placed a high priority on radio transmission, the radio was initially not a "household item," though the Dopolavoro (OND), the organization devoted to the development of tourism and leisure as a means of utilizing technology for managing workers, especially during their non-working hours, sought to encourage the low-cost production and circulation of radios.[8] The radio was used in schools for educational purposes and for mass communication in rural areas.[9] Audiences were thus becoming acclimatized to popular cultural forms including music, plays, and serial dramas. Equally important was the effect that the sound technology had on cinema, since technicians gradually learned to develop styles that relied entirely on sound, and particularly the voice.[10]

The "acousmatic image" is a "a sound that is heard without its cause or source being seen. . . . When the acousmatic presence is a voice, and especially when this voice has not been visualized—that is when we cannot connect it to a face, we get a special being, a kind of talking and acting shadow."[11] This hearing image is generative of a relation to an invisible figure that is highly affective, a remote and powerful being, and an ambiguous spiritual entity. The talkies, however, restored "voices to bodies," providing the illusion "that the body and voice cohere," while, in fact, the grafting of the two via synchronization is arbitrary.[12] Synchronization became a critical, not ancillary, ingredient of the medium, altering modes of acting and thereby enhancing or diminishing physical appearance, augmenting or contracting the sense of space, introducing new and specific traits unique to the star figure (e.g., vocalization), and creating through the artifice of synchronization an effect of greater naturalness.[13]

Other attributes of modernity became apparent in the cinema. In his discussion of *La telefonista* (1931), James Hay sheds light on a taken-for-granted image in these 1930s Italian films, calling attention particularly to another acoustic technology—the telephone. The telephone is not merely another decorative visual appurtenance belonging to modernity but a meaningful appurtenance of the *mise-en-scène* of a mediated world that marks significant technological and cultural transformations in the creation and reception of images. The relationship of the telephone to the cinema has far-reaching implications for rearticulating "various scales of social space—regional, urban, domestic space—and defining new relationships between public and private, civic and leisure spheres,"[14] and changing conceptions of national identity. This telephonic technology affected the image and performance of the star, highlighting her virtual entrapment within the cinematic medium, as this chapter recounts. Cinema offered diegetic and non-diegetic images that were instrumental in providing reflections on its status as a technology and insights into the contradictory conditions of modern life under fascism that were to transform Italian culture well after the demise of the regime in 1945.

With the coming of sound on film, already-existing economic crises in the industry intensified, though there were some interesting and successful films thanks to experiments with the medium characterized by the innovative work of such directors as Alessandro Blasetti, Mario Camerini, and Goffredo Alessandrini.[15] Filmmaking improved through further efforts at centralization, rationalization, investment, and technological improvement. New cinematic and narrative techniques became evident in the production of musicals, comedies, melodramas, historical films, biopics, and fables that became identified with types of stars different from those of the silent cinema. As the decade progressed, Hollywood films played a crucial, though not exclusive, role in the formation of stars[16] that were tied largely to genre production. The films had a "modern" look. There was an emphasis on tensions between city and country life evident in the films of Mario Camerini and Alessandro Blasetti. The automobile, the department store, and forms of leisure life figured prominently, as did images of peasants and workers. While aristocrats and the rich had not disappeared from the narratives, they were often presented in critical fashion. Blasetti's *Terra madre* (Mother Earth, 1931) starred Leda Gloria as a loyal and devoted peasant woman in contrast to decadent Isa Pola as an upper-class city woman. Camerini's comedies introduced new male and female stars in an urban context as they sought to find their way in the challenging, if not threatening, world of the modern city (e.g., *Rotaie* [The Rails, 1929–31] and *Gli uomini che mascalzoni* [Men, What Rascals! 1932]). The films occasionally adopt a fusion of fiction and documentary.[17] Among the films that introduced new faces, *La signora di tutti* (Everybody's Woman, 1934) established Isa Miranda as a major star and is an investigation into the birth of a star (in contrast to the diva of the teens).[18]

The cinema of the 1930s has surprises in store for those who expect that it is a simple reflection of the public policies, ideology, and rhetoric of fascism. To judge by the majority of films produced, the emphasis was on producing profitable entertainment films with only oblique political reverberations.[19] By the late 1930s and the early 1940s, certain films and writings on cinema began to assume a more critical posture toward conventional forms of filmmaking, if not toward fascist culture. Directed by filmmakers Renato Castellani, Ferdinando Maria Poggioli, Luigi Chiarini, and Mario Soldati, these films were dubbed "calligraphic" for their highly ornate and formalistic style.[20] Reliant on earlier literary texts, particularly nineteenth-century novels in the cases of Fogazzaro's *Malombra* and *Piccolo mondo antico* and Luigi Capuana's *Gelosia*, the films portray a hermetic world where landscape and décor are characters as much as the actor.[21] In their literariness, their antiquarian attitude toward history, their remoteness from overt politics, and their painterly treatment of décor, the calligraphers offered a dark and somber portrait of a world inhabited by obsessed, somnambulistic, and violent characters.[22] The films employed established stars and familiar character actors of the 1930s and 1940s, but revealed significant departures from the cinema of *Divismo* in their styles and in the portraits that they offered of their male and female stars.

Star Making, Camerini Style: Vittorio De Sica

Vittorio De Sica, a stage actor, became a major star of the early Italian sound cinema, and his *Gli uomini che mascalzoni* (Men, What Rascals! 1932) and the later
Il signor Max (1937) are seminal films for understanding the rise of the popular
Italian cinema comedy and its emergent star icons in the pre–World War II years.
"Without Vittorio De Sica," writes Pierre Sorlin, "would comedies have met with
such a unanimous approval? I doubt it."[23] Directed by Mario Camerini, *Gli uomini* appears at the beginning of Italian sound cinema, and, as such, its style provides a retrospective as well as prospective look on cultural continuities and dis-
continuities during the fascist period. Camerini, a major figure in 1930s cinema,
directed such popular comedies and melodramas as *T'amerò sempre* (I'll Love You
Always, 1933), *Darò un milione* (I'd Give a Million, 1936), *Il signor Max* (1937), *I
grandi magazzini* (Department Stores, 1939), and *Batticuore* (Heartbeat, 1939). He
was responsible for launching major Italian stars of the 1930s and 1940s such as
Assia Noris and Vittorio De Sica. His comedies and melodramas self-consciously
highlighted the nature and effects of cinematic technology, revealing a tension
between the public spectacles of fascism and mundane images of quotidian
existence.[24]

Gli uomini is instructive about the eclectic tendencies of a popular cinema
of stars. Popular cinema acknowledges and seeks to reconcile differences among
social classes, generations, genders, and regions without eradicating obvious distinctions. Foregrounding the technological instruments of modernity—trains,
trams, automobiles, airplanes, telephones, and occasionally television—this cinema exploited the potential of media to shape a mass society through spectacle.
After the commercial disasters of the late teens and early twenties, the film industry was in search of audiences through the creation of commercial cinematic
forms that could cut across different social groups, regions, and generations, and
rural and urban spectators. The Cines Studio, founded in Rome during the silent
era and headed for a brief time in the late 1930s by major exhibitor-turned-
producer Stefano Pittaluga, moved to the forefront of this attempt to restructure
and modernize the film industry. Cines was to boast a group of experienced directors, such as Alessandro Blasetti and Mario Camerini, and skilled technicians,
such as Massimo Terzano, Gastone Medin, and Ivo Perilli, who must be credited
for enhancing the look of the actors and the cinematic world they inhabited, contributing to the emergence of a form of star "system." Following Pittaluga's un-
timely death in 1931, Emilio Cecchi assumed the position of artistic director in
1932 at Cines and worked to raise the quality of its production.[25]

Though general output of films was not large, Cines, in the early 1930s,
experimented with genres and sound in such films as Blasetti's *La tavola dei
poveri* (The Poor People's Table, 1932) and 1860 (1934), Baldassare Negroni's

Due cuori felici (Two Happy Hearts, 1932), Goffredo Alessandrini's romantic comedy *La segretaria privata* (1932), Giudo Brignone's operatic *La Wally* (1932), and Mario Camerini's *Gli uomini che mascalzoni* (1932). The films cannot be characterized as exemplifying a unique "national style." This cinema was eclectic, drawing variously on Hollywood, Hungarian, German, Austrian, and even Soviet styles but also realism and modernism.[26] But it was evident that the cinema was in search of styles that could integrate the technical and narrative potential of visual image and sound, and Camerini's *Gli uomini che mascalzoni* is an exemplary text with which to explore this enterprise. Sound on film, particularly through the insertion of song, was an ally in the transformation of film narration and in the increased popular reception for Italian films. For example, *Gli uomini*'s theme song, "Parlami d'amore Mariù," written by Neapolitan composer Cesare Bixio, became a hit, helping to create connections between popular cinema and the music industry and contributing to De Sica's emergence as a film star of romantic comedy. In its treatment of the protagonists and in their relation to a contemporary milieu, the film offers numerous clues to the formation of stars different from those of the silent cinema.

Gli uomini, a comedy, features Bruno (Vittorio De Sica), a chauffeur who pursues Mariuccia (Lia Franca), a saleswoman who lives with her taxi-driver father, Tadini (Cesare Zoppetti). The film focuses on the tensions and dilemmas generated by the economic and social aspirations of its working-class characters. Both Bruno and Mariuccia appear to be driven by conflicting desires: social ambition and money, but also romance. Through the characters' struggles to mediate between the pressures of an older traditional society and contemporary urban life, *Gli uomini* highlights a fascination with modernity and mobility, especially in its focus on the automobile, the telephone, and images of technological wares displayed at the Milan Trade Fair. Furthermore, the film features contemporary working-class characters that struggle to survive economically in the modern metropolis. In contrast to his counterparts in the cinema of *Divismo*, De Sica is neither a masochistic doomed lover nor an incarnation of a heroic strong man, but a young man whose qualities reside in the ability of his exceptional physical traits and acting talents to convey the illusion of ordinariness, one of the contributions of De Sica and Camerini to the emerging stars of the 1930s.[27]

Like Frank Capra's films, as Gianfranco Casadio has noted, Camerini's films were "dunked in realism, populism, and an ingenious sentimentalism or, better, with optimism."[28] Hollywood played a critical role in the composition of Italian films though the choice of narratives, the youthful appearance of stars, the uses of sound, and the diegetic and extra-diegetic highlighting of technologies, but Hollywood was not the only source of inspiration in shaping the star persona. Europe offered influential models evident in Camerini's emulation of the films of René Clair and, to a lesser extent, Ernst Lubitsch. Camerini's urban landscapes derive from yet another tradition, that of the silent era and the experimental "city films" of Walter Ruttmann, Jean Vigo, and Dziga Vertov, which focused on traffic, commerce, industry, leisure, architecture, people on the move, and contrasts between stasis and movement. Camerini's actors maintained silent cinema's emphasis on gesture, physiognomy, and movement. *Gli uomini* offers a view of emergent stardom based on mundane and demotic images, looking backward to the comedy of early cinema but altered in narrative fashion to allow for more realistic situations and acting.

Critics have struggled to characterize the style of *Gli uomini*, describing it variously as a film of escapism, subtle accommodation to the status quo of the fascist regime, or as precursor to neorealism along with *Assunta Spina* (1915) and the later *Quattro passi tra le nuvole* (A Walk among the Clouds, 1942). Comparisons of *Gli uomini* with neorealism extend to the use of location shooting—the tavern at Lago Maggiore and the Fiera di Milano (Milan Trade Fair)—and to his use of actors. According to one commentator, Camerini's choice of actors was based on "realist" criteria. Vittorio De Sica was a theater and variety actor when the film was made and Lia Franca was an unknown actress selected because she was not "too actress-y an actress." Camerini wanted to "give a feeling of truth," which is why his preference for working-class characters has been cited as a neorealist precursor.[29] In any case, it is evident that Camerini was experimenting with less exotic theatrical actors. However, Franca and De Sica's performances are also indebted to silent film poetics. The images "speak" through the actors' gestures. Sound functions as more than support; it is a co-presence, a partner with the visual image, and a means of overcoming linguistic and local differences among audiences. In its camera work and editing, uses of continuity, and selection of actors, the film was a harbinger of forms of stardom to come.

Describing his film as "a very simple story, a human comedy," Camerini saw *Gli uomini* as "different from the current ones in Italy and abroad with their complicated stories."[30] Careful and detailed attention was paid to the framing of the characters' physical movements and to their milieu, and through close-ups to the emotional nuances of face and body. For example, taxi-driver Tadini (Cesare Zoppetti) has just finished his night shift and is ready to return home. This scene stresses milieu but not as mere background; it is inextricably tied to the identity, movement, and actions of a character identified with the urban and working-class life of Milan. The camera tracks the man as he enters and exits the office of the taxi company, gets a drink at a local bar, and takes a bottle with him as he leaves. He returns to his home, where he takes a drink in his kitchen before awakening his daughter, who is asleep in the next room, his movements suggesting that father and daughter have repeated this ritual often. Also visible is that this is a motherless household: its focus is on a paternal and recognizable "ordinary" world, an instance of what Buccheri terms "piccolo realismo."[31] Conflict and reconciliation depend on physically attractive and enigmatic protagonists operating in a recognizable landscape. Accordingly, the opening scene sets up a chain of incidents culminating in a meeting between Bruno (Vittorio De Sica) and Mariuccia (Lia Franca) that takes place outdoors at a newspaper kiosk. As in the later *T'amerò sempre* and *Il signor Max*, the kiosk is a place where different classes meet. Set amidst the city traffic, communication is exchanged via newspapers and chance encounters among people. While dialogue is minimal in these early scenes, the film establishes its characters in the urban milieu of the street, which will then be set in contrast to rustic scenes.

One of the most cited moments involves a love-struck Bruno who, smitten by Mariuccia, trails her on his bicycle as she walks and then rides a tram to work. De Sica's pantomime and gesticulations from the bicycle are intercut with images of Mariuccia at the window of the tram, she functioning as a spectator and on-screen audience to his performance, and he, in turn, focusing on her. The scene emphasizes the act of looking as the camera captures images of the couple with no dialogue exchanged. Bruno's pursuit of the young woman in the spirit of the comic chase scenes of silent cinema serves as a pretext to explore the potential of the camera and editing to capture De Sica's bodily presence and movement: Bruno on his bicycle is tracked by the camera as he seeks to maintain his speed in following Mariuccia on the tram; the camera also captures his obliviousness to the obstacles along his path as he concentrates on the "chase," and Mariuccia's amusement (along with the movie spectator's) in watching Bruno bumping into garbage and being sprayed by water. Franca's appearance radiates youth, energy, and playfulness. She is not glamorous; her costuming and makeup are unpretentious, and she is identified with other working-class women, underscoring her "ordinariness." De Sica's youthful appearance, too, his energetic movement, and his proneness to catastrophe renders the actor credible as "one of us," a major distinction between *Divismo* and stardom. Furthermore, the film provides a guide to the artifice entailed in the formation of a star, establishing those characteristics identified with De Sica's future stardom.

The comedy features encounters and collisions with machines: Bruno's frantic chase of Mariuccia on a tram, his reckless automobile driving as he races to return to Mariuccia in a tavern, the traffic jam he causes by refusing to drive his new employer's car, and a "collision" with play cars in an amusement park. The humor does not merely reside in a physical clash with the machine so much as it serves character and narration, establishing relations of power among the protagonists that are reinforced through the relay of gazes.[32] The machine (which he does not own but covets) is what identifies Bruno as being modern, of humble economic means, and is another mark of his ordinariness. Machines both separate and bring Bruno and Mariuccia together as he tries to impress her with his status as possessor of a luxurious vehicle that actually belongs to his employer. The car ultimately becomes the bond between himself and his future father-in-law, Tadini, a taxi driver, and this machine is also linked to other modern machines in the film. For example, what enables Bruno to make use of the car is another technological and communicational gadget—the telephone. When his employer telephones to see if his car is ready, Bruno misinforms him that the work is not complete, thus keeping the car at his disposal. And, ultimately, the cinema machine, like the telephone, highlights a tension between the real and the imaginary world essential to the functioning of stardom.

Thus, the spectator embarks on a double voyage—the movement of the car through space from the city to the country, and a movement of perception that juxtaposes fantasy and reality, work and play. Prepared to meet Mariuccia in grand style, Bruno drives to the shop where she works, and this episode provides images of the urban world, its architecture, streets, and signs of advertising that come to be associated with the characters. Bruno entices Mariuccia to join him, suggesting a ride to the country. The ride itself is another indication of the film's attention to milieu. The montage reveals images of Lake Maggiore, the shoreline, the open space of the countryside, and a tavern set in a bucolic landscape. This scene portrays rural life through the eyes of an urban spectator and emphasizes images of leisure and entertainment, eating, singing, and dancing as opposed to the routine world of work. The couple's encounter in the tavern, with Bruno's serenading Mariuccia and their harmonious dancing movements, offers a utopian image of pleasure, congenial to the formation of stardom. However, as inevitable in comedy, this idyllic moment is disrupted as the film adds to the chain of incidents that will separate the lovers before finally uniting them. In the inevitable play of chance endemic to popular storytelling, Bruno's employer's wife appears, seeking entertainment with her own social group. Tiring of the situation and discovering her car, she connives to have Bruno drive her back to town. Maintaining his impersonation, Bruno presents himself to Mariuccia as a gentleman come to the assistance of a "lady," promising to return after his benevolent deed. One of the consistent characteristics of De Sica's star persona, apparent in this early Camerini film, is his identification with role-playing and masquerade.

Bruno leaves the tavern and hectically drives his employer's wife to the city. In contrast to the tavern scene, a montage of images involves accelerated movement through close-ups of the speedometer and wheels of the car, suggesting the circularity that drives the narrative. Motion and speed are highlighted until Bruno collides, not with another car, but with a peasant's cart. Not only does this "collision" frustrate his plans to return to the inn and to Mariuccia, it also reinforces a contrast between the different rhythms of country and city life as well as social distinctions between the wealthy woman, working-class Bruno and Mariuccia, and the peasant in his cart. Bruno's "masquerade" produces a series of situations that hinder the possibility of union with Mariuccia and that must ultimately be overcome. Mariuccia, left alone in the tavern, does not have the money to pay for food nor a way to return home. Since she is concerned to be home before her father returns from his night shift, the proprietor graciously invites her to spend the night, and reassures her that her son will get her home on time. The narrative movement, like the rotation of a wheel, returns her to Tadini's lodging, but with a difference. The repetitive pattern of the life of father and daughter is ruptured, producing another collision as Tadini discovers Mariuccia's deception and lectures her on sexual morality. Not only has this family relationship become problematic, but Bruno's situation has also become precarious: he has been fired from his job.

In a new job, Bruno is exposed in his subaltern role when his wealthy employer offers Mariuccia a ride and Bruno is the chauffeur. When she sits in the rear of the automobile with the rich man, she is framed through the rear view mirror as Bruno nurses his jealousy. The images of him looking at the couple through the mirror reinforce the film's preoccupation with expressive "framing" and "mirroring" through two optical apparatuses, the car mirror and the camera. Camerini's comedies are often quite reflexive, playing humorously with the medium and its capacity to reveal or impersonate, and both questioning and reinforcing the artifice of cinema. The trope of collision is again introduced and, once again, associated with the automobile. Bruno stops the car in the middle of traffic and shouts at his employer to drive the car himself, castigating Mariuccia for accepting the ride and accusing her of being interested in rich men. As a star maker, Camerini introduces through his direction many of the ingredients that unite genre forms to stars. Through the interplay of disruption and equilibrium, De Sica and Franca metamorphose from the familiar and banal to the extraordinary, maintaining a necessary tension between artifice and reality.

The climax of the film takes place at an industrial fair in Milan (La Fiera Campionaria) where, after being fired from her prior job, Mariuccia has found work. The fair is a culmination of the many images of industry and locomotion inserted throughout earlier moments in the film. Here one sees an abundance of images of movement: bicycles, merry-go-round, and industrial machinery—a hub of activity. Bruno again encounters Mariuccia, who, upon discovering that Bruno is out of work, agrees to find him a job at the Fair as a tour guide, but Mariuccia accepts an invitation from the industrialist who agreed to the hiring. Once again, a rich man is interposed between the couple, and, once again, the prospect of their uniting is retarded as the element of theatricality is emphasized. Bruno's role as tour guide highlights the attractions of industrial/urban life and is tied to the ongoing aspects of the splitting of his character. Wearing a megaphone (a reminder of the enhanced vocalization of his voice and of sound amplification) and looking slightly ridiculous, he calls attention to the various mechanical apparatuses. At the same time, he is a guide to a cinematic carnival, intertwining industrial and film technology. The siren marking the end of Bruno's workday is a reminder that work, including the work of the film itself, is determined by time and by the necessity of an ending. The carnivalesque restaurant scene is theatrical melodrama as Bruno affects indifference, and Mariuccia conveys strong affect. The performances take place in public settings where casual witnesses become involved as observers, eavesdroppers, and surrogates for the film's audience.

The requisite "closure" returns the figure of the taxi-driver father to the narrative. The reintroduction of Tadini, playing the stern but benevolent patriarch, is not to be taken simplistically as endorsement of the fascist regime's emphasis on the power of the patriarchal leader. Tadini, the taxi-driver, like a surrogate for the director, moves the narrative forward and drives it toward closure. Fortuitously, the two lovers get into taxi driven by Tadini, and the film undergoes a further revolution in the repositioning of the characters. The narrative has been propelled by a circular movement, like the wheels of a car or the machinery at the fair. Like a ratchet, each segment that pushes the movement of the narrative forward also returns it to earlier episodes: the scenes in Tadini's lodging, the restaurant scenes, the various car episodes, each recollecting an earlier situation and, finally, moving forward in such a way so as to enable a new situation to emerge through repetition and difference. In this form of narration, the film joins with the cinema of the pre–World War II era, expressing a modest faith in the power of action to alter situations through the potential union between man and machine. The doubling of the narrative with the cinematic apparatus complicates the audience's relations to the visual image and to sound. In repeating in reverse movement the earlier scenes of the film, the film introduces difference into sameness through consistently highlighting the tension between theatrical illusion and the semblance of everyday life without finally "resolving" one at the expense of the other. *Gli uomini* exposes its strategies in the interests of dramatizing for its audiences the power of cinema in its illusory dimensions: "appearance" relies, in this film especially but also in others of the 1930s, on allowing the Italian audience to gain a sense of how the cinematic machine, like other machines, has introduced new and contradictory forms of perception into modern life and how stars are its agents.

Films such as *Gli uomini* are not the mere products of a "dream factory" and of commercial cinema's tendency toward escapism. They offer the illusion of a world wherein characters act *and* react so as to modify their milieu and their relation to other characters. Through De Sica's role, *Gli uomini che mascalzoni* created a dynamic sense of possibility and optimism, establishing a relationship with the audience through forms of spectacle largely realized through

De Sica's impersonations, which combine the familiar and the extraordinary. Highly dependent on self-conscious forms of artifice, Camerini's films playfully foreground the illusory strategies of the cinematic medium in accessible images ultimately appealing to the spectator. A film such as *Gli uomini* invites reflection on the complexity of society and of the spectacle as a medium that promises a modest mediation between the "tensions created by modernization and the ambivalence of Italy's middle and working classes toward their changing cultural environment."[33] De Sica's film persona captures this ambivalence.

De Sica's roles in *Gli uomini* and in subsequent Camerini-directed films such as *Il signor Max* and *Darò un milione* solidified his romantic comedy persona. His popularity derived from his versatility as romantic lead and as singer in ways that caused him to be compared to Cary Grant. De Sica often impersonated a benign, slightly awkward, but charming rogue who, after being tamed by circumstances, finally becomes a respectable member of the petite bourgeoisie. He differed from emerging Italian stars such as Amedeo Nazzari, who was identified with melodramas and with historical and adventure films, and in publicity releases and reviews was compared to Errol Flynn. Also, in contrast to Fosco Giachetti, a popular version of the fascist "strong man" in the style of 1930s cinema who was identified with a stiff bodily deportment and a disciplined moral stance, De Sica's youthful and engaging image was capable of appealing to different female and male, middle- and working-class segments of the audience. His screen image was enhanced by his ability to play double roles, as a working-class figure with aspirations to the high life and to pleasure rather than to work, or as a millionaire masquerading as a worker as in *Darò un milione*. He may have been typed as "a sort of ordinary Joe, the typical middle-class or working-class guy,"[34] but his frequent impersonations of a wealthy or upper-class figure helped to endow his stardom with more protean characteristics. As a petit bourgeois, he conveyed the "provincial customs of the small (and grand) Italian bourgeoisie of the 1930s."[35] Quintessential to his popularity were his crooked smile, courteousness, aura of benevolence, and worldliness, as well as his identification with the street life of Naples. Under Camerini's direction, he emerged as an ideal type who incarnated the Italian everyman with sufficient complexity so as also to reveal his pretensions and discontents, so integral to the essence of his stardom.

The doubling and impersonation with which De Sica became identified is satirically dramatized in *Il signor Max*, which featured him in the two roles of Gianni, a newsvendor, and Mr. Max, an aristocrat, affording him the opportunity to spoof and expose both working-class aspirations to wealth and luxury and the pretensions and vanity of the upper classes. Briefly, Gianni on vacation becomes entranced with a leisurely and extravagant lifestyle and with the charms of Lady Paola (Rubi Dalma). In pursuit of her, he squanders his money gambling and buying expensive flowers, undertakes lessons in horseback riding, tennis, golf, and bridge,

2.1. Vittorio De Sica impersonating an "Italian Everyman" in *Darò un milione* with Assia Noris. *Courtesy of Museum of Modern Art Film Stills Collection.*

assumes affectations in behavior and speech, and dresses like an English gentleman in dark sweater, neatly creased trousers, and an ascot at the neck, or in evening dress. As Mr. Max, De Sica is able to convince Lady Paola through his good looks and charm that he is a member of her class, but his acting is sufficiently awkward and self-conscious to communicate to the audience his lack of credentials for the role. His doubling, rather than relying on overacting, depends on tensions, potential slips, and concealments in his moving between two worlds until he reaches the limits of his knowledge of and finally desire for the upper-class lifestyle.

In his life as Gianni, he moves between his place of work on the street and the unassuming quarters of his family to the ship, the train, and the hotel, thus forcing a class distinction that emerges from the landscape. The comedy arises from De Sica's communicating Max's ineptness in playing the games of Lady Paola and her friends but also from observing their indifference to affairs of the heart. The life of the wealthy is portrayed as highly mobile, ultra-"modern," and identified with travel on ship and train, with hotels rather than apartments, and with theatrical poses, while Gianni's life revolves around the urban space of the newsstand, his uncle's apartment, and the modest forms of leisure identified with the working classes. He dresses modestly and is identified with the virtues of family, sobriety, and collective social rituals associated with the Dopolavoro (the fascist after-work organization). As part of his desired ascent into the upper reaches of society, he does not disdain to exploit servant Lauretta (Assia Noris) to gain access to Lady Paola. However, his roguishness is never treated as malevolent, since he becomes the butt of both his own schemes and his attempts at overcoming them. His transfer of affection to Lauretta has an interesting twist that enables him to maintain the upper hand when he withholds from her his identity as Max at a time when a confession might be anticipated.

If judged solely by a narrative that involves misrecognition, the uneven course of romance, and then the "happy ending" with the protagonist restored to his proper place in the social order, the film is indeed formulaic, even "escapist." Given the abundant revaluations of the cinema of the era between politics and profit, it is no longer tenable to argue for a cinema that "reflected" a unified ideology and style consonant with fascism or with escapism via Hollywood. A view of the range of stars during the sound era reveals variety in narrative forms, in acting styles, and in the uses of landscape, rural and urban—and a surprising variety in their relation to reigning conceptions of culture under fascism. Audiences of the time were becoming accustomed to and were fascinated by the star-driven world of commercial cinema, its images of modernity, technology, mobility, commodity pleasures, youthful energy, and social class tensions. *Gli uomini che mascalzoni* and *Il signor Max* offered one form of masculine stardom of the era, one in which De Sica's acting, his physiognomy, his lanky body, his crooked and dazzling smile, and his familiar speaking (and sometimes singing, as in *Gli uomini* and Palermi's *Napoli d'altri tempi*) voice become markers of the star quality that endeared him to female viewers.

De Sica, thanks especially to his work with Camerini, offered an image of masculinity, or rather two images of masculinity, that addressed the mundane and the cosmopolitan, the everyday world and that of fantasy. He was largely identified with the urban milieu and his doubled images of masculinity captured ambivalence not only about "modernity," but also about traditional forms of social life and representations of action in cinema. In most of his roles for Camerini, he was conflicted about his identity, prone to accident and error, and physically vulnerable but resourceful. De Sica was largely a romantic comedy actor, and in his roles he rebels against but finally accommodates to events. As "aristocrat" and as "worker," he learns to adopt the right tone to respond to situations. The humor and pathos arise from difficulties he encounters in his various and competing roles. He not only impersonates different identities but also becomes the agent, as in many of Camerini's other comedies, to share with the audience the role of cinema as the instrument *par excellence* for creating illusions concerning identity.

Italian stardom is often connected to the star's identification with specific regional and urban locales, and Italian audiences (and perhaps also Italian-Americans) regarded De Sica as belonging, along with other comedy stars of the time (e.g., the De Filippo brothers and Totò), to the regional world of Naples. Furthermore, De Sica's star image is augmented by his role as director, adding to the reputation of his versatility as actor, director, and distinctive personality that would increase rather than diminish during the post–World War II era. In the early 1940s, he turned to directing with such films as *Rose scarlatte* (Red Roses, 1940), *Maddalena, zero in condotta* (Maddalena, Zero for Conduct, 1940), and *Teresa Venerdì* (1941), comedies in which he also starred. In *Un garibaldino al convento* (A Garibaldian in the Convent, 1942), he elected to play a supporting role. His penchant for impersonation continued throughout his career to be a key aspect of his persona. In *Maddalena* he plays three roles, grandfather, father, and son, and Roberto Rossellini would later exploit his skill in playing multiple roles in *Il Generale della Rovere* (1959, see chapter 3).

The abiding constituents of De Sica's stardom are indeed indebted to his work with Camerini, revealing the role of the director as an important, though obviously not the only, determining ingredient in the creation of a star. Camerini's comedies starring De Sica met several requirements: They promoted new images of actors and acting. They offered innovative and sophisticated uses of sound and visual imagery. Above all, they engaged with critical issues concerning the cinema as an instrument of modernity, foregrounding problems of identity, belief, and reality and illusion. In the comedies that followed *Gli uomini che mascalzoni—Il signor Max, Darò un milione* (1936) and *I grandi magazzini* (1939)—the paring of De Sica with Assia Noris further enhanced the stardom of each. Their films together reiterate the motif of masquerade, duplication, and spectatorship that contributed to a bonding between actor and viewer, animated by a dual recognition of the star as both resemblance and simulation.

Camerini, Comedy, and Assia Noris

Assia Noris might be considered another cinematic version of the star as "everybody's woman," and her screen image, thanks to her work with Camerini, tended largely in the direction of comedy. She is not an embodiment of stereotypic Italian identity, though her image does express a type of ingénue popular in 1930s cinematic comedy, identified with Hollywood and as northern European. Born in Russia of an aristocratic family, Noris first appeared in Italian cinema in 1932. Her first film for Camerini was *Giallo* (1933), and, though during the 1930s and early 1940s she made films with other directors, her greatest successes were with Camerini. Noris did not have a long career in cinema: she only made two films after the demise of the regime, but her image contributed to expanding and diversifying the forms of stardom of the era. Her marriage to Camerini lasted seven years, and the films she made for him were the quintessence of a certain form of light comedy. "With her light blonde hair," Noris was "the very image of a cinema of filmic artifices" that generated interest in popular stars.[36]

Her role in *Il signor Max* confirmed her as a star who specialized in domestic comedy. Blonde, slight, she largely played the role of ingénue. Compared to and billed as a Carole Lombard type, she could do screwball comedy, as evident in her role in Camerini's *Batticuore*. She could play saleswomen, maids, and governesses as well as upper-class and aristocratic women (e.g., in *Una donna tra due mondi* and *Dora Nelson*). In *Il signor Max*, her character is set in contrast to Rubi Dalma's sophisticated upper-class role. While Noris's aristocratic background played a role in publicity about her, in this film she plays a modest and wide-eyed daughter of the petite bourgeoisie. Her costuming and makeup is modest, and she is filmed in close-ups that highlight the unblemished quality of her skin and her sparkling eyes. Unlike Isa Miranda, Noris was generally filmed as neither statuesque nor glamorous but rather as a "wholesome" image of femininity.

In her role as Lauretta in *Il signor Max*, her character serves to expose the hypocrisy and vanity of her upper-class employers and to undermine the preoccupation with theatricality that Camerini's films spoof. Her popularity is a sign of the transformations wrought in stardom during the fascist era. The dominating image of the diva has receded, if not disappeared, to be replaced by a more familiar and accessible image of stardom reminiscent of Hollywood stars of the era. Her image relies on an appearance of ordinariness and youthfulness. There is nothing highly exaggerated or mysterious about her appearance. Her popularity derives from her own (and her director's) ability to create a character with whom female members of an audience could identify despite, or perhaps because of, her foreign accent.

One of the integral elements of Camerini's films is their self-conscious exploration of theatricality and artifice, and in *Batticuore* Noris plays a dual role that highlights the tension between the artifice of cinema and "reality." As Arlette, Noris is a student of a school for thieves. Upon graduation, she undertakes to put her learned skills into practice, but her first attempt to display her ability as a thief is inept as on an elevator she seeks to steal a man's jeweled tie pin, and she is exposed. The victim of her theft, a count, follows and apprehends her in a movie theater, where a film of Astaire and Rogers mirrors her dilemma. Her "punishment" is to masquerade as an aristocrat. She is to attend a ball where she will blackmail the ambassador of Stivonia. Dressed in an elegant gown bought by the count and reminiscent of Ginger Rogers's attire in the film clip, she is told to dance with Lord Salisbury (John Lodge), a British diplomat, and to steal his watch, which contains a photograph of the ambassador's wife. Lord Salisbury, having seen her remove the photograph from the watch, is determined to discover her identity. She attempts to escape him and seeks refuge in a hotel befitting her assumed upper-class identity, but he follows her. Her excuse for having no luggage prompts him to have a stylish wardrobe sent to the hotel. The two spend time together, and their relationship replays the vicissitudes of scenarios associated with Hollywood roman-tic comedy and culminates with their marriage, celebrated in the presence of members of high society and the school for thieves. While the film adopts the req-uisites of the genre, it is a revelation about stardom, Camerini-style, that capitalizes on Noris's star persona. The enigma of identity is critical to the film and to Noris's image, but the emphasis is on performance as theft. Introducing parallels with Hollywood stars and genres, focusing on photographs as "evidence" of misrepre-sentation, the film presents Noris as a novice in dissimulation. Her role as thief and aristocrat situates her in two worlds, the lower-class world where she is clothed plainly and the world of aristocracy where she dresses like a glamorous Hollywood star. Hence, she appears both commonplace and extraordinary, embodying a major characteristic of stardom (but not *Divismo*), that it is performative and not an essential indicator of identity. The qualities contributing to Noris's stardom are, as in the case of De Sica, a consequence of Camerini's adept direction, if not cyni-cism about cinematic production. Along with publicity about the film and its star, Noris's stardom is indebted to the director's familiarity with the conventions of ro-mantic comedy: its theatricality and artifice as well as his sophisticated reflections on the limitations of the genre. Noris is a "star" pupil not only in the narrative but also in her emulating the star-driven Hollywood comedy of the 1930s with its por-traits of transgressive social class and antagonistic gender roles. More importantly, her persona (via the trope of thievery) is a joke to be shared with the audience. Moreover, the internal audience plays as critical a role in the film as does the extra-filmic viewer in affirming Noris's persona.

Audiences of the time would be familiar with publicity concerning Noris's personal history and might derive pleasure from seeing an aristocrat imperson-ating a lower-class character masquerading as an aristocrat. Camerini was proud that "in a country whose regime boasted of its nationalism and racial su-periority (especially in the late 1930s), an actress who spoke the Italian language faultily could gain the throne of popularity."[37] Her appeal with audiences is validated by her being voted in these years the most popular female star ahead of competitors Alida Valli and Isa Miranda.[38] Her changing identities belong to a carnivalesque world in which social class and economic positions can be temporarily transcended. Furthermore, the film's reiterative focus on looking via surveillance by the camera (as in the opening sequences), the introduction of the movie theater, the use of television during the ball scene, and the linking of the narrative transformations to the use of a photograph, finally comes to rest on the figure of Noris. As Arlette, she is the creation of a system and of a director who relies on her physical appearance to perform in protean fashion. Thus, her persona introduces a reflection on cinema as fiction, offering a meditation on the cinematic image as unstable currency in relation to her on-screen creation of the character and her off-screen reputation.

In the same year, 1939, *Dora Nelson* was released, directed by Mario Soldati, who had worked with Camerini. It also starred Noris in a dual role as a shop girl, Pierina, and as a movie star, Dora Nelson. Similarly to Noris's character in *Batticuore*, her character here does not aspire to the upper reaches of the social register but is drawn by coincidence and chance into that milieu. While *Batticuore* does not focus explicitly on stardom, *Dora Nelson* does. As Dora, Noris embodies the inflated, passionate, and transgressive behavior identified with *Divismo*. Dora, like Noris in real life, is a former Russian aristocrat, a willful princess who cannot accommodate to bourgeois existence. The film begins with the convention of a film within a film, of which Dora is the star. Dora is given to tantrums, and when she walks off the movie set the director is forced to find a replacement, a familiar device for introducing the future star by means of contrast with a pretentious and temperamental star figure and by calling attention to the "naturalness" of the true star. Thus, the look-alike Pierina is hired to substitute for Dora, and thus the familiar motif of doubling through reflective devices introduces the necessary qualities of sameness and difference, ordinariness and exceptionality. Though in appearance Pierina/Noris resembles the star Dora/Noris, her personality is completely different, reminiscent of her ingénue role as Lauretta in *Il signor Max*. While Dora as diva is temperamental, imperious, smitten with the world of the aristocracy, and hostile to a bourgeois life that entails conjugal responsibilities, Pierina is a loyal, devoted, and maternal figure (as Noris had described herself in interviews despite her numerous marriages).

When Dora runs off on one of her many extra-marital escapades, Pierina is seen by Dora's industrialist husband on the set to which he has come to bring Dora home, and he is struck by her resemblance to his wife. Pierina is asked by him to impersonate Dora for a family celebration of the engagement of his (and Dora's) daughter so as to provide the illusion of gracious and harmonious family life for this festive occasion. Pierina agrees and saves the family, and, as might be predicted, Giovanni, the husband, falls in love with her. Since Giovanni is a married man, Pierina determines to leave him; however, the news arrives that a former husband of Dora, believed dead in a train crash, has reappeared and therefore her marriage to Giovanni has been dissolved. The film ends with Pierina and Giovanni united and riding off together. When they pass a movie set where Dora is making a film, the couple stops and looks, laughs, and rides off.

As is evident, the film capitalizes on the fact that the dual roles assigned to Noris are a caricature of commercial filmmaking and stereotypes of stardom, revealing how the cinema of the 1930s was forging a language that differed from the cinema of *Divismo*. Further, *Dora Nelson* draws on the extra-filmic elements in Noris's life, allowing her to caricature her own role as a star and to inhabit, through Pierina, a less inflated, more commonplace image of a star. Similarly to other Camerini films, this film expresses condescension toward popular cinema as well as toward the upper-class life often conveyed through the so-called "white telephone" films of the 1930s that focused on the foibles of the upper classes. *Dora Nelson* also uses the phenomenon of stardom to puncture the cinema of *Divismo* from the perspective of the emerging cinema of the late 1930s, proffering another more mundane image of cinematic spectacle via stardom. Noris's image is that of a modern star in the Italy of the late 1930s. The film implies an audience familiar with filmic conventions that is able to share in the increased, more "modern" forms of theatricality and fictionalizing of social life.

Dora Nelson was not the first time or the last that Noris was enlisted to play spoiled foreign, upper-class women. In *Una donna tra due mondi* (1936), she plays Miss Daisy Elkins, the American playmate of a Maharajah. In *Voglio vivere con Letizia* (1938), she is the capricious daughter of a once-wealthy family who bridles at a marriage arranged by her mother and designed to restore the family's fortune. The quasi-screwball comedy arises from her misrecognition of the identity of the young man selected to be her husband. He, having hired an affected person to assume his identity, almost succeeds in thwarting the marriage. However, his ruse is finally exposed, and, after Letizia enacts a playful punishment on him, the couple is united. Noris's role in this film evokes similarities to screwball comedy, involving gendered combat, parental obstruction, disguises, deceptions, and counter-deceptions. However, Noris's acting, as directed by Camillo Mastrocinque, lacks the frenetic energy intrinsic to his type of comedy. Noris's role does not actually transgress or unsettle cinematic images relating to social class and family.

Unlike her other roles, where her playfulness is tied to the reflexive character of performance, in this film her persona is somewhat wooden and disingenuous. The kind of artifice associated with her other comic roles is theatrical, often intertextual, and reflexive, and the theatricality serves to confound the boundaries between artifice and reality, cinema and life. In *Voglio vivere con Letizia* (under Mastrocinque's direction) this tension is missing. Her acting appears merely as acting and does not convey to the spectator a shared knowledge of character or role-playing. Her body movements are awkward, and her facial expressions rather bland. Moreover, her outfits are rather dowdy, even nondescript, underscoring that costuming in many films of the era was arbitrary, often left to the actress rather than to a costume designer. In general, unlike those of Isa Miranda, Noris's costumes were quite modest, except in historical films where more expensive costumers were utilized. Noris was not a glamour queen and was rarely identified with the latest fashions, but what linked her to American films of the decade, other than her blondness and her lithe physical appearance, was her youthful image. The one reflexive element in *Vivere con Letizia* that perhaps calls attention to her star image is the painting of her made by the man destined to become her husband.

In 1942, Noris played in *Un colpo di pistola*, directed by Renato Castellani, where she again plays a Russian aristocratic figure that is the source of two men's sufferings. Though given top billing along with Fosco Giachetti and Antonio Centa, her role in this costume drama is secondary to the conflicts between the men, though her costumes in the film were more elegant than in many of her other films. She is an icon of the upper classes, proficient at music and games, and capricious. In this men's melodrama, she serves mainly as an agent in their competitive and tormented relationship. Similarly in an earlier film, the comedy *Darò un milione* (1935), Noris assumes a secondary role opposite De Sica and the tramp played by Luigi Almirante. The film focuses on the bored millionaire Gold, played by De Sica, who decides to escape his social life and assume the character of a tramp. He ends up in the circus, where he meets Anna, played by Noris in another of her working-class roles, who after some misunderstandings convinces him that there are generous people in the world who are not merely after his money. The much-reproduced shot of Noris as Anna, standing on a float during a performance, became a distinguishing image in publicity about her. Semi-clad, with a crown on her head from which hung a long veil, Noris presented an image of the star as visual spectacle in contrast to her more modest appearance elsewhere in the film. Noris's stardom, her popularity with audiences, consisted in her exceptional ability to render the character of stardom as mortal, not divine, and accessible, not remote.

Alessandro Blasetti: Stars and Genres

If Camerini created new forms of film comedy (along with his historical films and melodramas), Alessandro Blasetti rivaled him and was also responsible for the turning around of Italian cinema by the mid-1930s. Critical of the state of Italian cinema, Blasetti set about inventing new forms in a variety of genres and styles that, correspondingly, introduced new images of stardom. His influence was in large part connected to his awareness that the cinema was in desperate need of renovation. Recognizing that cinema was both an art and an industry, he attempted in his writings and in the many films he directed to steer an intellectual, cultural, and stylistic course that took account of the changing technological and industrial imperatives of the cinematic apparatus as well of the politics of the fascist regime. In his writings he stressed that the old cinema was dead and a new cinema was in need of being born, one that was more attuned to the Italian people and nation. Writing for *Il mondo allo schermo*, its name later changed to *Cinematografo*, he promoted a cinema that could confront portraits of Italian culture and social life. His indefatigable commitment to a rejuvenated cinema brought a group of men together, such individuals as Umberto Barbaro, Ferdinando Maria Poggioli, and Raffaello Matarazzo, among others, who became central to the new cinema Blasetti was advocating. Other than his aspirations to create a national cinema, he was committed to the primacy of the director to enhance the visual and auditory properties of the cinema.

Educated in the forms of other national cinemas, he experimented with cinematic style, with types and typing of actors, and with narratives. From his first silent film, *Sole* (Sun, 1929), to such early sound films as *Terra madre* (Mother Earth, 1931), *La tavola dei poveri* (Table of the Poor, 1932), and *Vecchia guardia* (Old Guard, 1934), to his *1860* (1934) (considered by many critics to anticipate neorealism with its use of location shooting and non-professional actors), to such costume dramas as *Ettore Fieramosca* (1938), *Un' avventura di Salvator Rosa* (1939), *La corona di ferro* (The Crown of Iron, 1941), and *La cena delle beffe* (The Feast of Fools, 1942), Blasetti experimented with cinematic form and created star-driven narratives. His *Quattro passi tra le nuvole* (A Walk among the Clouds, 1942) has, along with *1860*, been considered to be exemplary of the new direction taken by the Italian postwar cinema. His career continued in the post–World War II era, ending with his directing a TV science fiction series in 1978. The overriding motifs of his films involved tensions between tradition and modernity, rural and urban life, as well as Italian historical subjects and events, often in the form of biopics, and mythic narratives that featured stars particularly identified with his films.

He had his own group of actors, among whom were Luisa Ferida, Osvaldo Valenti, Gino Cervi, Elisa Cegani, and Rina Morelli. With the exception of Ferida and Valenti (who were executed by Partisans for their collaboration with the puppet fascist republic set up by the Nazis at Salò after their dramatic "rescue" of Mussolini from imprisonment), these actors were not at the top of the lists of the most popular stars but became stalwart and popular supporting actors. Not particularly a devotee of the star system and more concerned to experiment with narration, utilizing European and even Soviet montage, Blasetti nonetheless contributed much to the creation of star figures. His use of professional actors testified to his careful selection of actors that could embody the physical properties of the historical figures they played. Of the female actresses he featured in his films who became prominent stars of the era, two are most notable—Elisa Cegani and Luisa Ferida. The antithesis of dark-haired, passionate, working-class Ferida, Cegani was blond, slight, and featured in largely aristocratic roles, a mythic figure of romance, desirability, and quintessential femininity. Not a diva, she played roles that were in keeping with the fantasmatic and mythic conceptions of *Divismo,* though they signaled the emergence of a popular conception of stardom in the era that downplayed the transgressive and defiant dimensions of the diva and instead highlighted her beauty and spectacular costuming.

Her first major role was in *La Contessa de Parma* (1937), and the familiar convention of doubling so central to Camerini's films plays a critical role as well in this Blasetti film. Cegani plays a fashion model who passes for an aristocrat and who, after obstacles, is united to her young man, who, though penniless, has a wealthy uncle. Cegani's impersonation adds a reflexive dimension to her star status wherein through the artifice of cinema an ordinary person becomes extraordinary. Moreover, the presence of the device of doubling in both directors' works suggests that this transformation can be shared by an audience now familiar, via Hollywood and the Italian comedies of the 1930s, with such transformations and with their production of star images. In this film, as in Alessandrini's *Cavalleria* (Chivalry, 1936) and Blasetti's *Ettore Fieramosca* (1938) and *La corona di ferro,* she is bejeweled and clothed in furs, flowing gowns, and veils (thanks to such costumers as Marina Arcangeli); she is a creature of illusion. Filmed in exotic surroundings, she embodies a form of beauty that is unattainable but fascinating. She is the princess of fairy tale brought into modernity by means of the cinema. Her appearance has been described as "hieratic, antibourgeois, and classical."[39]

If, in the majority of her films, Cegani is the proverbial ice maiden, Luisa Ferida, "the black star of Cinecittà," is only too human, energetic, and passionate. As Tundra in *La corona di ferro,* Ferida was cast in competition with Cegani. If Cegani's Elsa is a static figure, identified with lethargy, veiled, and isolated from others, Ferida is a sexually ambiguous and wild warrior imperiously commanding those around her. She was largely cast in roles in which she played a *popolana,* a woman of the people, though she also undertook roles in which she incarnated a vengeful and domineering diva, as in *Nozze di sangue* (Blood Wedding, 1941), directed by Goffredo Alessandrini. Her role as the exploited peasant woman Agrippina in Poggioli's *Gelosia* (1942) was similarly tempestuous and tiger-like, though muted by her passion for the Marquis (Roldano Lupi). Her star image departs dramatically from the maternal figures sentimentalized in films of the era, including Palermi's *La peccatrice* (1941), starring Paola Barbara, who was a popular star of the late 1930s and early1940s. Barbara was often cast in motherly roles. Her short career waned in the postwar era, though she continued to appear in films made in Spain and in Italy, including three spaghetti westerns in the 1960s.[40] By contrast, Ferida's popularity with audiences derived from her incarnating a transgressive image of femininity and also from her growing notoriety in association with Osvaldo Valenti (on- and off-screen) and with the regime. Her much-vaunted wild beauty, her defiant character, and the fantasy roles she embodied, especially in the adventure films, melodramas, and biopics directed by Blasetti, gave full rein to her theatrical and flamboyant image. Through her relationship with Valenti, she was identified with the excesses of Salò, with orgies and wild parties, and with the activities of Nazi torturers that remain attached in memory to the turbulent dimensions of her star biography.[41] Blasetti's adventure films were identified with Valenti and to a lesser extent Gino Cervi, Amedeo Nazzari, and Massimo Girotti.

In *La corona di ferro* (The Iron Crown, 1941), along with the contrasting figures of Ferida and Cegani, Blasetti cast Massimo Girotti in a fairy tale (and parable) of power run amok that features him as a strong man, in the mould of Tarzan, set against a decadent Gino Cervi. An aristocrat exiled from childhood, Girotti as Arminio lives with a lion in a semi-clothed primitive condition until he returns and destroys the tyrannical and inglorious reign of King Sedemondo. At the beginning of a long and illustrious career, Girotti would graduate from this strong man image to more romantic and melodramatic roles in the 1940s. His career was immeasurably advanced by his role as the nomadic Gino in *Osessione* (1943, see chapter 5). Blasetti featured Gino Cervi as the ill-fated mythic paternal figure whose tyrannical obsession with power leads to his defeat. Prior to Blasetti's *La corona di ferro*, the popular Cervi had appeared in comedies and melodramas for various directors, including Bragaglia, Guazzoni, Mastrocinque, and Palermi, in which he revealed his versatility as an actor. As Cervi plays King Sedemondo in *La Corona*, he is not a totally unsympathetic character. In his refusal to listen to reason and in the flawed judgment that ultimately anticipates his madness, he is one of a long line of Blasetti male characters that belong in fairy tales and in Hollywood swashbucklers. His acting is stylized, cartoon-like, and campy, in the manner of Errol Flynn, thus giving rise to the judgment that in Blasetti, the hero finally "can exist only as a joke."[42] Cervi's booming voice and his histrionics border on the comic. Trailing slightly behind Amedeo Nazzari and Fosco Giachetti in popularity polls,[43] he was capable of acting in historical spectacles as well as in more contemporary dramas. In general, Cervi's star qualities were based on an ambiguous sense of dominance and virility. Often placed in a position of power gone out of control, he was able to communicate vulnerable masculinity.

In *Quattro passi fra le nuvole*, Cervi as a representative of the petite bourgeoisie acts in chivalric fashion to save the reputation of a young woman from the countryside. Consistent with other of Blasetti's films, *Quattro passi* conveys nostalgia for a simpler, more rustic life against the pathos of entrapment in a claustrophobic milieu, thus revealing another dimension to the "two faces" of the director, one as the maker of innovative films, the other as a popular genre filmmaker with his goals set on the prestige and commercial success of the Italian film industry.[44] Thus, over the course of his career, Blasetti was identified with socially oriented films that were geared to realism and others that were tied to adventure and historical spectacle, films that exploited costuming, architecture, and monumental landscapes, and which, like those of Camerini, if often contrary to Blasetti's reservations concerning the use of stars, were responsible for creating or enhancing stardom.

Goffredo Alessandrini and Amedeo Nazzari

Aside from Amedeo Nazzari's starring roles in Blasetti's films, his major roles in the late 1930s and early 1940s were for Goffredo Alessandrini, a director who was drawn to spectacle, comedy, and adventure and whose films are further evidence of the influence of Hollywood swashbucklers and comedies on the cinema of the fascist era. Nazzari appeared in Alessandrini's *Cavalleria* (1936), *Luciano Serra, pilota* (1938), and *Caravaggio* (1941), films that established his stardom. If the direction of Augusto Genina, Guido Brignone, and Carmine Gallone gave visible form to Fosco Giachetti's physical appearance, deportment, and acting as incarnating an Italian fascist model of masculinity, Nazzari too was formed on the basis of an Italian cinematic culture which had an eye on Hollywood models as well as on fascist gendered iconography. However, the films in which he appeared, the characters he played, and his acting style were affectively charged and melodramatic, presenting him in situations that threatened his masculinity. In publicity, he was often likened in his appearance and in the parts he played to Errol Flynn, though his personal life was hardly as tempestuous and scandal-laden as Flynn's. Born in Sicily, Nazzari began acting in the theater, and turned to cinema in 1935.[45] He made a large number of films during the Ventennio, and his career in films carried on beyond the fascist era until his death in 1979, leaving behind a legacy of over 120 films. His popularity was enhanced in the post–World War II era by his roles in such successful "rosy neorealist" melodramas as *Catene* (1949) and *Tormento* (1953) (see chapter 4). But he also acted in biographical films, costume dramas, and epic spectaculars in the 1960s.

His career burgeoned after the release of *Cavalleria*. Playing the debonair but ill-fated Captain Solaro, he loves an aristocratic woman whom he cannot marry for reasons of his inferior class and economic status. Arranged marriages among the upper classes and the attendant suffering to the couples were still a popular subject for melodrama. *Cavalleria*, as the title suggests, features Nazzari as a dashing but broken-hearted cavalry officer who turns to aviation. Colored with a strong nationalist and military tinge, set in an earlier historical moment between the Umbertian and Giolittian eras, the film dramatizes changes from an earlier traditional society to modernity, although not without nostalgia for the past. Nazzari's stardom was established through both *Luciano Serra pi-*

lota and this film, which was a success at the box office. His persona was aided by his appearance: he was tall, handsome, and graceful in movement, but in the roles he played, his characters were sensitive, dutiful, often religious, and patriotic. From *Cavalleria* onward, he is a highly romantic figure inclined to deep feeling, particularly melancholy. His sense of duty is linked to his chivalric demeanor; he is a protector of endangered femininity. More than that, he is often in the position of being accused wrongfully of criminal behavior, as in *La grande luce* (or *Montevergine*, 1939), a film that anticipates the later post–World War II *Tormento*. A masochistic figure, decidedly emotional in his acting, he perseveres in the face of numerous obstacles to redeem his honor. Though he is often portrayed in antagonistic relations to male figures, a striking characteristic of his films is his ambivalent but often idealized relationship to female characters.

In *Cavalleria*, Solaro is a leader of men but remote from realizing his personal desires. Unfulfilled, he leaves the cavalry and assumes a commanding role in the world of aviation, a role Nazzari reprises in *Luciano Serra, pilota*. Nazzari would become associated with the romantic image of the aviator so popular in the cinema of the thirties and forties.[46] Aviation also figures in *Centomila dollari* (1940) and *Giorni felici* (Happy Days, 1943). In *Cavalleria*, an historical film set in World War I, the heroism and national glory earlier identified with the cavalry is transferred to aviation and embodied in the modern role of the daring pilot. The aviator thus serves as a modern reincarnation of the traditional romantic hero, transported in space and time by both the camera and the airplane. If in the silent cinema the divas and divos confronted a world of desire expressed through their bodies in their struggles to transcend the mundane world, Nazzari's star persona expresses another mode of transcendence. His physical body is metamorphosed into a machine, becoming a virtual body, lending itself to the abstract moral imperatives of heroism, patriotism, and family honor. Solaro's death at the end, as his plane plunges to the earth in a field of flowers, must be seen in this light: not as the death of the body but as its apotheosis. In a similar vein, the ending of *Luciano Serra, pilota* highlights that sacrifice and transcendence of the body for the nation through technology is a passport to immortality.

Even when not featuring war and aeronautics, Nazzari's star image is identified with action rather than contemplation. For example, *La grande luce* features Nazzari as Rocco, a worker and devoted husband and father, who is wrongfully implicated in a murder by a former lover of his wife. Rather than facing the police and the court system, Rocco flees, ending up in Argentina, where his desire to return to his family is constantly thwarted by new forces that keep him away from Italy for over a decade. However, thanks to the testimony of a mute and the aid of a priest, Rocco is exonerated. Rocco finally returns to Italy and is determined to seek vengeance on Pietro, the man responsible for blighting Rocco's life. In a scene in church, Rocco, ready to stab Pietro as they both kneel before an image of the Madonna, drops his knife and grasps Pietro's hand as the film ends in images of religious transcendence (the church, its dome, and the clouds).

This film is revealing about the elements contributing to Nazzari's stardom that would appeal to contemporary viewers, especially female viewers. Aside from his physically attractive face and strong body, he presents an image of a heroic working-class rural male who is a victim of injustice. That he is forced to emigrate serves to connect his plight to the hardships of immigration, a theme evoked in other films of the era (e.g., *Passaporto rosso* [Red Passport]). In a culture that places a high value on the family, Nazzari is denied the solace and compensations of family life, forced to live without his wife and child, and imprisoned in an alien culture. Moreover, his reputation as a religious man and the intense religious imagery of his films—the Madonna in the church, the incarnation of the Madonna in the image of Rocco's wife, Lucia, and the religious festivals—provide yet another index to Nazzari's myth and to the positive character of audience responses to him. While Nazzari can be said to be a consummate version of the Italian strong man of the Ventennio, a man of honor and moral rectitude, a savior of the oppressed, and a man of religion, he is also portrayed as a passionate figure engaged in a struggle between vengeance and justice that had resonance with audiences of the 1930s and early 1940s. In *La cena delle beffe* (The Feast of Fools, 1941), Nazzari plays against Osvaldo Valenti, who is an unscrupulous scoundrel. This grizzly tale of attempted rape, torture, madness, and revenge set in the Renaissance is hardly a glorious evocation of an earlier moment in Italian history. Nazzari's role as the beleaguered Neri is as a man who is inevitably trapped in events that overwhelm him, reveal his melancholic disposition, incite him to retaliation, and are identifiable as reiterative characteristics of his stardom.

Since the perception of stardom relies on its capacity to evoke affective responses in a mass audience, audiences of the time would, no doubt, have been engaged in selecting diverse attributes of his persona. Some might have perceived him as the quintessence of the fascist hero, bearing similar qualities to the idealized image of Il Duce and its affiliation with nationalist identity. For others, his identification with the church may have been a source of his appeal. In place of the traits of a superman, his melancholy stance and his misfortunes in love, including his deep intense mourning for his wife in *La donna della montagna* (The Mountain Woman, 1944), might have generated sympathy for his character and mitigated the more conventional aspects of public heroics, particularly for viewers who might see his character as the antithesis of patriarchal authoritarianism. For still others, he may have generated nostalgia for earlier moments in Italian cultural history that were now under threat from the new order of modernity. What-

2.2. Amedeo Nazzari in *La donna della montagna. Courtesy of Museum of Modern Art Film Stills Collection.*

---

ever the explanation, it can be established through audience polls of the time that Amedeo Nazzari was a major star at the box office and would continue to be so in the late 1940s and 1950s (see chapter 4).

The Mythic Fosco Giachetti

If polls are to be trusted, Fosco Giachetti was second only to Nazzari in popularity at the box office in the late 1930s. As was characteristic of many cinema stars, Giachetti came to films via the theater and was originally resistant, if not hostile, to the medium of film, considering cinema an "inferior art" and preferring to work in theater.[47] However, in a career that peaked during the Ventennio, though he continued to appear in films until 1973, Giachetti was a major icon. He starred in melodramas and war films and offered an instance of the transformation of the male star in the sound era from a physically powerful *uomo forte* to an icon of a disciplined and controlling leader of men respected for his superior moral recti- tude and his stiff and unyielding resistance to temptation. One of Giachetti's major roles in a war film during the fascist era was in Augusto Genina's film set during the war in Ethiopia, *Lo Squadrone bianco* (The White Squadron, 1936), as the mythic captain Santelia, a model of military discipline and patriotism to his men and responsible for the conversion of a playboy, Ludovici (Antonio Centa), who is addicted more to romantic love than to military duty. If Camerini assisted in De Sica's rise to stardom, Blasetti in Ferida's, Cegani's, and Valenti's, and Ales- sandrini in Nazzari's, then Genina must be credited with Giachetti's.

Giachetti's craggy facial contours and expressions, his stiff posture, and his deportment remained constant in his films, whether in melodramas such as *Napoli che non muore* (1939) and *Noi vivi/Addio Kira* (We the Living/Goodbye Kira, 1942), in biopics such as *Giuseppe Verdi* (1938), or in war films such as *L'Assedio dell' Alcazar* (The Siege of the Alcazar, 1940). Giachetti was a model of seriousness, as he himself acknowledged in his interview with Francesco Savio. His sculptured face was a key to the stylized character of his perfor- mance, underlining his control even in extremely emotional moments. His body movements were stylized, if not mechanical, almost like the poster art most evident in the war films, where he embodied the virility that was exalted in the propaganda of the time and identified with Mussolini. He was Italian cinema's answer to the perceived image among Italians of the "effeminate" Rudolf Valentino and Ramon Navarro,[48] embodying a form of masculinity that was stoic, reserved, and restrained, not exotic.

If he qualifies as a version of the strong man, his strength resided in his unwavering moral authority and power. His was a heroic model of self-sacrifice comparable to the theatrical postures of Il Duce's stardom. Giachetti's best role was as a communist with a conscience in *Noi vivi* (We the Living, 1942, reissued in 1986 and rarely discussed by writers on the cinema of the era). In this film, in a role secondary to Rossano Brazzi, Giachetti is a consummate example of a man committed to a cause for which he is willing to sacrifice love but not honor. Speaking of his part in that film, he described the character as "an ideal- ist, not only a communist, but perhaps even Christian,"[49] which suggests that the character of Andrei was in many ways a part compatible with Giachetti's perception of his star persona as an "idealist," during the years of fascism. It is this image of the masculine star that will be subjected to scrutiny and revision in the films of the post–World War II era. His customary unwavering devotion to duty is tempered by his love for Kira, played by Alida Valli, one of the popular stars of the fascist era, who appeared in a variety of roles in comedy, melodrama, historical dramas, and musicals. Her long and varied career continued until the 1990s, but despite major roles in Reed's *The Third Man* (1949), Visconti's *Senso*

(1954), and Argento's *Suspiria* (1977) she was never able to regain her former popularity.

Everybody's Woman: The Faces of Isa Miranda

While Isa Miranda had appeared in Blasetti's *Il caso Haller* (1933), Palermi's *Creature della notte* (1933), and Brignone's *Tenebre* (1934), this last being instrumental in helping her to gain the role in the Ophüls film, *La signora di tutti* (1934) propelled Miranda into the rank of stardom and has become an important film not only in Ophüls's oeuvre but in considerations of stardom. *La signora di tutti* was part of an attempt to create a cinema that appealed not only to the Italian but also to the international public.[50] The press office of Novella-Film made sure to create advance publicity favorable to the production and particularly to its star. Stories, photographs, and comparisons to American stars such as Greta Garbo, Katharine Hepburn, and Marlene Dietrich appeared in the publicity circulated about her. Her appearance was described by one writer in terms of her photogenic quality, stressing her face, and particularly the eyes "that illuminated her face and conveyed a secret interior torment."[51] Her career blossomed in the mid-1930s, but after a two-year period in Hollywood, where she was groomed as a Dietrich look-alike, she returned to Italy only to find that she was being disciplined as a "reprobate."[52] Her husband, producer Alfredo Guarini, helped her to rebuild her star image, but the roles she played were usually of French or German characters, not Italian.

La signora di tutti is a remarkable film for the light it sheds on popular culture in the pre–World War II era. Focusing reflexively on the production of stardom, the film is framed by images of the movie industry—the production of posters, photographs, publicity, and other artifacts associated with the business of filmmaking, including its tie-ins with popular music and fashion. Unlike the diva of the silent cinema, in this film, the star becomes an industrial assemblage of qualities who is captive to the director, an agent, a producer, the camera, publicity, changing fashions in clothing, makeup, and hairdos, and the box office. In this film the star is exposed as the "the sum total of a disembodied voice and an image (the two sensory registers of the cinema)."[53] Visibility and audibility, and their disjunction, are major tropes in the Ophüls film, heightening awareness of the star as a product of the cinematic apparatus.

The title of the film, "Everyone's Woman," suggests reproducibility rather than difference, as does the film within the film that bears the same title as the film itself. It also suggests a dominant characteristic of stardom as opposed to *Divismo*; namely, substitutability, accessibility, and mass dispersion. The film obsessively portrays the repetition of her image through the printing press that reproduces her poster. Rather than being identified with purposive action, Miranda's image offers a different sense of the star's body that suggests her entrapment in the narrative. The self-reflexive treatment of the star transpires through narcosis, a dream state, detached from the chronological events of the narrative. In her complete passivity, Miranda as Gaby differs most notably from the diva of the silent era, who projected a sense of force, energy, and volition. Hers is a newer image of stardom controlled by the medium rather than controlling it, as the film makes abundantly clear.

Miranda's roles in the film as wayward daughter, heedless companion to a maternal figure, and wife to Leonardo portray her entrapment and inability to escape institutional and familial constraints. As a parallel to her stardom (in the film within a film in her role as star) she is situated in a melodramatic narrative that traces her transformation from a sexually precocious schoolgirl to a tormented woman who repetitively finds herself in the position of home-breaker and destroyer of men. Her persona is developed through an emphasis on her deadly fascination to men: they cannot resist her. By contrast, she seems to be seeking a familial, particularly a maternal, environment but is thwarted by her inability to resist the seductions of a paternal figure. Like a sexual loadstone she draws men to her and like a somnambulist she is unable to resist them. As in the role she plays in the later *Zazà* (where she also plays an entertainer), Miranda seems doomed to inhabit the position of *femme fatale* even while she is drawn toward an unrealizable maternal role. Miranda's portrait of Gaby in the Ophüls film is carefully constructed to position her first as young student held responsible for the suicide of a teacher enamored of her; then as daughter subjugated to her father's disciplinary control; as seeker of pleasure, which brings her to the household of the young man to whom she is attracted; as a playful companion to his mother; as the object of the husband's seduction and unwitting accomplice to the mother's death; as guilt-laden wife to the widower; and as a lonely star deprived of love. Thus, she undergoes a series of transformations in the narrative that bring her to the summit of a career in film and finally to suicide. The changes she undergoes are marked repeatedly by a sense of fatality and of the role of accident rather than will in her encounters with others. She presents a portrait of a woman who is acted upon by others but unable to assume control.

Critical moments in the narrative are signaled by changing costumes—from schoolgirl dress, to ingénue gazing at her reflection in the mirror as she prepares for a party, and, later, again before her mirror image, to dark, svelte, decorously ruffled and stylish evening gown selected by the motherly Alma. Her costumes were designed by Sandro Radice. Her makeup and hairdos correspondingly undergo transformation, giving her the glamorous appearance of a Hollywood star. The critical issue that defines her role in the narrative (the film within the film and the melodrama that inspires it) is the parallel drawn between Miranda/Gaby, the character, and Miranda the star. In both instances,

2.3. "Everybody's Woman" in the 1930s, Isa Miranda. *British Film Institute.*

this parallel portrays a figure that increasingly is represented as deprived of agency. She appears to be hypnotized. Her two active moments are her leaving the now-broken Leonardo and her suicide. However, a clue to her unfulfilled and unrealized desires seems to be embedded in her last word before undergoing anesthesia—"Mama." If her relationship to Leonardo's wife seems to constitute an alternative of sorts to her choreographed destiny in relation to the men in her life (including later agents, producers, technicians, etc.), it seems that the inexorable movement in the film is toward a progressive voiding of her persona until she becomes reduced to an image, a poster, a photograph. The striking image of a dangling telephone conveys her inability to speak her desires, underscoring how the star as an industrial creation is at the mercy of technology and is isolated and deprived of the ability to speak for herself and to others. Furthermore, the film suggests (and this will characterize both the character and Miranda's star persona) that borders between star and "real" life become blurred: she will repeat these roles with variation, until she, in the popular imagination, is that persona.

Miranda the star is "devoid of intention or motivation: she floats from experience to experience without motivation."[54] She fulfills Parker Tyler's description of film stars who "seem to be sleepwalkers, the mirage of souls incarnate, their own shadow selves rather than real women."[55] The "real woman" is never at issue. What is at stake is not a "just image" but only "just an image" that in-heres, as Walter Benjamin has written, in the mechanical and dehumanized reproduction of the camera. The star seems to break with the strong affective character of *Divismo* and with the organic nature of the movement-image ex-emplary of a different relation to the spectator. The spectator is allowed to share a recognition of the star as artifact, and the film captures how the affective world of the star is now focused on appropriation, possession, and emulation of the star image rather than on the quasi-religious qualities of distance, remote-ness, wonder, and power. Miranda would largely continue to embody this image of stardom in other films and with other directors.

Among her other films of the 1930s, Miranda's role as Nennele in Cameri-ni's *Come le foglie* (1934) is also strongly inflected with the polyvalent dimen-sions of stardom that characterize her other films. In this film, she is placed in contrast to a flighty, socially ambitious, and opportunistic mother and aligned with an oppressed father, acting as a surrogate mother to her incorrigible brother. Her costuming is simpler in the Camerini film than in most of her other films, and her role often places her in the position of a viewer, unable to stem the disasters caused to the family by her mother and brother. She is con-fronted by disappointment and a failure to act and is driven to commit suicide. In a climactic scene, the father averts her suicidal jump from a bridge; the fa-ther and daughter embrace, bonding in their common plight, but she restores the integrity of the family through her potential marriage to a family friend and her admirer, Massimo, whom she had earlier rejected. In her identification with a paternal figure, she assumes a maternal demeanor often denied her in films and in actuality but desired, as portrayed later in *Zazà* and in the quasi-"auto-biographical" episode in *Siamo donne* (1953, see chapter 5). Camerini and the photographer Massimo Terzano sought to downplay the dramatic photogenic qualities of *La signora di tutti* and to present her as "modest, simple, and human," but in the final analysis she comes across as a "porcelain statue."[56] Evi-dent from this description is her passivity. Hardly a conventional *femme fatale* in *La signora di tutti*, Miranda's image projects a certain melancholy, if not ironic quality, and a statuesque deportment that infuses her other films. Her star image is linked to family melodrama, but in ways that are sufficiently com-plex to mitigate reductive ideological readings that would tie her star persona too tightly to the familialism and gender biases of the regime. Similarly, in *Pas-saporto rosso* (1935), a patriotic "epic" set like a Hollywood western in the South American frontier, she is portrayed as devoted daughter, then loyal wife and nurturing maternal figure, but also as a teacher, entertainer, and nurse. There is a continuity in the ways she is filmed, in terms of the uses of lighting on her mask-like face and the attention paid to her costuming and makeup to bring out the various but familiar dimensions of her star persona that have been characterized as highlighting her "division between two universes: the sump-tuousness and sad fragility of humanity."[57]

Miranda's role in *Scipione l'Africano* (1937) provides another chapter in the evolution of the figure of the diva to star. The film, a reprise of the earlier *Cabiria*, casts Miranda as Velia, a devoted patriotic Roman woman taken off by Carthaginian "barbarians" to be Scipione's concubine. Miranda is filmed so as to highlight her facial expressions and to convey the monumental Madonna-like quality of her stance and gestures, emphasizing her vulnerability as well as her determination to kill Scipio and save her lover. Her iconic presence, enhanced by means of the lighting, the classical simplicity of her gown, and her statuesque poses are in marked contrast to Sofonisba's Orientalist, drawn out, and decidedly perverse self-immolation. Francesca Braggiotti as Sofonisba appears as a parody of *Divismo* in her "extreme stylization," her appearance "like an Egyptian hieroglyphic." She is "both a distant, undecipherable letter and an exotic cliché, a trite character."[58] Like the diva, Braggiotti's Sofonisba is single-mindedly devoted to her personal desires and defiant toward authority, preferring a Cleopatra-like death to subjection. The lighting of the two characters is also different. Miranda's head is lit to so as accentu-ate her spiritual qualities, while the excessively bright light on Braggiotti's face ap-pears designed to accentuate her crazed look. The death of the cinematic diva is signaled here by means of this contrast. Thus the diva dies within the film's narra-tive and is replaced by a more psychologically determined, if not spiritualized, figure—the star exemplified by Miranda. A contrast between images of stardom was developed in *Una donna tra due mondi* (A Woman between Two Worlds, 1936), in which Miranda plays a working-class young woman to Noris's role as a princess, preferring romance with a young artist to the aristocratic world.

In *Zazà* (1944), a highly ornate film directed by Renato Castellani, Mi-randa is also a divided figure, a chanteuse admired by men and a seeker of love. She is the embodiment of a woman of two worlds, doomed in her body, a vision for others to devour visually but unable to do more herself than gaze on a world to which she is denied entrance. Controlled by others, she remains to the film's end a spectator herself as she stands at a window, alone, and watches her lover disappear from sight. Dynamic movement and gestures identify her role as en-tertainer, whereas her role as voyeur to family tableaus is consistently static. Her costumes in the film are distinguished by large hats that partially conceal her face and cast a shadow on it. However, when she visits Dufresne's family, her costumes are more subdued, if not severe. In general, her image is of a *femme fatale* manqué, a melodramatic figure controlled by director, narration, camera, a narrative that dooms her to be forever the object of vision but incapable of re-alizing her desires.

One of the successful directors of the Ventennio was Mario Soldati (1906–1999), a director identified not only with calligraphism but also with various film

2.4. A reluctant femme fatale: Isa Miranda in *Zazà. Courtesy of Museum of Modern Art Film Stills Collection.*

genres—comedies, historical films, and melodramas. His film credits during the fascist era include *Dora Nelson* (1939), *Tutto per la donna* (Everything for a Woman, 1940), *Tragica notte* (Tragic Night, 1942), *Piccolo mondo antico* (Old-Fashioned World, 1942), based on a Fogazzaro work of the same name, and *Malombra* (1942), also based on a Fogazzaro novel. His films starred actresses Juni Astor, Doris Duranti, and Alida Valli, who were described by Pierre Leprohon as "representative of a new school opposed to the sophisticated extravagance of the *dive*."[59] In contrast to the divas, these actresses were youthful, slim, and fashionable; they were meant to look ordinary, not exotic, but the costuming, the makeup, and the camera work enhanced their perfected ordinariness. In many instances, the films, particularly the comedies and melodramas, employed reflexive devices (allusions to novels, films, and theater) to call attention, within the films, to their artifice and intertextuality and to the notion of femininity as performance. Unlike the diva, these stars were captive to the director, the camera, genre narrative, publicity, changing fashions in clothing, makeup, and hairdo, and the box office.

Soldati's remake of *Malombra* adheres closely to the Fogazzaro novel in its evocation of the historical context for the events in the narrative, its religious dimensions, and particularly the symbolic role of landscape and the hermetic world identified with the d'Ormengo estate, but it differs in the director's treatment of the female protagonist. For his Marina di Malombra, Mario Soldati wanted to use Alida Valli for her affective acting style but was unable to sign her. Before accepting Isa Miranda, whom he considered to be identified with a restrained style of acting, he made her do a screen test.[60] He was uncertain whether she could capture his sense of Marina's character. The results of the casting were propitious for both star and director. Fogazzaro's Gothic novel, with its aristocratic setting, its reflexive allusions to poetry and music, and its highlighting of the *femme fatale*, was congenial to films of the silent era and also to the calligraphic films of the sound era. In Gallone's *Malombra*, the incidents from the novel are drawn selectively so as to elevate the role of Marina di Malombra and to allow for an operatic rendition by diva Lyda Borelli. The Soldati remake follows the trajectory of the novel more faithfully while also echoing specific images from the Gallone film, but Soldati employs dramatically different cinematic techniques to develop character and situation, whereby the star plays a different role. Miranda's portrait of Marina suggests the now-familiar attributes of modern stardom. In accounting for the distance between the silent film and its remake during the sound era, the metamorphosis of *Divismo* into the star system is crucial. Too often, the diva has been considered similar to the star; however, the two forms of cinematic expression differ. While historians of Italian cinema acknowledge stylistic differences between the two films and of both films from the novel, they attribute distinctions less to divergences in Borelli's and Miranda's interpretations of the role of Marina than to inevitable differences between the technology and grammar of the silent cinema and those identified with sound on film.[61]

Further differences between the roles of Borelli and Miranda are determined by the cinematic apparatus and by economic, social, and cultural imperatives. The quality of the differing portrayals arises from changing historical conditions and modes of production articulated through the distinctive physical appearance of the two actresses, their styles of acting, the uses of the camera, lighting, editing, and *mise-en-scène*, as well as the presence or absence of synchronized sound, of spoken dialogue and other ambient sounds. The diva was not a passive agent of the narrative: she was a significant determining factor. Gallone's *Malombra* as interpreted by Lyda Borelli is manifest through her omnipresence, her every gesture, the movement of her body, her way of literally and metaphorically touching everything about her and using her gestures to convey nuanced affective states. In Borelli's portrayal of Malombra, classical gowns drape and cling loosely to her body, enabling her to move easily through the different moments of her mental metamorphosis. Her makeup and hairdos do not call attention to themselves but reinforce the theatricality of her moods, actions, and reactions. Like her costumes, they are important visually but are secondary to her acting style.

In contrast, elaborate costumes define Isa Miranda's role. While meant to approximate period costuming, they are a blend of nineteenth-century and contemporary fashion, modish enough to be admired, if not emulated. Her clothes are designed by Maria De Matteis, who also designed *Zazà* and was responsible for the outfits of other major stars during the years of fascism and after the war. The gowns worn by Miranda serve to define the historical landscape but to underscore the protean elements of her role, and to delineate her relations with the other characters, her inner conflicts, and the growing stages of her conflict between control and rebelliousness. They are designed to call attention to her slim figure and enhance the contours but not the movements of her body. Her makeup and hairdos, like her costuming, are an outward and visible sign of her commodification status in the world of commerce. Her hair is often piled tidily and fashionably atop her head when conveying her public persona. By contrast, when she sits alone in her room at the piano or during the storm scene with Silla, her hair is loose and windswept. Her makeup is sculptured and mask-like, delineating her eyebrows, heavy eyelashes, and painted full lips. In her descent into madness, her expression is frozen rather than animated.

Gallone's film abstains from signs that would connect the diva to the mundane world: her world is spiritual. Borelli's Marina, from the beginning of the film to the end, belongs to another world that "partook more of ritual than fashion: the diva was at once goddess and priestess."[62] In operatic fashion, the film identifies the protagonist with a long tradition of *femmes fatales* whose power was undisputed and "whose personality and acting overshadowed every other factor." Through "the scenario, the directing, the lighting, the photography—the diva went in front of the camera for a solo performance."[63] In keeping with the diva's paramount position, the Gallone film is more invested in her dreams and visions than in the historical milieu. The film transformed an elaborate historical and political novel into a vehicle for the diva. In the lexicon of silent cinema, the absence of synchronous and ambient sound allowed the diva's image to concentrate on an interior world of female subjectivity that destabilized the other characters over which she wielded power. In the Gallone film, the natural and cultural world retreats before the diva. The images of the palazzo, the gardens, and the lake are identified with Borelli's character. She is mistress of the milieu and draws sustenance from it, as in the scenes of her on her boat or walking in the garden. The scenes in her bedchamber focus on her rather than on her surroundings, emphasizing through her gestures the varying stages of her struggle with confusion, pain, and rage.

In contrast to the omnipresence of Borelli on the screen in Soldati's *Malombra*, Miranda's presence is judiciously and economically controlled and more attention is devoted to the other characters. She is the hinge on which events turn, but her actions are those of a somnambulist, her power diminished. Hers is a portrait of female abjection. Though a source of fascination and curiosity, her power is contained by her juxtaposition to the other characters. The change of titles of the book that Miranda reads, from A *Dream* to *Specters of the Past,* is revealing of the remake's muting issues of spirituality and the latent powers of female subjectivity. The diminution of focus on Marina's states of mind is reinforced by the greater attention paid in the Soldati film than in Gallone's to the other characters: the Count, the Countess Salvador, Nepo, Steinegge, the curate, and Don Innocenzo, as well as a number of lesser characters. Symbolic of her alienation from the Count, Soldati's Marina spends her time playing the piano, especially opera music, reading poetry, writing letters, taking long walks alone in the garden, and sailing frequently on the lake. Miranda's power is further contained by her juxtaposition to Edith. The Soldati remake's formalist techniques subordinate the characters, even its star, to a comprehensive, oppressive, and dark vision of the world. Calligraphic films like Soldati's that appeared during the war focused less on action and more on the texture and character of a disintegrating world.

The filming of Miranda as she stands immobile before the window and as the camera glides past her, capturing images of the passing seasons, suggests Marina's entrapment and her straining for escape. These images are emblematic of the film's strategy for conveying her emotions and thoughts through visual correlatives. Marina's discovery of Cecilia's letters and other memorabilia is largely conveyed through camera work and editing rather than gesture. She is filmed in close-up as she reads the text aloud, and the scene is intercut with close-ups of the letter. She does not rise and pace about the room but remains rooted to her seat, picking up in turn each object that belonged to the unfortunate Cecilia, first a brooch, which she attaches to her dress, then a lock of blonde hair. She loosens a strand of her own hair to match it with Cecilia's. Yet, while she caresses her own hair, she does not move nor make any gestural sign of disturbance. Instead, the camera cuts to an image of rain hitting the pane of the window, suggesting perturbation.

Ironically, the enigmatic and fascinating character of the star's image is further conveyed through Miranda's visual absence. For example, Silla's curiosity about Marina is conveyed not through her visual image but by sound: her voice in the corridors and her loud playing of the piano. Also, his discovery of a copy of Baudelaire's *Fleurs du mal* with her name written on the cover incites his and the spectator's curiosity to see and learn more about her. In keeping with the depersonalized, even disembodied, image of the star, Miranda is often filmed by repeated shots of her at the window and from the camera's point of view on the world outside the house. Rather than focusing on her face and her bodily gestures, the camera moves past her, to reveal a foggy and wintry view of the outdoors that dissolves into an image of a flowering tree, signaling the arrival of spring. Rain can be seen in yet another shot of her gazing from her window. These shots, more than her gestures, suggest her solitude, her identification with the natural world, and the ability of the world of nature to define her internal states. Soldati's Miranda is a creature divided, this struggle visualized through the use of landscape. Natural surroundings are associated with her desire for freedom, whereas the labyrinthine and elaborately decorated palazzo sheds light on her feelings of imprisonment.

Character vies with landscape. The image of the star competes with but is also defined by the milieu. *Malombra* was filmed on Lake Como at the Pliniana palazzo, and an image of the lake appears under the initial credits, focusing on the play of light on the water.[64] Throughout, the film connects the world of the house and its environs to Marina and to Silla. Like the novel, this film relies heavily on the atmosphere of a world far removed from the contemporary metropolis. The D'Ormengo house is situated amidst lake, mountains, and exotic flora, all of which Fogazzaro identifies as a "paese sconosciuto" (an unknown country) that comes to be identified by Marina with a world of dreams and the occult that is unknown in terms of the everyday. Ultimately, Miranda has served the filmic narrative and the requirements of stardom. She has shifted from object of desire to suspicious object of scrutiny.

The narrative's preoccupation with the historical past in Soldati's film, in its reliance on the Fogazzaro novel and in its remaking of the earlier silent film, is illustrative of a world which is preoccupied with, if not critical of, the limits of action. In both cases, Miranda's role is circumscribed. The distance of a quarter of a century between the Gallone and the Soldati films is marked by two world wars, the ascent and decline of the fascist regime, the passage from tradition to modernity, and the transformation of the silent cinema into sound. The world of Fogazzaro, like that of Gallone and of *Divismo*, is another "piccolo mondo antico," and Soldati's return to that world is laden with ambiguity about its relation to Italy in the late nineteenth century and in the early moments of the twentieth. The retreat to the past on the part of the calligraphers, as exemplified by Soldati's remake, can be regarded as a reaction against the cinema of the fascist years (prior to neorealism), as a veiled critique of the contemporary political and social situation, as a further exercise in experimenting with cinematic form, and as a contribution to a different use of the human body through its treatment of the star. The most unsettling dimension of the Soldati film concerns the portrait of femininity embodied by its star. Isa Miranda is not a diva, though her character in *Malombra* bears a resemblance to the *femme fatale*, a recurrent figure in the films of the calligraphers (e.g., Castellani's *Un colpo di pistola* [A Pistol Shot, 1942] and *Zazà* [1944], and Poggioli's *Gelosia* [Jealousy, 1942]). However, the focus in these films tilts from the spectacle and power of the woman to the weakness and disintegration of the male figure in Soldati's *Malombra*. If the figure of the diva as portrayed by Borelli was a celebration of the power of femininity even at its most self-destructive, femininity in Soldati's film is a portrait of oppression and victimhood.

The Marina of the film remake is portrayed as a divided character. Contrasted to Edith, her alter ego, an acceptable figure under fascism as an embodiment of familial devotion, Marina can be identified with the aggressive and "masculinized" women censured by the regime. If Marina becomes a demonic figure, Edith is an angelic incarnation of spirituality. Alternatively, Marina can be regarded as the film's vehicle for questioning connections between aesthetics and politics. Offering a different portrait of femininity from the Gallone film, the remake highlights investigation and crime detection (derived from the novel). Where Borelli's presence invited the spectator to regard and experience her ecstatic transports, Miranda's becomes the occasion to investigate and decipher her precarious state of mind. Thanks to the highly stylized presentation of her character via her costumes, makeup, hairdos, and deportment, the editing, and her juxtaposition to other characters, in this remake of the earlier film of the Fogazzaro novel, Isa Miranda becomes the embodiment of a different order of representation, that of the star and not the diva, and Miranda's role in its style of acting, iconography, and uses of costuming and makeup offers reflections on the changing image of stardom.

In her publicity photos and in the films, lighting becomes the essential ingredient in conveying the mysterious and elusive character of the star. Her face shines forth from the darkness, and while she is praised for her employment of gesture, the dominant impression she conveys is of a statuesque quality. Her figure is clearly delineated while the landscape is often hazy or out of focus. Her stance and dreamy gaze suggest her being posed in a position to be seen and admired, qualities also characteristic of her appearances in Brignone's *Passaporto rosso*, Gallone's *Scipione l'Africano*, Chenal's *Il fu Mattia Pascal* (1937), and Castellani's *Zazà*. In *Malombra*, Miranda's Marina reflexively plays on a spectatorial desire to penetrate her elusiveness. For example, after the Count's mysterious illness, Marina becomes a passive object of scrutiny, investigation, and discussion on the part of the other characters. Like Gaby in *La signora di tutti*, she is a source of curiosity and fascination eliciting interpretation. Miranda's portrayal of Gaby in *La signora di tutti* would seem to validate the change of conceptions of female beauty away from the "languid poses, slow gestures, affected speech, dress of classical and exotic orientalizing" of the teens and twenties.[65] Miranda's *femmes fatales* of the 1930s and 1940s belong to a different cinematic and social world. As exemplified in *Zazà* and strongly implied in *La signora*, there is melancholy associated with her image that is often linked to an unrealized desire for maternal femininity. Her stardom provides further evidence of the influence of Hollywood, and to a lesser extent of European images and styles, revealing a fusion of Italian and foreign

2.5. Reflections of stardom: Isa Miranda in *Malombra. British Film Institute.*

models as they contributed to the rise of stars. Her star image is a validation that the stars were not mere expressions of fascist propaganda and also that they testify to the power of the cinematic body of the star to express tensions between the actual and virtual reality.

Many stars, with the exceptions of Assia Noris, Luisa Ferida, and Osvaldo Valenti, had careers that extended into the post–World War II era, including Amedeo Nazzari, Vittorio De Sica, Alida Valli, Massimo Girotti, Clara Calamai, and Isa Miranda. If their later careers did not match their popularity during the years of fascism, this is attributable to the war, to discontent with and reactions against the fascist regime, and, correspondingly, to changing conceptions and expectations of the cinema, particularly articulations of the "new realism" as exemplified by writings in the journal *Cinema* and by the films that were produced under the rubric of "neorealism." However, in the present critical climate involving the ongoing revaluation of the films produced during the Ventennio as well as of those identified with neorealism, it is evident that the much-vaunted rupture between the cinema under fascism and the postwar cinema is not as clear as it once was.

The stardom established in the 1930s did not disappear but underwent a metamorphosis that had already been signaled by several cinematic events tied to the transformation of the national imaginary even before the end of fascism and the war. The calligraphism in the late 1930s and early 1940s of such directors as Soldati, Poggioli, and Castellani offered images of stars that, while highly artificial, contributed to introducing darker portraits of femininity and masculinity. Visconti's *Ossessione* (1942) has been long identified as a significant contribution to the changing directions that were emerging in the commercial cinema. *Ossessione* featured two significant stars of the fascist era: Clara Calamai and Massimo Girotti. Calamai had appeared as a seductress in such popular films as *Ettore Fieramosca* (1938), *Addio Giovinezza* (1940), and *Sissignora* (Yes, Madam, 1942), and Girotti had appeared as a popular romantic star in comedies, adventure films, and melodramas such as *Dora Nelson* (1939), *Tosca* (1941), *La corona di ferro* (1941), and *Harlem* (1941) and was to have a long career (until 2003). Visconti's film draws on Calamai and Girotti's earlier star personas but undermines them, situating them within a different social context and through a style reminiscent of the "calligraphers."

Other films also gave indications of a changing course in filmmaking that was to make an impact on Italian stardom—Poggioli's *Sissignora*, Mario Bonnard's *Avanti c'è posto* (Before the Postman, 1942), Blasetti's *Quattro passi tra le nuvole*, and De Sica's *I bambini ci guardano* (The Children Are Watching Us, 1943). In the physical portrayal of femininity and masculinity, and in acting, one can already detect alterations in conceptions of the star. Both Gino in *Ossessione* and Paolo in *Quattro passi* unsettled the virile images of stardom that frequently characterized the masculine persona of the era; similarly, the female characters Giovanna in *Ossessione* and Maria in *Quattro passi*, through two portraits of femininity, serve to destabilize the glamour of such stars as Isa Miranda or mythic figures such as Elisa Cegani. These films, in ways similar to *Ossessione*, especially in their uses of contemporary stars, offered a different world that conveyed a "crisis of the movement-image," where standards of truth, beauty, and identity were undermined and where the stars were to assume less idealized personas.

Similarly, the star image of Mussolini underwent a change that paralleled the vicissitudes of cinematic stardom. If in the early years of the 1930s, his political cinema appeared to be one of uncontrolled enthusiasm and of interaction between the leader and the people, Mussolini's image in the late 1930s and early 1940s signaled that "the credibility of an eternally youthful Duce was crumbling."[66] The image of the virile and invincible leader was gone. Instead spectators were confronted with images of an aging body, an old man suffering stomach problems, a victim of depression and insomnia. The last stages of his public drama involved arrest, escape, and finally, an ignominious ending at Mezzegra, where he was shot and strung up by his heels with his mistress, Clara Petacci. His muti-

lated corpse, trampled by a crowd at the Piazzale Loreto, was buried in an un-
marked grave at the Musocco cemetery until it was exhumed and hidden from
1946 to 1957 at the convent of Cerro San Maggiore. It was to remain there until it
was returned to his family and entombed at Predappio, now a place of pilgrimage
for followers, fans, and curiosity-seekers. His death did not put his ghost to rest; it
fuelled books, newspaper articles, and oral legends that revealed that Mussolini
had not ceased being a star but was a center of a drama that would involve the nation for years to come.[67] The Italian cinema of the postwar era was engaged in altering, dismantling, or seeking to memorialize what remained of fascist virility,
leadership, and power. Similarly, icons of femininity as incarnated by the female
stars of the decade were further transformed.

Stars amidst the Ruins:
The Old and the New

The term neorealism was born with the success of Roma, città aperta—*a belated action success, like a time bomb. When the film was shown in Cannes in 1946, it went quite unnoticed. It was discovered much later, and I am not yet sure its message has been fully understood.*

Roberto Rossellini[1]

At the war's end, Cinecittà was in shambles, suffering from Allied bombing, the Nazi removal of valuable equipment, and its use as a place of detention for refugees, but Italian filmmaking did not cease,[2] though the number of Italian films in production and available for distribution diminished significantly. In ways reminiscent of early cinema, production was decentralized, relegated to small companies in regional locales.[3] The American occupation played a critical role on the film scene through its dumping onto the market of Hollywood films that had been boycotted during the latter years of the regime. American films, alongside films imported from Britain and France, constituted the largest share of the movies accessible to Italian audiences.[4] In addition, prewar films or films reminiscent of this type of commercial genre production were distributed. Economic and political factors along with direct and indirect censorship practices on the part of the state and the Catholic Church played a significant role in the development of the postwar popular cinema and particularly in any assessment of the evolution and impact of neorealism. Furthermore, many of the directors, writers, actors, and technicians were inevitable carryovers from the prewar period.

In this chapter, I look closely at reigning conceptions of neorealism with an eye to investigating its significant, if often misunderstood, contributions to the resurgence of a popular commercial cinema and, with it, the role of stars, some of whom were familiar faces and others of whom were to populate the postwar cinema. Neorealism was responsible for new stars in the context of a changed cultural and political landscape. In effect, the hybrid character of neorealism, as exemplified by such films as *Roma, città aperta* (Rome, Open City, 1945), *Vivere in pace* (To Live in Peace, 1946), *Il bandito* (The Bandit, 1947), and *Riso amaro* (Bitter Rice, 1949), played a significant role in revivifying and enhancing popular actors from previous years such as Anna Magnani, Aldo Fabrizzi, and Massimo Girotti and in producing a new galaxy of stars through the use and enthusiastic reception of such actors as Vittorio Gassman, Sophia Loren, Gina Lollobrigida, Silvana Mangano, and Marcello Mastroianni. Moreover, *Paisà* (Paisan, 1946), *Sciuscià* (Shoeshine, 1946), *Ladri di biciclette* (Bicycle Thieves, 1948), *La terra trema* (The Earth Trembles, 1948), and *Caccia tragica* (Tragic Pursuit, 1948), while utilizing non-professional actors, contributed to the emergence of a different iconography of male and female stars in the cinema of the postwar years. The presence of both kinds of stars is revealing of what David Forgacs has termed a "popular culture in transition."[5] While there are critics who acknowledge that there were not one but many realisms,[6] the character and impact of neorealism may still be, as Rossellini claimed, "not fully understood."

I attempt to bridge the chasm between the high political and moral ground assigned to neorealism as committed, elite, and canonical and the often condescending, if not pejorative, assessment of popular Italian cinema and of its connections to stardom. My object here is not to elevate the cinema of genres and their stars at the expense of neorealist texts. Rather I hope to create a genealogy that brings neorealism and the popular cinema into closer dialogue even at the risk of disrupting long-standing conceptions of each. Among the myths I seek to lay to rest in rewriting Italian cinema by way of stardom is that neorealism was a short-lived phenomenon, finished off by the mid-1950s, an evaluation that relies on a reductive identification of its aesthetic and philosophic characteristics. Also, Gilles Deleuze is among those critics who maintain the myth that the Italian cinema of the postwar years began from zero, a view that disregards significant elements of continuity. According to him, the Italian cinema "could point to a resistance and to a popular life underlying oppression, although one without illusion. . . . Films such as *Roma, citta aperta* began again from zero, questioning afresh all the accepted facts from the American tradition. The Italians were therefore able to have an intuitive consciousness of the new image in the course of being born."[7] This "new image" situates neorealism within parameters that are larger than a national tradition and more all-encompassing than the reductive notions of neorealism as "redemption" from fascism. Deleuze's situating of a postwar zero degree from which neorealism emerged can be refined through a backward glance that qualifies the notion of a radical break from the past. Both the popular and the art cinema were engaged in a redefinition of cinematic culture that involved reflections on the body of stardom, its past, present, and future. The popular cinema addressed contemporary culture, cinema history, and stardom within a metacinematic exploration of personages and events often couched in elliptical narratives, disconnected spaces, and afflicted characters that were symptoms of a world unsettled by war and its aftermath and of a cinema that had played and was to play a future role in a struggle over the evolution of images. Hence, the body of the star is integral to meanings concerning political and cultural representations.

An analysis of these neorealist texts and of their particular and contradictory ideological formations reveals that they do not escape complicity with the texts that proceeded and those that follow them. I contend that neorealism is a hybrid form that, while expressing discontent with preexisting cinematic forms, cannot, for better or worse, ignore them, though using them for different ends. In the texts of neorealism a metacinematic dimension is evident in the films' self-conscious allusions to popular culture (cinema, theater, romance magazines, and photo-romances),[8] and in their selection and treatment of actors to play the major or supporting roles that elevated certain actors to stardom. Neorealism, then, did not disappear as so many have claimed, nor did the phenomenon of stardom, but evolved in directions that shed light on the presence of residual and emergent elements that are an inevitable concomitant of evolving forms and concepts. One expression of neorealism survived and re-animated the popular cinema. The other, through its experimental character and identification with particular directors, is evident in what Deleuze describes as the regime of the time-image, exemplified by the films of Rossellini, Fellini, Antonioni, and Pasolini (see chapter 5). These directors developed and augmented the critical and conceptual aspects of "neorealism" that also characterize the oft-disparaged "popular cinema." Even in the works of these directors the star plays a significant role, albeit as a critical reflection on the state of cinematic culture.

Looking at Neorealism

Rossellini's assertion that neorealism was "born" with his film, and that this cinematic phenomenon has not been "fully understood," is still debatable today. Nonetheless, *Roma, città aperta*, in the view of many critics, stands as "a prototype, a model, and even today, an unavoidable starting point"[9] in many ways for the Italian post–World War II cinema. Gian Piero Brunetta attributed the film's determining role on postwar Italian cinema to the social and political momentum characteristic of the time: "Most aspects of the postwar Italian cinema derive from *Roma, citta aperta*, direct testimony of the fight for liberation and a tribute to the will for rebirth among the Italian people."[10] And, following Benedict Anderson's description of nation as "imagined community," Angelo Restivo has written,

> [N]eorealism can be looked at as just such an attempt to create an imagined community to replace (the equally media-constructed) imagined community of the fascist period. That this project—the neorealist project—seems so vital within the neorealist texts itself attests to the profound disarray that Italy found itself in at the end of the war, a disarray marked precisely by the collapse of a coherent national narrative that could be taken as meaningful by Italians.[11]

This chapter seeks to account for this "disarray" in the context of profound changes in postwar Italian culture and society and the contradictory roles played by neorealism in creating narratives and forms of acting that constituted attempts to "imagine" a national community. There is no doubt that external historical events played a critical role in establishing the crises and the successes of the cinema produced in Italy in the 1940s and 1950s. These crises involved the physical and social effects of the war itself, the contested role of the Resistance, the increased presence of the United States via the army during and after September 8, 1943, the struggle over governmental power until the election of 1948 that brought the Christian Democrats to power, and with them U.S. economic and political interests that were to accompany the new regime. "America's long march in Italy" was intensified and "for a long period after the war Italy continued to be the biggest importer of American films in Europe."[12]

The American presence, governmental and cinematic, had an effect on the production of neorealist films, for "a clearly visible process of contamination and assimilation gradually took place between this new native film form and the dominant one from outside."[13] This "contamination" was evident in two significant ways: it can be seen in the direct or critical treatment of images of America in certain of the neorealist films, and it can also be seen in the increased appearance of films that returned to the uses of popular genres and, with them, of stars. However, if we want to understand the hybrid character of this "new native form," as Angelo Restivo is quick to point out, "we must look not simply at 'representations' of Italy within the films, but also, more importantly, at the enunciative strategies of the film"[14] in which stars were a significant factor.

The style and subject matter of neorealism have been described by many film critics as residing in a predominant use of location shooting, deep focus and long take photography, non-professional actors, a loose form of narration, a documentary look, the intermingling of fiction and non-fiction, the privileging of marginal and subaltern groups, and a focus on contemporary situations. Not that there had not been "realist" filmmaking in the cinema in the 1920s and 1930s, with such films as *Assunta Spina* (1915), the lost *Sperduti nel buio* (1914), and such Blasetti films as *1860* (1934). According to Pierre Sorlin, "After the Liberation, Neorealism was much sharper and more systematic in its critique of injustice or inequality but its techniques were those tested in late 1930s."[15] Hence, it is necessary to abandon too rigid a distinction between the cinema under fascism and the cinema that followed it. In fact, writings in *Cinema, Bianco e Nero,* and other publications featuring such writers as Antonioni, De Santis, and Barbaro called for a return to an earlier form of "realism" exemplified by the writings of Giovanni Verga (Verga's work was to play a critical role in the cinema of the latter days of the regime and particularly in the films of Visconti). In addition, critics and filmmakers cited American writers such as Ernest Hemingway, William Faulkner, and John Dos Passos for their innovative modernist treatments of language, style, landscape, and characters, which were to play an influential role in the further developments of cinematic form.

One of neorealism's major spokespersons, Cesare Zavattini, described neorealism as a reaction to the cinema of the fascist years and to Hollywood's commercial cinema with its "invented stories," its tightly controlled scenarios, uses of stars, and stylized treatment of character and situations. "Substantially," wrote Zavattini, "the question today is, instead of turning imaginary situations into 'reality' and trying to make them look 'true,' to make things as they are, almost by themselves, create their own special significance. Life is not what is invented in 'stories': life is another matter. To understand it involves a minute, unrelenting, and patient search."[16] But this "search" has been complicated by the mythology of realism, making it difficult to grasp its genealogy, its evolution, and its persistence in the critical literature.

Similarly, French critic André Bazin lauded the work of the neorealists as giving back "to the cinema a sense of the ambiguity of reality."[17] This cinema "reveals to the anxious and alert spectator a world alive with possibilities, where perception results in care and where aesthetics finds its fulfillment in morality."[18] A film such as *Roma, citta aperta* was "to be the repudiation of an industry as wedded to rhetoric as the Mussolini regime under which it flourished. The filmmaker's most obvious antirhetorical ploy was to dispose of all the physical trappings of prewar cinema, making a virtue of the necessity imposed on him by the straitened circumstances of a wartorn industry."[19] "Neorealism, according to Millicent Marcus, is first and foremost a moral statement with all the ethical responsibility that such a vision entails."[20] Thus, despite the differing styles identified with neorealism, the filmmakers shared a common concern not merely to record the past but also to find a philosophical, social, and aesthetic form to explore "what lies beneath the surface of events," to suggest their moral significance.[21]

In the first segment of his documentary film *Neorealismo*, as an introduction to his exploration of this cinematic movement, Carlo Lizzani asks, "What was neorealism?" Based on a discussion of a range of films from 1943 to 1954, he offers the answers to this question in terms of the dominant figures involved on-screen and off and of the critical issues generated by a group of diverse filmmakers and critics such as Alessandro Blasetti, Mario Camerini, Renato Castellani, Giuseppe De Santis, Vittorio De Sica, and Luchino Visconti. The three major traits Lizzani singles out as a basis for commonality, despite differing styles, are (1) the treatment of the collective life of crowds as active and as a vast territory to be explored; (2) the use of the urban landscape as a periphery that leads in horizontal fashion to infinity; and (3) variations, an interchangeability of the roles of women and children in relation to their social functions. Identifying further qualities associated with neorealism, Alberto Farassino lists the films' topical concerns: a suspicion of historiography; a partiality for geography, topography, and social criticism; and a predilection for such themes as war, Resistance, and their aftermath, Americanity, criminality and banditry, labor and unemployment, popular culture, sports, and theater. Instead of passive, choreographed, familiar, and orderly images, the cinematic world became a vast territory to be explored, as in the films of Rossellini, De Sica, and Giuseppe de Santis.[22] This territory was brought to life through a profound revaluation of the geographical and social landscape. Interior life was expressed through an exterior milieu that included rural, suburban, and urban peripheries. The Italian cinema of the postwar years was involved in redeeming Italian "reality" from the ravages of fascism and World War II, and Italy as part of this process became identified with particular locales, rural and urban spaces, and physical and linguistic characteristics intrinsic to this "redemption" as these are embodied in the human figures located and struggling within this milieu.

The overarching image that governed these films was the road, through focusing on a journey that is both physical and psychic as in *Quattro passi tra le nuvole* (A Walk in the Clouds, 1942), *Ossessione* (1942), and *La strada* (The Road, 1954). In keeping with the conception of time-image, space becomes disconnected; destinations are uncertain, the characters' line of travel lost in infinity. The structure of these films presents a contrast to the vertical and closed design of classic cinema and of the commercial cinema of the fascist years. Not only has the milieu been rendered unfamiliar, but also expectations of action and resolution have been undermined. Furthermore, neorealism expressed a mobile sense of social, gendered, and institutionalized roles. One sees the appearance of children who behave as adults, as in *Germania anni zero* (Germany, Year Zero, 1948), *Roma città aperta*, *Sciuscià*, and *Ladri di biciclette*, portraits of women challenging marital and familial models and expectations, and portraits of priests who eschew ecclesiastical conformity, sometimes becoming militants, if not communists.

Not surprisingly, these transformations, evident in the choice of a contemporary setting for narratives and in the choice of marginal, ambiguous, and unstable characters, were to have a transforming effect on stardom, reinvigorating it and producing different cultural models. While stars of the cinema of the 1930s and early 1940s make their appearance in the films of the post–World War II era, notable changes become evident in the filming of the human body and gesture, and the uses of verbal language and of narration. Indeed, one of the more neglected aspects in the debates over neorealism is the role of stardom. The familiar texts of neorealism took a critical look at the glamour and artifice associated with stardom during the years of fascism, and such films, particularly *Roma, città aperta* and *Riso amaro*, either drew on established stars or were responsible for the creation of new ones that highlighted the changing bodies of femininity and masculinity that were to effect the postwar cinema. The selection of actors to play roles was determined as much by their availability, despite their association with the cinema under fascism, as by their suitability to express a radically transformed world. Thus, the presence of stars would serve a different function than in earlier cinema, becoming a reminder and exploration of their roles within the preceding cinema and a critical reflection on the inadequacy of their models for the postwar cinema, as well as harbingers of things to come.

While neorealism has been theorized as remote from the ever-present threat of the mass market of cultural production, the particular films identified with it were burdened with remainders of a past with which they had to reckon and which were inevitably fused to political and cinematic memories of fascism. This description is applicable to *Roma, città aperta* and to Anna Magnani, who is a critical figure in subsequent cinematic interpretations of redeeming the national landscape through images of the feminine body. In fact, as an aftermath of this film, Magnani's stardom became consistently identified with the Roman landscape, and, by extension, with the Italian nation in peril. Similarly, *Riso amaro*, starring Silvana Mangano, was a film that bridged "the neorealist experiment and the popular cinema of the 1950s."[23] This film, with its emphasis on "landscape and the human presence in it, rather than constituting a radical break with neorealism, became the basis for the commercial cinema of the 1950s and beyond."[24]

The transformations in stardom were effected through a focus on the human body, particularly on the bodies of female stars, in which they "are represented . . . as *operators* of a new national identity and physical characteristics, bodies, and gestures . . . become landscape."[25] Stardom was re-territorialized in affective images linked closely to region, nation, and class, with a particular emphasis on the value of being oneself, offering now the promise of authenticity. The cases of Anna Magnani's and Silvana Mangano's meteoric rise to international stardom are instructive for an understanding of the confrontation of the old and the new in relation to postwar cinema as well as for identifying the contradictory character of various forms of neorealism. Neorealism would appear to take different, seemingly disparate routes by bifurcating into the popular star-driven genres, particularly the comedies and melodramas of the 1950s and the cinema of auteurs identified with the 1960s, but a closer examination of stardom reveals the malleable philosophical, cultural, and political character of the neorealist aesthetic as it inflects the postwar cinematic landscape. Thus, stardom permutated yet again, offering a different, egalitarian sense of performance that, rather than abandoning the star, paradoxically created the conditions for its "redemption."

An Italian Icon: *Roma, città aperta* and Anna Magnani

The figure of Anna Magnani looms large in identifying how neorealism played a role in the creation of stars. Her long career began in variety and cabaret theater, and in her early films she reprised her music hall persona, one that combined comedy, caricature, and vulgarity in appearance and dialogue. In the sixteen films she made prior to *Roma, citta aperta* she was largely cast in supporting roles. Her roles as a chanteuse were distinctive and praised by critics, though, by comparison with Isa Miranda, Magnani, a vaudeville performer, was still a lesser luminary in cinema.[26] Given her background in variety, she portrayed a singer in *Cavalleria* (1936) and in *Teresa Venerdì* (1941). Her role as entertainer and mistress to Vittorio De Sica in *Teresa Venerdì* has been described by one critic as volcanic, smoldering "like Mount Vesuvius,"[27] but such an assessment is retrospective, since the film became a vehicle for Adriana Benetti, who also starred in *Quattro passi tra le nuvole* among other roles in the 1940s. Only later did Magnani come to represent for many critics and fans a symbol of Italian-ness associated with organic forms of representation, identified with her iconography, stocky body, use of gesture, unique laughter, and inimitable voice.

The role that might be considered to prefigure her metamorphosis into a Roman icon in *Roma, città aperta* is in *Campo de' Fiori* (The Peddler and the

Lady, 1943). In that film she plays a fruit vender, Elide, at the Campo de' Fiori market, an out-spoken, choric commentator on the romantic fantasies of Peppino (Aldo Fabrizzi), a fish vendor and a Don Juan figure who seeks to "fare un bella figura" (make a good impression) with an upper class woman, Elsa (Caterina Boratto). In his obsession with Elsa, he taunts Elide, scorning her affection for him. In contrast to the blonde, fashionable, and mysterious Elsa, Magnani is dark-haired, untidy, and outspoken ("When I see the truth, I speak it"). Her working-class status is reinforced by her appearance. Though identified largely with proletarian characters, Magnani is not from the working class but from a middle-class but itinerant background. In *Campo*, she is dressed in nondescript skirt, sweater, and apron, with tousled hair and minimal makeup. Her voluble responses to events are emotional: she is contemptuous and angry about Peppino's antics, though she also expresses concern for his welfare. "You are all heart," the barber Aurelio (Peppino de Filippo) tells her. The Magnani image that was to be her signature as a star is evident in her boundless energy, her defiant stance, characterized by the position of her hands placed boldly on her hips, and her refusal to be silenced and subdued. However, at the end of the film, her appearance and manner is altered. She is fashionably attired with a tidy coiffure that contrasts to her earlier unkempt locks, but while somewhat subdued, she remains audacious. She is an image not of passive and submissive femininity but of defiance, willfulness, and garrulousness.

In *Abasso la miseria* (Down with Misery, 1945), she was cast in a maternal role that further underlined her abrasiveness and garrulousness but also her underlying benevolence. Her husband brings home an ostensibly homeless child and a dog that she tries vainly to rid herself of until she discovers her affection for the child and his pet. In this film she sings, not as the public performer with which she had been identified in her earlier film roles, but in the home, to accompany music on a radio, her prize possession, thus inserting an extra-diegetic element but also indicating her love of playfulness. In retrospect, Magnani's star image resided in her identification with the Roman working-class and maternal figures she played in many of her films. In certain ways, this maternal persona was not a dramatic departure from her previous performances "as a *popolana* whose identity is very much bound up with her community," and whose "colloquial language" is a sign of her belonging to a different landscape.[28] Her image in *Roma, città aperta* was realized in a text that elevated her type of strident femininity by situating it for audiences in a world that had experienced the sufferings of fascism and war, redeeming cinematic images of femininity and maternity from the clichés to which they had been subjected, establishing a persona to be identified with the dishonored and dismembered city of Rome. Magnani as Pina offered the illusion of "the female body, intact and uncontaminated by the look of Fascist ideology"[29] through the illusion of being "herself," a persona different from the clichés of fascist femininity, an "authentic" star.

Roma, città aperta provides a map to trace Rossellini's contributions to the language and forms of postwar Italian and world cinema. The film introduces different cinematic conceptions of landscape, character, action, situation, femininity, and masculinity than had characterized many films of the previous era. The canonical status of the film resides not in its adherence to documentation but in its challenge to forms of realism that uncritically assume that "to see is to believe." Rather than resting on fidelity to actual sights and sounds, the film is an instrument for questioning memory and belief in what is seen and heard. While the film provides documentary-like images of a city in the moribund grip of its occupiers, it questions and subverts familiar images and sounds associated with newsreels, documentaries, and commercial feature films. The suffering body of the city of Rome, its inhabitants, and cinema itself become a text for the spectator to contemplate as an impetus to critical thinking about the cinema of the past and one in the process of change.

Roma, citta aperta appeared in 1945 at the end of World War II. For twenty years, Italy had been subjected to the power of the Fascist regime under its dictator, Benito Mussolini, or to German occupation. The path of the regime led to Italy's entry into World War II on the side of Germany and resulted in the ouster of Mussolini in 1943 by the Fascist Grand Council. The war that Italy had joined under Fascist leadership had already brought about devastating losses for the Italian populace. The country was divided in two. In the south, the Allies fought against the Germans to liberate the country. In the north, partisan groups comprised of Socialists, Communists, and Catholic Action militants fought to liberate cities and countryside from Fascist and Nazi occupiers, and their actions were, for many, identified with heroic bravery and sacrifice, attitudes that translated well onto film and literature.

While Rossellini's *Paisà* (1946) traced the actions that took place throughout Italy to liberate the country, *Roma, città aperta*, as its title indicates, takes place in Rome during the last months of German occupation, but the events are emblematic of the broader situation confronted by the nation. The phrase "Roma, citta aperta" was not Rossellini's. The conception derived from the conventions of warfare that decreed that "international cities" were "open" and, thus, protected from destruction; however, the notion of "openness" was not observed by the German occupiers, who destroyed buildings, imposed severe martial law on the city, and wantonly slaughtered inhabitants.[30] Dire consequences were exacted from those considered enemies of this occupation. In particular, German brutality was directed against those who supported the Allies and were identified with Resistance and leftist activities. The conception of "openness" emerged as central to the style and motifs of *Roma, città aperta* and in particular to the conceptions of the characters of Pina, the Partisan priest, and the martyred Manfredi. The film's treatment of character and landscape underscores the distinctions between open and closed conceptions of a cinematic world as embodied in characters that will become a dominant characteristic of the emerging postwar stardom.

Roma, città aperta was produced under most adverse circumstances.[31] The Germans had only recently departed, but the effects of their social and economic devastation were evident everywhere. Not only were filmmaking facilities destroyed, the social infrastructure was in ruins. Money was hard to come by, as was raw film stock, but Rossellini and his associates were able to put a script together, hire professional actors, and film the sequences on the desired locations. The film was shot on the streets, in churches, in scriptwriter Sergio Amidei's apartment, and in Capitani Studios. Further problems occurred when crowds appeared during the filming, hostile to the sight of Nazis, while other problems entailed lighting difficulties and conflicts among actors.

Despite the difficulties encountered by the filmmaker, *Roma, città aperta* need not be mythologized as a narrative of cinematic adversity transformed to international good fortune. Pierre Leprohon believes that "the film would bring out the hoary truth that scant resources and difficult conditions of work are often beneficial to art."[32] And David Forgacs, while acknowledging the impact of *Roma, città aperta* on postwar filmmaking, regards it as a transitional film—"for Rossellini, for the cinema, for a society coming out of two decades of Fascism—rather than a wholly new work."[33] The film is a compendium of strategies and images that are assumed to belong to the cinematic narratives of the fascist era with their star images. These images are presented in Rossellini's film in a style that renders them familiar but at the same time uproots them from their familiar milieu in the commercial cinema of the Ventennio. The eclecticism of the film brings past and present cinema and culture into conflict through stark juxtapositions between the characters.

In the history of Italian cinema and in critical biographies, Roberto Rossellini is presented as an enigma, an image he helped to create. In 1937, after a playboy existence, Rossellini turned to filmmaking, writing scripts, assisting directors on productions, and finally creating his own films.[34] His first cinematic creations were short and poetic documentaries of natural life. His first feature-length films, a trilogy of war films, appeared in the early 1940s: *La nave bianca* (The White Ship, 1941), *Un pilota ritorna* (A Pilot's Return, 1942), and *L'uomo della croce* (The Man of the Cross, 1943), all considered to be anticipatory of the neorealist aesthetic. In the spirit of the war film, the trilogy relied on a fusion of fictional elements, focusing on personal hardship, sacrifice, and romance, and on documentary footage, conveying the brutality and machinic character of war on sea and land. The films undoubtedly reveal the character of and demands on both commercial and state-sponsored cinema under the regime. They also reveal the filmmaker's idiosyncratic and changing treatment of cinematic narrative, perspective, and star images, which were to develop over the course of his career as exemplified in his uses of Anna Magnani and Ingrid Bergman (see chapter 5).

In one sense, *Roma, città aperta* is not a drastic rupture from the cinema that preceded it, since the cinema under late fascism was already engaged in a critique of the status quo through the films of Vittorio De Sica (*I bambini ci guardano* [The Children Are Watching Us, 1942]) and Alessandro Blasetti (*Quattro passi tra le nuvole* [A Walk among the Clouds, 1942]). However, *Roma, città aperta* was able more directly and more freely to tackle the nature and consequences of fascism and war. No longer reliant on the mode of production that had distinguished commercial and state-supported cinema during fascism, Rossellini had to generate his own sources of funding. He had also to find producers who would invest in the film (e.g., Chiara Politi, Giuseppe Amato, and Aldo Venturini), hire popular theater and film actors (Anna Magnani and Aldo Fabrizzi) who were willing to lend their names to such a project, locate and purchase hard-to-find film stock, and enlist the talents of professional screenwriters (Sergio Amidei and Fellini) and a world-class photographer (Ubaldo Arata).

The final film script focused primarily on eight characters: a working-class woman, Pina (Anna Magnani); her fiancé Francesco, a typesetter and member of the Resistance (Francesco Granjacquet); Manfredi, a communist Resistance fighter (Marcello Pagliero); Don Pietro, a Partisan priest (Aldo Fabrizzi); Nazi commandant Major Bergmann (Harry Feist) and his German henchwoman, Ingrid (Giovanna Galetti); Lauretta, Pina's sister (Carla Rovere); and Italian actress Marina (Maria Michi). These fictionalized characters were either based on actual individuals of the time or were conflations of several figures, and the various threads of the narrative are woven together to portray the desperate conditions under the Nazi occupation, culminating in scenes of betrayal, torture, and execution.[35] In certain ways this description of *Roma, città aperta* would qualify it as a wartime melodrama, and critics have commented on its conventional dimensions.[36] However, the style and method of the film reveal that its focus exceeds generic categorization as war film, melodrama, or fictionalized documentary, though it includes reflections on these genres. The innovativeness of the film resides in the subtle stylistic treatment that I define as "conceptual realism," one that depends on a metacinematic treatment of images that situates them within an identifiable and specific narrative but calls attention to their status as artifacts. This self-conscious preoccupation with cinematic form is central to the cinema of the postwar era—in certain instances treated indirectly, in others overtly. The film's anastomosis of fact and fiction through its characters is an invitation to regard cinematic realism as based not on literal reproduction but on the encounter between events and their invented significance.

Roma, città aperta's method is to invoke the memory of earlier cinematic narratives and their images, but to re-situate them in a new context to cast doubts on them and to signal to other meanings. Instead of being familiar, transparent, and fixed in their meaning, the images solicit new and multi-faceted associations. The method of conceptual realism resides in producing unfamiliar encounters with commonsensical and clichéd images that are unhinged from their conventional moorings. The film has not diminished the specificity of place or the tragedy of events that transpire in it, but has used the landscape to challenge the spectator to explore their implications. In the case of Pina, her figure undergoes a metamorphosis that will transform her from an ordinary victim to a figure whose dying will acquire a power that will not only remain indelibly in cinematic memory but will also consolidate Magnani's position as a star.

The context for the narration is the quotidian landscape of the poor. In this manner, "the film in effect reappropriates Rome for its ordinary citizens and erases traces of the regime, freezing the city in the moment of occupation and resistance."[37] The emphasis is not on mere documentation of the milieu but on the camera's and the viewer's observation of the events within that milieu. *Roma, città aperta*'s treatment of landscape emphasizes mobility and the constraints on movement identified with the characters' difficult passage through the city's Roman milieu, dramatizing restraints imposed on the inhabitants by the occupying forces and also the strategies of the populace in evading capture, so that there are sustained differences in the angles of vision. The first half of the film emphasizes distinctions between interiors and exteriors conveyed through shots of characters as they gaze out of windows. Manfredi's landlady peers out to discover the arrival of the Nazis in search of Manfredi, and on the morning of the wedding, Pina observes the arrival of the Nazis for the roundup of the residents of the tenement from a window in her flat. The youths observe the arrival of the Nazis from their hideout in the upper reaches of the apartment house.

The film relies on several views of Rome, one involving a view from above and one a view from below, corresponding "to two different types of power and two different intentions: that of domination and that of resistance."[38] The former type is associated with the system of domination instituted by the Nazis via the establishment of the "Schroeder Plan," which mandated the division of the city into fourteen zones. These zones were coordinated through centralized intelligence operations and permitted the surveillance and rounding up of suspects dramatized in the film by Bergmann's activities. The latter type of power, associated with the Italian populace, is decentralized, "hidden from the occupiers' gaze . . . full of hidden routes on foot" that include escape routes over rooftops, and through basements and alleyways.[39] The Nazis' mode of surveillance is based on remoteness from their victims and a detached observance of their images.

In conjunction with the motif of surveillance, Millicent Marcus commented: "The several maps that recur throughout the film serve to remind us of its thematic importance and the different meanings attached to the city,"[40] to the people, and to Magnani's stardom. However, not only do the maps offer different aspects of city life but they also evoke different forms of cinematic viewing. Bergmann's maps of Rome that hang in his office are blueprints of his power and control over the movement of others. By contrast, the world of the Resistance is dispersed and identified with images of constantly shifting movement linked to the varying moments of the narration and the various characters. Allusions to vision predominate throughout *Roma, città aperta*, suggesting connections between the events filmed and the role of the cinema in generating ways of seeing. Bergmann's reliance on surveillance is also suggestive of forms of cinema wherein the viewer is given a unified sense of the cinematic milieu. The maps of the city function not merely as a thematic device to underscore a contrast between mastery and contingency but as a strategy for providing commentary on forms of visual control involving a closed system of interpretation. Similarly, the photographs he uses to identify and trap Manfredi are emblematic of a hermetically sealed world antithetical to an open form of narration.

The openness of the film's style, especially in its episodic character, creates spaces through which to regard the characters and events. When space is no longer unified but fragmented and dispersed, chance and opportunity can be entertained, if not by the characters then by the spectator. The potential for the open text introduces the potential for allegorizing, for creating layers of meaning that extend beyond the specific events portrayed in the film and that will be central to the sacralisation of Magnani's persona. As critics have acknowledged, the images in the film resonate beyond their contemporary context. The image of the "eternal city" is one of ruin and devastation, like the world of destruction and death that Major Hartmann invokes in his drunken speech to Bergmann. The ruins are historical and also cinematic, the consequence of fascism's devastation of the cultural and political landscape written on the ruined bodies of Pina, Manfredi, and Don Pietro.

Specifically, the film's treatment of Pina's death on the Roman street resonates with allegorical significance, as she becomes a tragic example of the many victims of the Germans. The filming of her death is metamorphosed from a material to an emblematic event. Her image merges with religious iconography particularly associated with the death of Christ. After she falls, Don Pietro cradles her body in Pietà-fashion. At this moment, Pina evokes general associations with martyrdom but in strikingly different terms than in conventional religious iconography and its spiritualized landscapes. Her death is endowed with a historical resonance that identifies her with the fate of Rome as a nation. The maternal body is fused to the city of Rome, and by extension to the Italian nation, reinforcing connections between the feminine body and the Italian cultural past. The film's allegorizing of landscape proposes strategies that orchestrate a complex sense of time, bringing past, present, and future into consideration, spilling over into the films' reconfiguration of the bodies of masculinity and femininity and their connections to the potential resurrection of the nation (and of the cinema).[41]

The most memorable, often reproduced, and enigmatic image in the film, if not in all of cinema, is that of Magnani, as Pina, shot down in the street as she races after the truck bearing Francesco away, but she is not the only female figure in the film, and she actually disappears quite early in the narrative. Pina and the other female characters in the film, Ingrid, Marina, and Lauretta, are an index to the method of the narrative and its designs on the viewer. Femininity is central to the film's transforming of cultural clichés. The spectator is given familiar associations with woman as maternal figure, lesbian dominatrix, actress, or prostitute as inherited from the archives of stardom. The female characters are not conceived in the language of technical realism as rounded and individuated characters. Instead, they are ciphers, provoking uncertainty about the quality and direction of their position in the narrative.

Peter Bondanella, Peter Brunette, and Angelo Restivo have identified elements of the film as "melodramatic,"[42] and the concept of melodrama is a starting point to understand how the film treats characters in dual fashion: as evocative of commonsense and cliché and as exposing the limitations of these. Melodrama is associated with affect, often with femininity; it is also identified with the ubiquitous existence of clichés that circulate not only "in the external world, but . . . penetrate each one of us and constitute his internal world."[43] However, unlike traditional melodrama, *Roma, città aperta* does not reinforce clichéd and predictable responses to suffering and injustice but rather subjects them to investigation. Surprisingly, in a film identified as "realistic," the female characters are drawn in stylized fashion, leading critics to regard the film as still tied to classical cinema, as a "transitional" film. However, in keeping with the film's self-reflexive method, the female characters are central to its investigation of relations between the cinema and fascism and influential in contributing to altered forms of stardom in subsequent decades.

Magnani's Pina seems a cliché of an idealized maternal figure, but her presence raises a number of enigmas about her "martyrdom" which ultimately coalesce in the iconic image of her body cradled in the arms of the priest. She is initially portrayed as a defender of the family, then an opponent of the Nazis, a penitent, and finally a sacrificial victim. The brief images establish Pina not as a narrative agent but as a figure acted upon by other forces, especially by the filmmaker. Specifically, Magnani's ample body, her disheveled look, husky voice, and passionate acting are indicative of the film's departure from earlier

3.1. New star bodies: Anna Magnani in *Roma, città aperta. Photofest.*

cinematic conceptions of femininity. Although the cinema of the fascist years had featured working-class women, they were largely erring figures in need of redemption whose star appearance reflected Hollywood images of beauty.

Rossellini's choice of Magnani to play Pina (though he had originally wanted Clara Calamai, who had starred in Visconti's *Ossessione*) went against the grain of her past performances in variety theater and film comedy. Consonant with the film's allegorizing, Pina's role is a reminder of ideological constraints on the cinema of the fascist era as they inflected representations of women. Documentaries by LUCE (the state-sponsored organization for the creation of propaganda) and certain commercial feature films had focused on the project of returning women to the domestic sphere and to their "primary" role as mothers. Government campaigns were waged to enhance the birth rate as well as to promote the primacy of the family, presumed to be under siege.[44] The valorization of motherhood was a response to feminist aspirations. The maternal figure was often presented either as a paragon of self-abnegation or as errant and destructive. Magnani's portrait of Pina does not annul these cultural clichés but endows them with new properties that speak to residual and emergent elements in relation to the role of the Italian mother.

Though Magnani's character may seem to bear cinematic affinity to portraits of the mother in earlier Italian cinema, her portrait is more ambiguous. The eloquent filming of the manner of her death was a critical factor in her subsequent elevation to stardom, making her the "sacred" monster of the postwar cinema. Classical representations of the Pietà are inverted by placing Pina in the position of Christ, and Don Pietro in the position of the Madonna, setting Pina apart from the other feminine characters and from dominant cultural representations of femininity. Her association with religious iconography serves to metamorphose her figure from one of ordinariness and renders it sacrosanct. Moreover, her precipitous removal from the narrative, while due, in part, to the film's adherence to actual events (based on the shooting of the pregnant Maria Teresa Gullace), anticipates the film's reflections on the deaths of Manfredi and Don Pietro. No more than their deaths can hers be reduced to formula as is often done in films that purport to elevate figures identified with "great actions and deeds."[45] Though visually absent later in the film, her presence continues in elegiac fashion to have an impact, offering an unforgettable memory rooted deep in the culture of stardom and identified with a form of sacrality that poses an alternative to clichés inherited from the fascist era and that is slated to become a permanent attribute of Magnani's stardom.

Pina's character is also distinguished from the other female figures that invite speculation on preexisting cinematic clichés and further enhance her figure. In contrast to Pina, Lauretta, her sister, offers a rather unspectacular image of prostitution and is portrayed as a pleasure-seeking and unthinking collaborator. She embodies a mundane and cynical view of the world. She is antagonistic toward her family and hostile toward criticism about her collaboration with the Nazis. Her vulgarity is revealed in her clichéd response to seeing Francesco on his wedding night. Unaware of Pina's death, she laughs and asks him if Pina has already chucked him out. However, as if to temper her callousness, the script has her say to Marina, "Perhaps Manfredi is right. Maybe we are stupid." Unlike Marina, whom she seeks to emulate, she is not malignant, but, as Pina describes her to Manfredi, "Stupid." Clearly, her image is diminished through her awkward physical appearance and her identification with a melodramatic world that comes to be associated with the banal choice of personal survival. In a film that places emphasis on looking, her figure is identified with a form of blindness: she is cast as a viewer to events but one who does not see.

Marina, the actress, played by Maria Michi, provides a familiar cinematic portrait of femininity—the *femme fatale* identified with theatricality. In contrast to Pina, Marina conjures up different associations with the earlier Italian cinema. Marina is a scaled-down and pale version of the pre–World War I image of the cinematic diva, a melodramatic figure associated with or desirous of belonging to an upper-class world identified with decadence, passion, and resentment. Her role evokes ironic associations with a form of melodramatic filmmaking connected to the stars in the cinema of the fascist years. Marina is identified with certain props of the comedic and melodramatic from the "white telephone" films of the fascist era. Her apartment, her clothes, and her attention to her appearance are contrasted to the cramped world of the tenement and to Pina's unadorned physical appearance and plain clothing. Like the feminine characters in film noir, she may be attractive but she is deadly. She introduces the viewer to the world of the Nazis, and she acts as informer and collaborator. Theatricality dominates her interactions with Manfredi as she plays the dual role of pursuer and betrayer.

The repeated images of Marina seated or standing before a mirror contrast to those that situate Pina before a window, looking out and aware of impending disaster, and suggest Marina's inability to see anything other than her own image. Her occluded vision is further evident after the death of Manfredi. She looks at his mutilated body and collapses onto the floor like a deflated balloon. She becomes objectified as an inert body, shorn of the fur coat that was the price of her betrayal. The material objects she sought to enhance her image are the ones that finally reveal her as an empty cipher of femininity. She emerges in the end as a somnambulist or a marionette set in motion by external forces rather than operating independently. Marina is exemplary of the film's double critique of politics and power: of the destructive power of fascism and of a form of cinema that had been reduced to cliché. If Pina becomes a harbinger of regenerated forms of stardom, Marina's is a portrait of its desired demise.

Ingrid conveys another register of femininity, expressed through an association with masculinity. Her clothing and her movements reenact the cliché of masculinized feminine figures often identified with melodrama and film noir. Ingrid's dress, hairdo, and makeup are, like her mannerisms, severe. Her movement is restricted to interiors: she is not seen in the city. Her character is expressed through innuendo in her sudden appearance at the theater where Marina performs, in mirror shots of the two together, and in images of Marina's reclining against Ingrid as Ingrid strokes her. Like the mirror shots, the telephone is their depersonalized form of contact and a further sign of their function as flattened and disembodied images that, though they look and speak, can neither see nor hear. The stylization and clichéd nature of Ingrid's character is not merely a device to identify her as incarnating "evil." Her character, like Marina's, further implies that theatricality is inherent to fascist culture. Ingrid's character may not "explain" the abuses of power, but it dramatizes its reliance on staging and the potentially dire consequences of performance. However, the contrast between Pina and these other characters also served to elevate Magnani's stardom, underscoring her difference and uniqueness.

Magnani went on to star in a range of films, not only in those directed by Rossellini but also in comedies, melodramas, and historical films by Visconti, Renoir,

Camerini, and Monicelli, winning an Oscar for her role in *The Rose Tattoo* (1955). Not only did she become the prima donna of cinema in her work for certain directors, but her off-screen life was correspondingly newsworthy and publicized in her marriage to and divorce from the director Goffredo Alessandrini, the illness of her son, her affairs with Massimo Serrato and Roberto Rossellini. However, hers is certainly a case where the films of neorealism created the stuff of stardom that was to be evident in the films of the next decades. In the wake of the horrendous events that had transpired as a consequence of fascism and World War II, images of landscape, masculinity and femininity, the body, and seeing and hearing could no longer to be taken for granted, and Magnani's stardom occupied a critical role in the regeneration of Italian identity not only for Italians but for international audiences. *Roma, città aperta*'s treatment of her character and the Roman landscape enlists the power of cinema to create images that facilitate the possibility of regarding gestures and words differently as an invitation to thinking through images. In the case of *Roma, città aperta*, this thinking involves a sustained reflection on the screen images that flash before spectators but that they, despite being surrounded by a world of images, do not often see and hence may not think about. In this reflection, the body of the actor plays a critical role.

Magnani's most successful role financially was in the postwar film *L'onorevole Angelina* (1947), in which she again plays a militant working-class but dutiful wife and mother who mobilizes her community against exploiters and speculators. To that role as well, Magnani brought the same wild energy, brashness, and raucousness that would be forever imprinted on her performances and persona. Described as "a one woman show,"[46] she literally realizes this description in *Una voce umana* (The Human Voice, 1948), directed by Rossellini, where she is the only character on screen, delivering a monologue into a telephone, once again confirming the cinematic importance of the telephone as a reminder of the importance of the star's voice and of her physical presence and, by implication, of cinematic apparatus as comprising both visual and sound images in tension with each other.

In *Il miracolo* (1948), she portrays a slow-witted shepherdess impregnated by an itinerant (Federico Fellini) whom she assumes to be St. Joseph. In an inebriated state, she disports herself with him and falls asleep. When she awakens, he has, like an apparition, disappeared. She gives birth to her "holy infant" to the vilification and abuse of the townspeople, but the poignancy of her acting as a suffering Virgin Mary further consolidated the sacrality of her star persona. The film became a scandal in the United States and was banned for a time until the courts ruled that it was protected under the First Amendment of the U.S. Constitution. But, once again, the film draws on the combined portrait of transgressive femininity aligned to religion integral to Magnani's stardom. But her star persona would also become a vehicle for critically exploring the illusory but real character of cinema. For example, Francesco Casetti asks, "What happens when a film speaks to us in some way or other about itself, about being cinema, about the universe it inhabits? When it tells a story which takes place in Hollywood or Cinecittà, when it shows how show business works, or tells the life story of a star?"[47] These questions are embedded in the films of many of the directors associated with neorealism, if not always explicitly treated.

Bellissima (1951) is a film that exploits Magnani's stardom (and the commerce of stardom more generally) to investigate the phenomenon of the star in the commercial cinema. Directed by Luchino Visconti, it stars Magnani as Maddalena Cecconi, a star-struck mother who regards the cinema as a way for her young daughter Maria to escape from their working-class life and for Maddalena to participate in the dreams offered by popular cinema. Obsessively she sets out on a campaign to ensure that the girl will be selected for a part in a Blasetti movie. She takes her to Cinecittà to enroll her for a studio test. She provides the child with clothes and elocution lessons, hires a self-serving "agent" at great expense to facilitate entry to the competition, and argues with her husband over the expenditures from a meager income designed to cover household expenses. Oblivious to the difficulties that her fantasy of cinema creates for her child, she persists until finally the child is chosen for a screen test. Having convinced a young woman, a former actress and aspiring star, to allow her to view the test from a projection booth, Maddalena is horrified as the director's aides laugh at the child's performance. The director, Alessandro Blasetti as himself and as an avatar of commercial cinema, decides however to select Maria, but Maddalena takes the child away and rejects the offer that she has worked so hard to receive.

Of the film Geoffrey Nowell-Smith writes, "at its highest level it is a denial of all stereotypes, about Visconti, about Italian films, and even about that sacred monster, Anna Magnani, who is the star of the film."[48] Visconti's use of "sacred monster" is significant for its adherence to the star's identification with portraits of working-class life and with the images derived from *Roma, città aperta* and *L'onorevole Angelina* of a maternal figure. This evocation of Magnani as a "sacred monster" captures the ambivalence toward Italian maternal figures incarnated by the star's persona but also inherent to Italian culture. The film is an incisive and complex investigation of stardom as inherent to the production of fantasies by way of the commercial cinema. Magnani, the star, is placed in a familial context but becomes an instrument to explore the boundaries between spectacle and reality, maternal responsibility and personal desire, from which her own stardom cannot be exempted.

Magnani, both as the character Maddalena and as the star who realizes this character, is complicit in the illusions manufactured by cinema that are inherent to Visconti's complex exploration of the nature of entertainment and spectacle and their paradoxical relation to reality. Magnani's star image is invoked through

3.2. The uses of stardom: Anna Magnani in *Bellissima*. *Photofest*.

two scenes, one in which she sits mesmerized before Howard Hawks's *Red River* and another where she dresses before a mirror. In the first, she is a spectator seduced by the reflection from the screen, and in the second she is a spectator seduced by her own image but also an image offered for the spectator: "Magnani exchanges her role with us and puts herself in the position of an (invisible) spectator, thus turning her own reflection into a spectacularized image. She doubles herself, being at the same time, her own spectator and the actress she looks at."[49] In this way, the film complicates Magnani's image, enabling spectators to identify with the film's star but also to resist complete immersion in spectacle, thus allowing for a critical engagement with spectacle while also intervening in its powerful hold on spectators.

Thus, the appropriation of a star persona seems consistent with Visconti's exploratory treatment of spectacle in other films where the spectator is invited to contemplate the power of these images but also to regard them differently as moments of reflection on what is seen and heard. *Bellissima*, thanks to its direction, its camera work, and especially Magnani's star presence, is an indication of how reductive and binary assessments of neorealism fall short of accounting for its dynamic contributions to both the popular and the auteur cinema of the postwar era. The film further reveals the conceptual dimensions of neorealism, which are often neglected in schematic discussions of the neorealist aesthetic. In a film such as *Bellissima*, through its uses of Magnani, and the fictional portraits of the older star and the unsuccessful actress, Iris, the everyday and spectacle are blurred rather than set in insuperable opposition, the real and the imaginary interpenetrate, and clichés are once again put under pressure, so that through reflection on the star and on artifice, the cinema "becomes an analytic of the image."[50] Thus, in Visconti's film, the star is not obliterated, nor is the cinema divested of its spectacular and fictional character. Rather, the film reveals how "fiction provides points of articulation for life. It punctuates it (moments of spectacle inside daily life) and transforms it (everyday life itself becoming spectacle)."[51] And the portrait of Magnani's star-struck Maddalena and the inescapable allusions to her own star persona serve to underscore more self-conscious and critical uses of the star, not only in a film such as *Bellissima* that directly focuses on cinema, but also in popular and auteurist forms of stardom that were to emerge in the 1950s and 1960s. Furthermore, neorealism is revealed in practice and theory as intimately confronting the question, "What is Cinema?" and this film specifically and reflexively confronts neorealism in the context of the phenomenon of stardom.

The five-part *Siamo donne* (We Are Women, 1953) offers a further reflection on the character and persistence of stardom in the early postwar years. The film features sketches by five directors who focus on four prominent stars, Alida Valli (Gianni Franciolini), Ingrid Bergman (Rossellini), Isa Miranda (Luigi Zampa), and Anna Magnani (Visconti). The initial sketch, directed by Alfredo Guarini, involves a group of actresses seeking to win a screen test to appear in a film featuring the four established stars. The prologue establishes the pre-life of the star, the preparation for stardom or for exclusion from it. It emphasizes the roles of beauty, personality, age qualifications, and the different motives of the aspirants for seeking to enter the movies. It also focuses on those who are rejected: the number of aspirants is finally reduced from a large number to two, Anna Amendola and Emma Danieli (playing themselves). Two of the sketches involve two extremely popular stars from the prewar cinema, Alida Valli and Isa Miranda, and (as with all four of the sketches of the stars) are preceded by a montage of posters publicizing their prominent films. In the case of the Valli sketch, she is portrayed in familiar terms as a glamorous star bored with her duties as celebrity. Invited to an engagement part by her masseuse, she indulges in fantasies of what her life might have been. Recognizing that she no longer can inhabit domesticity, she escapes from the party. Stardom is presented as a cliché, glamorous, socially demanding, but personally constraining, thus reiterating the conflict between "real life" and the cost of stardom. The episode seems a replay of a clichéd melodrama.

The sketch of Isa Miranda begins and ends with the star alone in her home. The camera moves freely through her house, capturing mementos from her long and stellar career through publicity stills of her in *Passaporto rosso, La signora di tutti,* and *Zazà.* Ultimately, because of the films advertised, she is portrayed not as a star but as a lonely woman who has missed out on the pleasures of maternity. Similarly to the Valli sketch, what is emphasized is a portrait of a woman whose commitment to career has barred her from maternal fulfillment. Briefly, the sketch portrays the older star coming to the aid of a young boy who has been wounded, taking him first to the hospital to be treated and then driving him home, where she finds his siblings waiting for the return of their mother from work. With their help, she tends to the boy's needs and to those of the youngest child. When the mother returns, Miranda is framed by the camera observing the pleasures of the reunion, commenting in the voice-over that she has finally understood "mother love." The final shots portray her, once gain alone at home, sitting on the edge of her bed and refusing to answer the ringing phone. Thus, the sketch recapitulates her film persona but also folds back to the first episode of the film with its portraits of eager pursuers of stardom, naïve to the "sacrifices" it entails.

The Magnani sketch directed by Visconti is different. It is a comedy, and the humor is generated by placing the actress in a seemingly inconsequential incident that "reveals" her persona. The incident is blown out of proportion and enables her to make fun of herself. The episode is an opportunity to exploit elements that inhere in Magnani's star persona, namely, her association with the Roman landscape and, even more, her reputation as someone who is feisty and hard to get along with. The spectator is treated to a tour of various Roman landmarks (with the star as guide and the taxi driver as foil of the joke). The conflict concerns whether her dachshund Babal is or is not a lapdog. If not, according to the taxi driver, she must pay an additional fare for the canine. She, dressed in a rather garish fur stole, refuses to pay the minimal one lira fee out of "principle," and, as a consequence, she is willing to spend more money and time to establish (vainly) that she is being overcharged, despite her being late to her performance in the theater. The outspoken character of the star in this instance is not aligned to a major violation of social justice but involves her refusal to accede to the unjust demands of a Roman taxi driver, who insists that she pay a fare for her lapdog.

As appropriate to a star identified with the Roman milieu, the sketch takes her through a tour of major sites in Rome—the Royal Place, the police station, and, finally, the Quattro Fontane Theater, culminating with her performing at the cabaret theater identified with Roman popular entertainment. As the curtains part, she appears on stage singing a melancholy song about "bella Roma" as the camera moves from long shot to middle distance to extreme close-up to capture her persona as a theater performer, which evokes for the audience her earlier career before becoming a major star. Thus, in this sketch, Visconti situates Magnani in a real location and in a context in which she is acting at non-acting, identifying familiar aspects of her personality and, thus, recapitulating the blurred boundaries between real and fictional situations integral to the character of Magnani's power as a performer, in this film as in her others. Unlike the other sketches cited, this one does not dwell on the cliché of the heavy burden of fame, but focuses on a major attribute of the star—her outspoken, garrulous, and energetic character as well as her talent as a comedian. It underscores Visconti's fascination with and ambivalence about commercial cinema, if not stardom (see chapter 5 for Rossellini sketch).

Pier Paolo Pasolini was also to capitalize on Magnani's stardom, and most particularly on her role in *Roma, città aperta*, in effect to produce a form of remake. In his choice of Anna Magnani to play the title role in *Mamma Roma* (1962), Pasolini returned to the postwar allegory of the maternal image and its connections to the hoped-for regeneration of the nation, albeit from a critical vantage point. In his film, Pasolini exploited Magnani's star image in the interests of de-territorializing it, attempting to de-fuse traditional conceptions of stardom and their links to a problematic nation/state identified with a sacrificial maternal image that the film seeks to expose as destructive. Thus, in *Mamma Roma*, Magnani the star was appropriated not as an "uncomplicated earthy, joyous, and sensuous creature" but as a prostitute. "Far from representing the glory of Italy, the word 'Roma' is at first uplifted by the association with the mother—indeed one of the sacred signifiers in Italian culture—and then degraded as the name of the prostitute."[52]

Magnani is indeed presented as a "sacred monster" in a film that links the star's maternal image to the vanity and destructiveness of middle-class aspirations for offspring. The "monster" is created by the elevation of maternity to a sacred position in the culture, but the Pasolini film tears away the illusion of sacrality, exposing it as a form of economic exchange (prostitution and theft) and as a form of coercion. Coming from an impoverished setting where survival involves prostitution for women and where illegitimate children are not uncommon, Magnani's character in the film unmasks the idealism of maternal self-sacrifice, the heterosexual norms it presupposes, and the class bias that it represents. Despite her fantasies of upward mobility, Mamma Roma is a woman of the streets where she sells her fruit, where she unsuccessfully tries to locate her son, who seeks to elude her, where she and her friend Fiore observe Ettore working at the trattoria, and where, forced to return to plying her trade on the darkened streets, she walks accompanied by her "clients." However, the filming

3.3. Framing Magnani's maternal iconography in *Mamma Roma. Photofest.*

of her "street-walking" is designed not to particularize and "psychologize" her character but rather to allegorize her role, albeit in the vein of demythologizing.

Magnani's role serves the allegory in several ways: (1) it draws on and inverts the canonical images of Magnani in the Rossellini film; (2) it invokes religion in critical fashion in relation to Mariolatry and motherhood; (3) it presents the dilemma of maternal-son relations in a context more expansive and critical than melodrama; and (4) it uses the iconography of Magnani as the film's instrument to question not merely the characters and events dramatized but "what a character sees" and, further, what and how the spectator sees.[53] The film relies on shots of Magnani framed by a window (or by the shots themselves, which act like windows) to reinforce the film's probing of the neutrality, technical realism, and normality of what we see on screen via its interpreters, the stars. The film exploits aspects of the "star," especially those that play with the star as "authentic" when, in fact, she is the incarnation of a process of visualization and simulation.

Despite Pasolini's attempts to "degrade" this "mythology," Magnani's star image in Italy and internationally persisted through his films and through the films of other directors. Magnani's persona was now so overwhelming, thanks to her defined appearance, her mode of acting, and the melodramas associated with her personal life, that her cinematic image far outstripped the narratives in which she appeared. Magnani would continue to incarnate an image of the Roman world until her last film, her brief and crusty appearance in *Fellini's Roma* (1972). Her funeral in Rome, where she died, was an overwhelming tribute to the star, in which dignitaries and massive crowds paid homage to the actress and to the world she had represented.[54]

Beauty Queens Become Stars: The Case of Silvana Mangano

The films directed by Vittorio De Sica, Rossellini, and Giuseppe De Santis not only reflect on the status of past and contemporary culture via the cinema but also indicate the emergence of new images of the female body. De Sica's *Ladri di biciclette* (1948), with its use of the Rita Hayworth poster for *Gilda*, had introduced "ties between the star and the pin-up as symbols of leisure, of prosperity, and consumption, all of which were desired in a country marked by war damage, unemployment, homelessness, and hunger."[55] De Santis's *Riso amaro* (1949) similarly invokes in critical fashion this type of star image through the role played by Silvana Mangano, who was to contribute to establishing a new and significant iconography of the "Italian" star nationally and internationally. Mangano's seductive dancing in *Riso amaro* (and in *Anna*, 1951) provides a spectacular display of her legs and her shapely body swaying to the popular music of boogie-woogie. The film further links her femininity to popular magazines and photo-romances, with their narratives of escape from the banalities of everyday life and their visual images of glamour. The popularity of pin-ups was a sign that spectacle and stardom had never disappeared from the screen, but also that it now assumed new forms.

Mangano (the winner of the Miss Rome beauty contest in 1947) and other beauty queens such as Gina Lollobrigida, Sophia Loren, and Lucia Bosè were the vital signs of the coming "restoration" of the erotic female Italian body to the body of film.[56] Mangano's films further capitalized on her successful modeling career. Her marriage to Dino De Laurentiis was also not unusual: other female stars were to marry producers (e.g., Loren to Carlo Ponti). Her body, synonymous with "sex appeal," was identified with erotic movement, displayed often through her dancing in *Anna* (1951), *Il lupo della Sila* (1953), and *Mambo* (1954). Like the other emerging stars mentioned above, Mangano was neither the mystical diva of the teens nor "everybody's woman" of the 1930s and 1940s. Stars of the 1930s and 1940s, such as Isa Miranda, were forged from a cinematic machine that theatricalized and depersonalized both masculine and feminine bodies. The stars of the late 1940s hinted at a new life to come in the cinema of the 1950s and into the 1960s.[57] Mangano, like Magnani, returned the body and gesture to the screen, producing fascinating but also threatening attitudes toward feminine sexuality shared by both the right and the left in their differing concerns about the ethical imperatives of cinema. Similarly, Loren's bouncy street strolls in L'oro di Napoli (1954, repeated in many films in which she starred), Lollobrigida's fiery and seductive bodily movements in the Pane, amore films (1953 and 1954), and Mangano's dancing in Riso amaro returned the sexualized body to the cinema. Theirs was a body with proper measurements: narrow waistline, full breasts, and shapely legs, that communicated desire and defiance, by way of gesture, and spectators within and without the film admired what they saw. De Santis's Riso amaro is a harbinger of the union of neorealism with the cinema of the body, and it is not accidental that it features stars that were to become an important part of the future cinematic landscape in what later came to be known (pejoratively, usually) as "rosy" or "pink" neorealism, considered to be a betrayal of the earlier neorealist impulse.

Riso amaro (1949) is an exemplary text to assess the hybrid character of neorealism in its permutations and specifically in relation to the development of Italian stardom. Along with Roma, città aperta, Riso Amaro is an instance of how neorealism combines melodrama and documentary in its uses of professional and non-professional actors, landscape and character, a focus on the present with allusions to remnants of a past associated with the acting and styles of Hollywood/Cinecittà. Roma, città aperta injects traces of earlier films but subjects them to critical treatment. Riso amaro introduces other elements from popular culture (e.g. fotoromanzi, music, and dance). The film presents a portrait of a society in crisis and in transition, trapped between the urban and rural worlds, tradition and modernity. Combining melodrama and realism, the film's self-conscious allusions to facets of popular culture indicate that the film's investment is not only in portraying the economic and political oppression of the world of the migrant workers but also in characterizing the forms of culture that obstruct social change by holding out deceptive images of escape.

Silvana Mangano plays Silvana, a young woman from a peasant family who has bourgeois aspirations to free herself from the bondage of the working class. Her fantasies are derived from mass cultural magazines and film. Her attempt to achieve the easy life is predicated on her fantasies of romance, aligned to images of sexuality and luxury, that she transfers to the rakish and unscrupulous Walter (Vittorio Gassman). As is evident in the oft-produced image of her seductive dancing to popular music (an image that will be repeated in other films such as Anna and Mambo), her body becomes a contentious but critical

3.4. The ascent of the beauty queen: Silvana Mangano in *Riso amaro*. *Photofest*.

element in the film's (and increasingly cinema's) exploration of sexuality. Her full breasts, revealed through her tight T-shirts, her undulating body, and her seductive smile helped to win her the opprobrium of the Church as a sex symbol but also popularity with audiences for the brash eroticism of her image. Describing De Santis's choice of Silvana Mangano, Antonio Vitti writes, "In the director's mind, she had to be the physical counterpart of Rita Hayworth. She had to represent a girl with a head full of fantasies but also a very complicated character on a quest for something new. She is one of the most complex female figures of postwar Italian cinema."[58] De Santis treated Silvana Mangano's role as further (and ambiguous) evidence of the body of the nation in need of regeneration, and as a critique of the false promises conveyed in the photoromances, *fumetti*, and Hollywood cinema.

Mangano's image was to have moral and cautionary signficance also for the future of Italian cinema and especially for the production of stars. Not only would she herald new images of Italian feminine attractiveness and seductiveness, but also her image was testimony to the paradoxes of neorealism in its focus on the feminine body. As Antonio Vitti comments about this film and other De Santis films in their uses of the human body: "De Santis demanded of his actors that the body be an instrument and form of communication. Silvana, with her perfect and opulent form and personality of contrasts, is the visual embodiment of a modernity that the schematic patterns of the film's structure could not suppress."[59] The portraits of the other female characters are juxtaposed to her figure in the film and contribute to the unexpected consequences attached to her form of femininity. Though Doris Dowling (as Francesca), an American actress, had received star billing, the film became Mangano's entry into stardom. Dowling remained in Italy for several years, and appeared in supporting roles in other films, but she was never to achieve stardom. Contrary to the scenario of the moral woman's redemption and thereby the redemption of the nation, Mangano's transgressive image dominated the film, offering a contrast to familiar feminine images of that time: "She was neither Mediterranean nor a Nordic type, but a mixture of the two. She combined the sovereign indolence of a southern feline with a cool northern gaze."[60] If Silvana is, as Vitti indicates, one of the "most complex female figures of postwar Italian cinema,"[61] this must be due in large measure to her embodying "moral, sexual, and social challenges to the patriarchal order, as the female used her body to turn traditional notions of proper feminine conduct upside-down."[62]

These "challenges" are inherent to neorealism's critical preoccupation, if not obsession, with cinema as a means to probe connections between artifice and reality. What the film paradoxically reveals, therefore, is that its greatest strength relies on the disruptive persona of Mangano. The dominating physical presence of her melodramatic character created difficulties for socially committed critics of the time, who regarded the film as betraying its political impact. The film is more than a capitulation to "vulgar" taste via popular narratives. Rather, in its exploration of the politics of culture, its images exceed and overwhelm its narrative. Like *Roma, città aperta*, the film succeeded in breaking through cultural clichés of the time in which, paradoxically, the emergence of a star is an instrument for making these clichés visible. The film's double trajectory offers another instance of neorealism's abiding concern, either directly or indirectly, to link narratives of social reality to cinematic styles, in a sense that accords with what in the next decades (via the writings of Antonio Gramsci) will become a strategy for probing connections between culture and politics.

Similarly, in *Il lupo della Sila* (The Lure of the Sila, made in 1949 but released in 1953), a noir-esque melodrama of revenge filmed in Calabria and produced by Mangano's then-husband, Dino De Laurentiis, Mangano reprises the enigmatic and sensuous persona that brought her stardom. The film also highlights her fatal impact on the men who desire her. In *Il lupo*, as Rosaria, she is determined to avenge the murder of her brother Pietro (Vittorio Gassman), unjustly accused of killing a man, and of her mother. The man responsible for their deaths is Rocco (Amedeo Nazzari), who, fearing for the loss of his family's good name, refuses to allow his sister Orsola (Luisa Rossi) to testify that Pietro was with her at the time of the murder. Years later, Rosaria is found near-dead in the snow by Rocco, who rescues her. Unaware of her identity (which she withholds), he allows her to remain as a servant, and she seduces him and his son Salvatore (Jacques Cernas).

Her character is juxtaposed to that of Orsola, an embittered woman, who clothes herself in funereal garb and refuses pleasure. By contrast, Mangano is dressed in simple but clinging garments that accentuate her body, with the exception of a peasant-style costume given to her by Orsola to wear at a local festival. However, her presence incites the local men to compete for her attention, resulting in a fight. Her love scenes with Salvatore are passionate, and her seduction of Rocco climaxes in a night scene where she, dressed merely in a slip covered loosely by a shawl, seduces him. As in *Riso amaro*, her presence dominates the film not through dialogue but through her aloofness, secrecy, and brooding physical presence, which were to become the abiding features of her star persona from these earliest films to the ones she made later for Pasolini.

Another popular film made during her rise to stardom is *Anna* (1951), a melodrama directed by Lattuada, where she is paired again with handsome and sinister Vittorio Gassman. The film is framed by extreme close-ups of her as a novitiate in her habit, framed by a window in the Catholic hospital where she works as a surgical nurse. Through flashbacks, her prior life unfolds, one in which she is a nightclub entertainer (an oft-quoted segment of the film of Mangano's dancing is used by Nanni Moretti in his *Caro Diario* [Dear Diary, 1994]) who has struggled vainly to break the sexual hold that Vittorio (Vittorio Gassman) has on her. Completing the trio of actors from *Riso amaro*, Raf Vallone as Andrea also appears in the film as a counter to Gassman, offering Anna marriage, a family, and a life removed from the city. Vittorio is accidentally killed by Andrea, and Andrea almost dies after a collision with a reckless driver that reunites him with Anna. Rather than choosing marriage, Anna chooses to take her religious vows and dedicate herself to a life of service. The film, a commercial success in Italy and abroad, reprises elements of *Riso amaro*, focusing on femininity, particularly on a conflict between sexual desire and religious practice. The film "resolves" Anna's sexual dilemma through an image of feminine "liberation" from masculine domination while, at the same time, placing Anna within an acceptable alternative, namely service to others via religion.

Thus, for the viewer, a double pleasure is available in contemplating two sides of Mangano's image, as sinner and as saint, as transgressor and as penitent, as physical body and as spiritual icon. Her repeated appearances with Gassman and Vallone also contributed to her growing familiarity with audiences, reinforcing

3.5. From voluptuous to saintly body: Silvana Mangano in *Anna*. *Photofest*.

expectations of her character and personality on the screen. By the time that Mangano appears as a dancer in *Mambo* (1954), again under the spell of a narcissistic and predatory Gassman, she has assumed for audiences a familiar star persona in recognizable narratives. The third member of the triangle in this film, however, is not Vallone, but an aristocrat played by Michael Rennie. Mangano is again cast as a troubled figure, torn between desire, career, and marriage. The camera and editing highlight her through many close-ups, images of her supple dancing, and contrasts as she moves from lower- to upper-middle-class life. She undergoes a visual metamorphosis from a modestly attired saleswoman, to an ecstatic dancer of the mambo, to the svelte and fashionable wife of an aristocrat. These changes further mark the gradual transformations in her star image that will later culminate in her playing more refined, often upper-class characters.[63]

In 1959, Mangano played another wayward female in *La grande guerra*, directed by Mario Monicelli. As the prostitute Costantina, she is volatile and more verbal than in her other roles. Paired once again with Vittorio Gassman, she reveals a comic side to her persona. However, many of her films of the 1960s and 1970s reinforce a different image. Her image as a model of upper-class fashion, elegance, and remoteness is exemplified in her roles of the wife in Pasolini's *Teorema* (1968) and the Madonna in *Il Decameron* (1971). Her star image was sufficiently familiar and stylized to be used by auteurist directors in metacinematic and critical fashion, most especially by Luchino Visconti, who cast her as Cosima Von Bülow in *Ludwig* (1972) and as the aristocrat Marchesa Bianca Brumonti in *Gruppo di famiglia in un interno* (Conversation Piece, 1974), a role that she felt violated her conservative and desired maternal image. After the 1970s, Mangano appeared in only a couple of roles, including as the Reverend Mother Ramallo in David Lynch's science fiction *Dune* (1984). In her final film, *Orci ciornie* (Dark Eyes, 1987), directed by Nikita Mihalkov, she played opposite Marcello Mastroianni as his wife in a lesser role that revealed her gaunt and ill condition. She died in 1989.

The male actors who were paired with Mangano contributed to the further consolidation of her erotic and fascinating image. As object of their desire, eluding their demands, she dominated the narrative, as did other burgeoning female stars in the late 1940s and early 1950s such as Gina Lollobrigida and Sophia Loren. However, Mangano consented to star opposite Alberto Sordi (see chapter 5), a persistent suitor for her affections, in *Lo scopone scientifico* (The Scientific Card Player, 1971), a comedy in which she uncharacteristically played a cleaning woman and mother of five to great success. In the roles they played opposite Mangano, Gassman and to a lesser extent Vallone were to become stars in a changing cinematic landscape that in the next decades began in cinematic portraits to probe, even satirize, conceptions of Italian masculinity. In *Riso amaro*, Vallone as Marco played his first role in the cinema. He was identified with a more openly tendentious ideological agenda associated with social and cultural liberation. This would not be the last of such roles for the actor in De Santis's films as well as in the films of other directors. The selection of Vallone was fortuitous in that in his physical appearance he embodied (and would continue to embody in later films) a portrait of ethical solidity.

By contrast, Vittorio Gassman was to introduce a more transgressive image of masculinity than that which embodies in appearance and behavior the value of work, law, and justice—in short, respectability. His cynical masculinity was to characterize many of his future roles and those of other Italian male actors in the coming decades. Associated with classical theater, in the cinema he was destined largely to play the rake in the many films that he made over a long career in Italy, Europe, and the United States. His physical appearance, in contrast to Vallone's, was of a romantic seducer and of a cool ironist; he was thin, agile, and elusive, moved like a dancer, wore an enigmatic smile, and appeared to know how to manipulate women. While Gassman was initially typecast as a criminal, swashbuckler, and cynical opportunist in melodramas, police dramas, historicals, and adventure films, he was to become one of the leading male stars of the *commedia all'italiana* in the late 1950s and 1960s (see chapter 4). His amoral and cynical character was established by his roles in *I soliti ignoti* (Big Deal on Madonna Street, 1958), *La grande guerra* (The Great War, 1959), and particularly *Il Sorpasso* (The Easy Life, 1962).

Cinematic Realism and Stardom: An Interlude

Stardom is a conglomeration of economic and social factors sensitive to the box office and to philosophic and aesthetic considerations involving conceptions of how "reality" is understood, and acted upon, and experienced in relation to media. In considerations of the politics and aesthetics of neorealism, critical discussions are largely silent on the role of stardom, preferring to regard it as a sign of capitulation to commercial cinema. Thus, the opportunity is lost to understand how cinematic and now electronic technology has played a major role, for better or worse, in redefining reality in relation to human appearance, perception, behavior, and values. Among the major contributions of neorealism in writings and film to engage with Bazin's question "What Is Cinema?" and one of the most illuminating, theoretical texts on film about cinema is Rossellini's *La macchina ammazzacattivi* (The Machine to Kill Bad People, 1952). The film, a comic satire, is an investigation of a naïve belief in the power of realism against artifice. In *Il generale della Rovere* (1959), also, Rossellini undertook a critique of reductive conceptions of neorealism in which he blurred the boundaries between theater and realism. While *Il generale della Rovere* utilizes the star properties of Vittorio De Sica, *La macchina* does not, but both films explore artifice and theatricality not as an aberration but as revealing of the relationship of reality to a cinematic machine wherein the character of stardom is implicated by virtue of its commodity status and its obliteration of boundaries between the true and the false, the real and its simulacrum.

In *La macchina*, Celestino (Gennaro Pisano), as a photographer and surrogate for the film's director, is the film's instrument for probing cinematic history, theory, and style. Angular, scrawny, and naïve, he journeys from the challenging moments of the war's ending to the sobering recognition of the need to move politically and aesthetically in tandem with inevitable and growing social transformations wherein "the illusions of the post-war era came to an end." Rossellini's film offers a cinematic account of the need to find a style to confront this realization. As Rossellini indicated in a *Cahiers du Cinéma* interview, there is no "break" with neorealism: "[O]ne is moved to take up other themes, interest is shifted somewhere else, you have to take other paths: you cannot go on shooting in ruined cities forever. Too often we make the mistake of letting ourselves be hypnotized by a particular milieu. But life has changed, the war is over, the cities have been rebuilt. It was the story of the reconstruction that had to be told."[64] That this has been interpreted as an abandonment of neorealism reinforces Rossellini's enigmatic comment that neorealism was never really understood.

La macchina features certain familiar strategies of neorealism: the image of the road, location shooting, the use of non-professional actors, and a focus on the cinematic apparatus. The Americans who have come to Italy for mixed nostalgic and commercial reasons confront an enigma on the road on a festival day commemorating the patron saint. An old man (who may either be Saint Andrea or the devil) appears and disappears mysteriously, emerging in the shop of Celestino, a photographer. Celestino, on learning from the old man how to copy and freeze the photographic image of a subject, has now an instrument that does not merely record but is capable of immobilizing and hence killing the subject, and he undertakes a tour of the town. He is in a position of power to use the camera to punish evildoers, self-seeking and greedy individuals, former fascists, authoritarian parents, and thieves, and he enacts his revenge. However, he recants after hastily "killing" his one friend, a doctor and an honest man, and also upon learning that the old man was not Saint Andrea but a devil.

Clearly, the film is a parable concerning "engaged" cinema, but one that harks back, as Peter Brunette indicates, to the *commedia dell'arte*.[65] The characters are drawn in the stylized fashion of the *commedia* rather than in the quasi-documentary mode of films such as *Paisà*, *Sciuscià*, or *Ladri di biciclette*. The film is presented as a framed tale, beginning and ending with a sketch of a landscape framed by theater curtains, an image of a hand that is reminiscent of Michelangelo's "Creation," and a voice-over that parodies documentary introduction by offering the film as a fable and ends the film similarly. Using this traditional convention identified with the fable and with satire, the film removes the characters and actions from a naïve conception of film as reproducing external and "objective" reality. The film can also be understood as probing the nature of stardom.

Celestino is working with a copy of a copy; and in his naiveté, he is unaware that the apparatus he uses is an instrument that "reflects not reality but human subjectivity and error."[66] Put differently, the cinematic image is not a reflection of reality but just an image connected to the hand of the imperfect creator, as Rossellini's film visualizes. Further, in equating the apparatus with magic and superstition, the film indicts its uncritical uses. It also indicts naive notions of technology. In relation to the use of non-professional actors along with professionals, the film in its artifice does not valorize their everydayness and physical closeness to the real world so much as redirect attention for contemplating another sense of the "real" and of the everyday. Similarly, this conception of cinema accords with a view of stardom that conjoins the ordinary and the exceptional, and helps to account for recourse to the use of stars in films. From *Roma, città aperta* to the other films with Magnani, Ingrid Bergman, and Vittorio de Sica, Rossellini worked with non-professional, professional, and star actors. In the films with Anna Magnani (*Il miracolo, La voce umana*), and with Ingrid Bergman (*Viaggio in Italia, Europa 51, Stromboli*), Rossellini is not a star maker so much as a director (see chapter 4) who uses stars reflexively and perhaps autobiographically, exploiting their prominence, their physical traits, and their mannerisms, in the interests of exploring and undermining naïve, romantic, and sentimental conceptions of the characters' relations to a cultural, if not political, milieu.

In *Il Generale della Rovere*, a film that he deemed unsatisfactory, Rossellini used De Sica's star image (and actually further consolidated it) so as to illuminate, not reinforce, the element of theatricality in life and fiction. In this film, De Sica's many identities introduce the question of how to determine the star's performance: as counterfeit, as inauthentic, or as ultimately reliable, real, heroic, and "true." De Sica as Bardone is an obsessive gambler, a charming swindler, and a collaborator with the Nazis in order to ensure his own survival. However, in his enactment of the general, he appears gradually to assume another identity. Is this a conversion drama in which Bardone is "converted" to becoming the Resistance fighter, family man, and aristocratic Della Rovere, or is Bardone impersonating yet another role in the interests of survival? These questions cannot be answered with a simple "yes" or "no," since the film's uses of de Sica's persona are tied to the impossibility, in relation to social life and to stardom, of identifying the "real" persona and his or her authenticity and motives for performing. Furthermore, by using De Sica, an actor identified with the role of doubling and impersonation in many of his films, and by drawing on elements identified with his biography, including his addiction to gambling, his womanizing, and even his identification with left politics, the film further blurs reality and artifice.

The film does not make it easy to distinguish between performance and "authenticity"; it provides no firm guidelines and no access to determine the character's "actual" feelings, to answer the question of who he is. In fact, it challenges the belief in fixed identity and contributes to a rethinking of the properties of cinematic "realism" as being diffuse and open-ended along the lines suggested by Bazin. The ambiguous treatment of character invites the spectator to consider theatricality as a critical intervention in reductive interpretations of realism. Ultimately, it does not matter whether Bardone has been converted to "heroism"; what matters is that Bardone now adopts yet another persona that is socially acceptable, conforms to expectations of heroic behavior. In fact, the film places a burden on the spectator to examine, since it does not resolve, the dilemma it poses about the nature of impersonation; rather it as-

3.6. Exploiting De Sica's star image in *Il Generale della Rovere*. Photofest.

sents to the critical importance of impersonation as a strategy for unsettling long-standing ideas concerning selfhood and subjectivity. This is not to reduce the film to a cynical "statement," but to acknowledge that the contributions of neorealism as outlined earlier involve conceptions of the real that differ from the more sentimentally and morally driven films of earlier cinema. Furthermore, true to the metacinematic propensities of neorealism, the film implicates the role of its star in its investigation of artifice as challenging a naïve belief in representation. The "powers of the false" are an inevitable characteristic of the world of post–World War II cinema that shifted the focus from the "absolutely true" to a contemplation of its manufacture.[67]

De Sica and the Changing Faces of Cinema Stars: Mastroianni and Loren

The late 1950s was a time of greater cynicism than the immediate years after World War II. It became evident to many on the left that there were, after all, no dramatic alterations in governmental power and the makeup of social institutions. In cinema, comedy became a viable instrument with which to capitalize on this cynicism, functioning in a society that was increasingly geared to material success. Comedy became a permissible (and entertaining) weapon against the status quo, particularly in making public what was previously concealed, if not censored. It also became profitable commercially. Given its emphasis on the physical and national body, on sexuality, reproduction, aggression, and social hypocrisy, film comedy capitalized on greater sexual freedom, dissatisfactions with courtship and marriage, and, as Jacqueline Reich indicates, changing conceptions of gender and power. Commenting on the prominence of the city of Naples as a setting for comedy (but also of the south of Italy more generally), Reich indicates that the city provides the proper setting for an exploration of the uses and abuses of femininity and transgressions of the social order.[68] This trend was reflected in Sophia Loren's ascent to stardom in *L'Oro di Napoli* (Gold of Naples, 1954), which led to other successful popular comedy roles, often co-starring with Marcello Mastroianni as in *Ieri, oggi, domani* (Yesterday, Today, Tomorrow, 1963), and *Matrimonio all' italiana* (Marriage, Italian Style, 1964).

Italian stars were increasingly identified with the south of Italy, as we have seen with De Sica, or with characters whose origin is placed in the Mezzogiorno, as is the case with Mastroianni in the Germi comedies.[69] While one might assume that these films that highlight a regional and national scenario would not travel well internationally, Loren and Mastroianni were able to translate their roles for audiences beyond Italy and to become international stars. Their stardom can be attributed to their physical attractiveness, their effectiveness and compatibility as a cinema couple, and their identification with the cross-cultural dimensions of the taming of the shrew scenario. Their identification as stars was tied to the character of Naples as a disreputable but also carnivalistic place where morality can be suspended. Further, accounting for the cross-over potential of these stars, Reich suggests that the "deconstruction of gender mythologies arises from the social and political uncertainty of the postwar era as traditional gender roles became destabilized during Italy's transformation from the devastation of war to one of the world's major industrial forces."[70] While such an interpretation addresses significant economic and social realities, how does it mesh with the role of media of the time—namely, cinema, advertising, and fashion? The cinema, despite its vaunted origins in postwar neorealism, has come of age in terms of its relation to the heyday of the culture of consumption and a form of consumption that is identified in predominant ways with media via stars, their faces, bodies, hair, and maquillage, and with geographic and physical mobility via autos and motorbikes, television, and also bodily gyrations in song and dance. The star, as particularly exemplified in De Sica's *Ieri, oggi, domani*, is identified with virtuality.

Mastroianni: Comedy and the Anti-heroic Star

Mastroianni's stardom has largely been identified internationally with roles he played for Fellini (see chapter 5). The qualities identified with his work are his theatricality, the sense of his always performing, his willingness to expose his imperfections and to engage in self-parody, his identification with the non-heroic or even the anti-heroic, an image of "being devoured and spat out by his female leads,"[71] and a capacity for introspection. Though Mastroianni's international stardom has been identified with the popular Mediterranean image of the Latin Lover, his stardom rather relies on an "undressing" of that image. As Jacqueline Reich argues, he is not a "bella figura" but an anti-hero, an "inetto," a descendant of the *commedia dell'arte*.[72] His films have consistently capitalized on the insubstantial character of his identity as a star, as has the publicity that has circulated about him.

His stardom is more directly related to Deleuze's description of the time-image, in which the character "becomes animated in vain, the situation [where] he outstrips his motor capacities on all sides . . . is a prey to vision, pursued by it, rather than engaged in an action."[73] He is not, except in parody as in Fellini's *La città delle Donne*, the super-male whose appeal resides in his physical power and mastery. In *Divorzio all'Italiana* (Divorce Italian Style, 1961) and *Il bell'Antonio* (1960), he embodies conventional portraits of masculinity that backfire against him. In *Il bell'Antonio* we have a consummate image of the slippery boundaries between the real and imaginary, and of the indeterminacy of identity. Mastroianni offers in that film, as in *Divorzio*, further signs of how stardom disturbs and exceeds the sociological, psychoanalytic, and semiological interpretations assigned to it. His role reveals particularly how the qualities inherent to stardom have altered, engendering more fleeting and uncertain forms of affection and identification, becoming polyvalent and unmoored from conventional modes of signification. In his case and in that of Vittorio Gassman, it is evident how the popular cinema and its treatment of stars mirrored the changing social world through images that were able to reach both national and international audiences. What characterizes these stars resides in how they come to incarnate a fusion of the actual and the virtual through an implicit or overt reflexive treatment of the cinematic medium. For example, in *Divorzio all'italiana* and *Il bell'Antonio*, Mastroianni's characters are identified with mirrors, doubling, performing for others, and discomfort in accommodating established norms of behavior.

It is generally customary to regard neorealism as alien to these types of films: some critics have indicated that "Italian-style comedy—and the cinema in general—was out to conquer the country in those years of partial economic boom: the scope and pathos of neorealism has been replaced with a sense of irony and detachment."[74] However, it is a mistake to identify neorealism largely in terms of pathos when, in fact, the canonical neorealist texts convey "a sense of irony and detachment" inherent to their cinematic practices. Rossellini's, De Santis's, and De Sica's earliest films are distinguished by a metacinematic dimension through which the films are involved in critically examining the medium, proffering new and contrasting images of the masculine and feminine body in their uses of stars and non-professional actors, and are engaged in constructing new images suitable to the contemporary social and economic milieu. Once again, the straitjacket of technical neorealism works against an understanding of the character and quality of the phenomenon known as neorealism by disregarding the nature of its critical and self-conscious treatment of the cinematic image.

Loren: The Look of a Star

A look at the construction of Sophia Loren's star image is instructive for revealing the multi-faceted ways in which stars were created in the postwar era.[75] Initially her star persona stemmed from the comic uses of her shapely and seductive body that often border on self-parody, exposing her body in excessive and flaunting fashion, as in *L'Oro di Napoli*, and revealing comedy as a transgressive form that projects the battle of the sexes as one of power where the female can exercise her power through her voice, language, sensuous body, uses of dissimulation, trickery, and withholding her person. All of these qualities are in abundant evidence in *Ieri, oggi, domani*, one of the most perennially popular of the Loren comedies. The three-part compilation film offers vignettes of cinema history, of film forms, and of the types of stars that are identified with these forms, as these qualities can be considered in relation to the various transmutations in Loren's star persona, and, finally, as reflections on film viewing. Moreover, her appearance in her various roles indicates the protean dimensions of her femininity and how these are tailored, quite self-consciously, to the commerce of cinema and to the various discourses which inevitably play a role in stardom.

However, if Mastroianni exposes his persona as an *inetto* via invoking and puncturing the stereotype of the Latin Lover, what can be learned about the genealogy and typing of female stars as exemplified by Sophia Loren or Gina Lollobrigida? In Reich's view, the counterpart of the Latin Lover is "the unruly woman" who comes to exemplify several dimensions of gender conflict and female power and who is, in contrast to Hollywood stars of the 1950s, not purely fetishistic. Rather this form of femininity is "a site of empowerment, one that castrates the male at the same time that it refuses to completely domesticate the

4.11. The comic duo of Terence Hill and Bud Spencer in the Trinity films. *Photofest.*

Enzo Barboni's *Lo chiamavano Trinità* (My Name Is Trinity, 1970) starred another pair of actors who became stars in this genre: Terence Hill (Mario Girotti) and Bud Spencer (Carlo Pedersoli). Terence Hill was a student for a time of classical literature but later turned to acting. In 1963, he appeared in the role of Count Cavriaghi, the rejected suitor of the Prince of Salina's daughter, Concetta, in Visconti's *Il gattopardo* (The Leopard). But it was through the western that he became a superstar. Once again sports played a role in the creation of male stars. Pedersoli was a swimming champion, later a journalist, and then a film actor. The pair has been described by director Barboni as evoking the comic duo of Laurel and Hardy, whose humor, rather than being largely verbal, is conveyed visually through physical action.[82] Spencer, a physically stocky figure, with unkempt hair and beard and with a gruff demeanor, conveys unsociability and mistrust of others and plays the eiron to Terence Hill's alazon. Hill's persona is based on his agile movement, his trickster and deceptively childlike character that conceals his opportunism and animates his idealism. In the 1970s, he would star in *Il mio nome è nessuno* (My Name Is Nobody, 1973) in the role of "Nobody" against Henry Fonda's Jack Beauregard, the aging gunfighter admired by Hill's Nobody, who is determined to memorialize the legend of the western hero.[83] In this film, Nobody keeps Fonda's aging star persona alive in a film that reflects on cinema history and the role of the star within it. The film is also homage to Sam Peckinpah, whose film *The Wild Bunch* (1969) inspired the naming and actions of the outlaws and whose name appears on a tombstone in the film.

As Nobody, Hill embodies many of the characteristics of a *commedia dell'arte* figure, an itinerant figure whose verbal communication is equal to his bodily gestures. A sympathetic but rascally figure, his actions are reminiscent of the *lazzi* in the *commedia:* he works by trickery and cleverness, outsmarting his opponents while initially seeming to accede to their threatening demands, as in the scene in the bar where he pretends that he cannot shoot the glasses in the air but nonetheless undertakes the bet, only to win each time that he shoots despite his drinking larger and larger glasses of whiskey. Hill's body movements are agile and fast, and his actions are enhanced by the camera work that films him in his various gags, such as his evading his pursuers in a fun house where multiple images of him appear as he gaily skips from image to image.

Consistently, like a director, Nobody sets up the situations to guarantee that Beauregard will have a final chance to prove his skill as a gunman (and his stardom). Hill's identity as an actor and as a star, as a "nobody," aspiring to become somebody, establishes his star persona independent of an Italian identity, a feature inherent to the spaghetti western that undermines strict identification with nation. His star persona works differently from those of the Hollywood stars, apparent in the contrast between himself and Fonda. Nobody is talkative and curious, while Beauregard is economical in his use of words; Nobody is a clown, an acrobat, a dancer, and his movements contrast to the more static images of Beauregard astride his horse, seated in the barber's chair, and aboard a ship after Nobody has arranged his "death." The physicality of Hill's character is identified also with his eating and drinking, and with his nurturing of the legendary Beauregard/Fonda, suggesting a feminine quality to his appearance and behavior.

Whereas Fonda is the august, American, blue-eyed, largely silent hero of the western, he is studied through numerous close-ups and actually defined by and subject to Nobody' directions. Nobody is a storyteller who is a biographer and historian of the western, the lore of the gunfighter and of the star. He might be considered the surrogate for the director but he is certainly a star or, perhaps rather, a reflection on stardom. The film's focus on stardom comes across in the dialogue as well, where Beauregard accuses Nobody: "You shine like the door in a whore house," to which Nobody responds, "I like folks to see me." The allusions to vision range from the naming of the characters, "Beauregard" and "Nobody," to the obvious spectacles worn by Beauregard, and to the two viewing each other but also to the town looking on as Nobody "stages" Beauregard's death. Hill's persona is adequate to confronting and competing with Fonda's and establishing

differences between the Italian/European and Hollywood western as well as between the historical cinematic past of the "western" and the cinematic present.

Giù la testa (Duck You Sucker, 1971) is a hybrid film that employs a wide
range of techniques in its allegorical treatment of historical events, including references to anarchism and fascism, and to the nationalist struggle in Ireland and
in Mexico; allusion to other earlier and more contemporary films such as *Roma,
città aperta*, a parody of *Stagecoach*, and Peckinpah's *The Wild Bunch*; the use of
non-Italian actors, James Coburn and Rod Steiger, as the protagonists; and an allegorical trajectory that forges links between past to present. The film's transnational perspective is revealed not only in its featuring non-Italian stars, but also in
its embodying what Sergio Corbucci described as major differences in the roles
and acting of the Italian westerns from the American. The characters and the stars
who embody them have a modern mentality; they are "characters that sustain the
notion that the end justifies the means," demonstrating that "the past cannot be
recuperated, where it no longer exists."[84] In *Giù la testa*, Coburn as the taciturn
and ironic Sean and Steiger as the voluble, boastful Juan not only play on their
star qualities but also become a new entity as a comic duo.

A further indication of the financial success of the films and the drawing
power of their stars were the numerous parodies starring Franco Franchi and
Ciccio Ingrassia, including *Due Mafiosi nel Far West* (1965), *Il bello, il brutto, e il
cretino* (The Handsome, the Ugly, and the Stupid, 1967), *I due Sergenti del
Generale Custer* (General Custer's Two Sergeants, 1967), *I due figli di Ringo* (The
Two Sons of Ringo, 1967), and *Il sogno di Zorro* (The Sign of Zorro, 1975). These
two popular comics appeared in over one hundred of these parodies (as well as
parodies of every genre, including thrillers, spy films, historical films, and horror)
and are masters of the grotesque, their films and persona "ruining" every aspect
of beauty and fascination associated with classical genres by taking on the physical
appearance and mannerisms of stars who expose the seemingly normative world
they inhabit.[85] Their *Ciakmull: l'uomo della vendetta* (The Unholy Four, 1970),
starring Woody Strode, was also a parody of the westerns directed by Enzo Barboni, the creator of the Trinity films. The popularity of these comic stars validates
the star appeal of the western, since the films and their stars were sufficiently
popular not only to generate parodies but to produce stars modeled on the "origi-
nals," thus validating the idea that "imitation" is another measure of star appeal.

Thrills, Horror, and Demonic Stars

Another popular form in the 1960s and 1970s was the thriller. Constantly on
the lookout for successful forms to emulate, the Italian film industry turned to
the James Bond series, resulting in a number of imitations and also parodies. A

number of films featured secret agents, using actors modeled on the star images of Sean Connery and Ursula Andress. Umberto Lenzi directed Alberto Lupo, a TV actor, in *A00O8 operazione sterminio* (1965), while Gianfranco Parolini had some success with his creation "Secret Agent Walker," and even more with his *I tre fantastici supermen* (The Three Fantastic Supermen, 1967), modeled on *Goldfinger* (1964). Clearly these films, like the westerns and mythologicals, were geared to external audiences and were also indicative of the fare now being offered in Italian and international movie houses and on TV.

Similarly, the appearance of sex films was a concession to the changing times, to the existence of more diverse audiences, to a relaxed degree of censorship, and to more lurid forms of stardom. These films featured sensational stories that can be considered precursors to reality TV. They featured scantily dressed women, sexual encounters, nightlife, location shooting, and violence, purporting to reveal truths about sexual and social behavior heretofore suppressed.[86] The films too were not unique to the Italian scene but were also produced in other European countries (e.g., Sweden). Insofar as the films contributed to a redefinition of stardom, the ephemeral star images were linked to the tabloids and also, paradoxically, to more political and psychological treatments that included the role of media.

Filmmaking focused also on narratives of the Third World, particularly of Africa in such films as *Mondo cane e Africa Addio* (1966) that wedded documentary, horror, politics, and even parody. The films featured semi-nude women and violent dictators, presenting them as "a herd of bloody savages," and portrayed Africa as a site of primordial human instincts involving sado-masochism and other forms of violent behavior.[87] The films also share a fascination with sexploitation films of the decade. Significantly, other, more politically oriented filmmakers such as Pasolini turned to Africa and the Middle East as a corrective to the exploitation and sexual commodification he saw endemic to the west. It is evident that his films and the various forms of horror films (and even the films that parodied or were critical of them) shared certain traits: an international outlook, a focus on sexuality, an exploration of violent exercises of power, portraits of subjugation and abjection, and changing images of the human body.

A cinematic form that continues to captivate international audiences is the horror film, which has generated (or degenerated) its own stars. While many histories of Italian cinema only give a nod to these films, it is becoming increasingly evident that these films are no longer to be considered marginal and deserve closer examination for their contributions to cinema, aesthetics, and social history. Like the western and spy films, the horror genre is a transnational form with a long history, one often associated with a degraded view of mass culture as exploitative, but one earlier identified with earlier forms of Surrealism and, more recently, with considerations of cinematic representation as a site of historical and cultural contestation.[88] These films, even in their most gross forms, testify to the impact of events over the course of the twentieth and early twenty-first centuries that have altered our conceptions not only of the public arena and everyday world but of the cinematic image, and it is not surprising that these films continue to be reissued.

Classical Hollywood cinema boasted its output of popular monsters and stars that embodied desires and nightmares relating to vampires, monstrous creatures, spider women, and incestuous and power-mad figures via Boris Karloff, Gale Sondergaard, Bela Lugosi, and Vincent Price. The British cinema in the postwar era offered a very successful form of horror film produced by Hammer Studios and starring the attractive, suave, and sinister Christopher Lee, aided by the meticulous Peter Cushing as Dr. Van Helsing. The films were made inexpensively and were daring in their treatment of sex, becoming increasingly daring in the 1970s as the films engaged with lesbianism, homosexuality, etc.[89] An old house in the suburbs served as studio, the sets altered to suit various productions. The actors and technicians were regulars, and the studio became identified by these trademarks.

As is evident from an examination of the history of the popular horror cinema in Italy, it was, like Hammer, not constrained by intellectual pretensions: the films were designed to appeal to a mass audience. They were made inexpensively for profit and viewed in "third run" (*terza visione*) theaters for audiences seeking sensation and distraction. They featured both older and newer stars. But their powers of horror are connected to what Deleuze has termed the "crisis of the movement-image" that presumes a different, a mental, relation to the cinematic image, as happened with neorealism and French New Wave.[90] The loss of a sensory-motor response to narration does not eliminate affect; it eliminates the affect identified with causation in relation to situation and action. The time-image, as we have seen, blurs boundaries between the real and the imaginary, subjectivity and objectivity, presuming a viewer who records rather than reacts.[91] This regime of vision entails different orders of space and temporality brought into being through cinema's potential to align the virtual with the real. History becomes accessible through dream and nightmare.

The Italian horror film dates from Riccardo Freda's *I vampiri* (1957), a film that was made quickly in several days, according to Freda. Mario Bava, who became another successful director of horror films, photographed it. Freda describes this film as "completely baroque, surreal, and excessive."[92] Another film, perhaps influenced by the Quatermass films, is *Caltiki il mostro immortale* (Caltiki, the Immortal Monster, 1959). In 1961 Freda filmed *L'orribile segreto di Dr. Hitchcock* (The Horrible Secret of Dr. Hitchcock, 1962) and also *Lo spettro* (The Ghost, 1963), which are according to his own estimation his most famous works.[93]

These films introduced the "queen of horror," Barbara Steele, to the screen. Not only was she wildly successful in these films, she also acted for Hammer and, like Christopher Lee, became a cult figure and star in international cinema. Her role in these films was a major factor in their success, since she brought to the genre a necessary ingredient that differentiated Italian horror from other horror films: she was not merely a side element of eroticism but the critical fulcrum for all the incidents in the film. Her persona allegorizes the "wicked element that gives rise to evil or that awakens it after many years."[94] She is the embodiment of a past that returns to haunt.

Steele describes how she, like many actors and actresses in the 1960s, came to Rome to make a career in film. She looked quite different from the many other young women in quest of fame. She was tall, had all the requisite curves, and had extremely black hair but "with a face that did not seem that of a Barbie doll."[95] It was her face and her voice that caught the attention of such horror directors as Mario Bava. According to Steele's reminiscences of Bava, "I was a witch, but the magician was he,"[96] echoing the designation often used to describe her unusual star persona. She claimed to detest the likes of stars such as Doris Day, preferring to play more surreal roles where she could portray an aggressive character. She was a great fan of horror and the supernatural, though she also worked with such directors as Monicelli and Fellini.

In Freda's *Lo spettro*, she was "a true and proper queen of evil," but what gave her (and increasingly her audiences) the most pleasure and recognition was her role in Bava's *La maschera del demonio* (Black Sunday, 1960).[97] In this film, Steele played two roles, the witch Asa Vajda and her descendant, the endangered Katia, allowing her to portray both an archaic vengeful and wronged vampire and a more modern, dutiful, and hence threatened portrait of femininity. This was not the only horror film where she assumed a doubled identity. She played two roles in *Lunghi capelli della morte* (Long Hairs of Death, 1964), *Amanti d'oltretomba* (Lovers beyond the Tomb, 1965), and *Un angelo per Satana* (An Angel for Satan, 1966). Her dual identity was enhanced through her frequent identification with a painting or statue that she brought to life in her malevolent incarnation. She also appeared in films that were comedy spoofs of horror, as in *I maniaci* (The Maniacs, 1964). Freda described this "icon of horror" in terms of her versatility; in one film she was a victim, in another an assassin, and in many films both. She had a "beautiful but irregular face" in which her large dark eyes were prominent, enhancing the supernatural aspects of her roles.

If the melodramas of the 1950s were invested in conflicts between transgressive and subjugated portraits of femininity, Steele's roles as both victim and aggressor were appealing in their visual challenge to reigning conceptions of femininity. Her portraits of divided femininity function as "both a deep psychic threat to masculinity within a patriarchal framework, and concomitantly, though less overtly, as a gender that also threatens insubordination to patriarchal hegemony at a sociopolitical level."[98] Steele's stardom might be compared to that of the diva. She evokes the diva's sinister and transgressive quality; her sexual passion is transmitted through eyes "that promise exquisite sensual pleasure for her unsuspecting lovers, but with scorpions behind their dark stare, promising to strike. Her face in the cinema of horror is indeed an ambivalent one . . . promising love and evil simultaneously,"[99] and, more significantly, an invitation to rethink the world of fantasy and dream.

Christopher Lee, too, appeared in horror films as well as spoofs of them made in Italy; his first, a comedy directed by Steno, was *Tempi duri per i vampiri* (Hard Times for a Vampire, 1959). For Bava, he made *Ercole al centro della terra* (Hercules at the Center of the Earth, 1961) and *La frusta e il corpo* (The Whip and the Body, 1963), which capitalizes on Lee's sinister persona though cedes prominence to Dahlia Lavi who portrayed Nevenka's tortured desires for him. The film did poorly at the box office. It was identified as having "sado-masochistic" tendencies that were never overtly portrayed but were nonetheless called into question by the censors and some critics. However, the film was eventually released, distributed, and is now available on DVD. In this film, Lee as Kurt Menliff evokes the dark, threatening, sophisticated, and fascinating persona of his Hammer films. Initially appearing as the rejected son returned to reclaim his patrimony, Lee appears to be the destroyer of the family, though this family is already in decay, thanks to paternal authoritarianism, fraternal strife, female competitiveness, and sexuality aligned to violence. One-third of the way into the film Kurt is mysteriously stabbed, but he does not disappear. He becomes a ghostly presence viewed only by Nevenka, played by Dahlia Lavi, who revels erotically in Kurt's actual then fantasized violent whipping of her body. Even in death, Lee as "ghost" maintains his hypnotic hold over the woman, driving her to madness and murder.

Lee's stardom has been attributed to his suave, dark, and brooding presence, epitomized by his 1958 highly successful appearance in Hammer's *Horror of Dracula*, where he introduced a sophisticated version of the most celebrated of vampires. His role in Bava's film is enhanced not only by his acting but also by the sinister way he is filmed and often framed (as in the numerous window shots that highlight his ominous presence). Close-ups emphasize his enigmatic and hypnotic face. Lee's stardom, like that of Barbara Steele, challenges reigning conceptions of beauty and moral perfection. These stars evoke memories of buried desires and threats that invite a psychosocial reflection on their fascination for their spectators.

The historical, intellectual, and critical dimensions of horror are tied to a critical and self-conscious engagement with the nature and effects of media, particularly as exemplified in the films of Dario Argento. Argento's films belong to experimental conceptions of cinema in their uses of visual and sound imagery, narrative form, intertextuality, acting, philosophic predilections, special effects, a different treatment of established stars, and the appearance of new stars (see chapter 5).

New Faces: The Small and Big Screen

Following the turbulence of the 1970s with the increase of organized crime, the rise of terrorism by both the right and left, the murder of Aldo Moro, president of the Christian Democrats, by the Red Brigades, and the marginalizing of the Communists, the 1980s promised a period of prosperity and stability, another "economic miracle."[100] However, in the case of the film industry, deregulation and competition with television, difficulties in gaining access to funding, and the decrease in cinema-going were to alter further the contours of cinema. Italian commercial filmmakers had to compete not only with Hollywood but also with emerging global film and television production, which has had an effect on the types of films produced, particularly through the union of film and television style. While innovative filmmakers were struggling to find the resources for their films, television offered an outlet for filmmakers. With the competition between the public and privatized RAI and privately owned channels such as Berlusconi's Mediaset (initiated in the 1970s), the offerings were largely distributed among historical, melodrama, and comedy programs along with a large dose of foreign imports.[101] Television became an alternative for filmmakers, creating "a symbiotic relationship between the small and big screen . . . and a new generation of comics."[102] Moreover, TV became a venue for established stars such as Sophia Loren and newer stars such as Monica Bellucci.

Among this new generation of comics spanning from the late 1970s to the present are Adriano Celentano, Paolo Villagio, Renato Pozetto, Massimo Troisi, Roberto Benigni, Maurizio Nichetti, and Carlo Verdone. Many of them began in TV and have continued to work in TV and cinema, known for their versatility as writers, actors, producers, directors, and singers. Unfortunately, their work is largely confined to Italy, though all have appeared in international co-productions. Celentano, a singer whose career in film and TV spans from the late 1950s to the present, has appeared in character roles and as a performer, and has also directed a few TV miniseries and films. His persona depends on his reputation as a pop singer, and his comic persona on his stylized movements, gestures, and facial expressions. Celentano has been described as belonging to a category of celebrated freaks dating to the nineteenth century, capitalizing on his eccentric and grotesque behavior without alienating his audiences.[103] His popularity arises from his carnivalesque persona, which, after the success of *Qua la mano* (Give Me Five, 1980) was a great success at the box office. His appeal lay in his improvisational style, his timing, and, above all, his penchant for a surreal form of nonsense. His frenetic and mad persona seemed attuned to the unsettled cultural and political milieu of the 1980s.[104]

Paolo Villaggio, a former TV stand-up comic, has starred in a number of comedies, westerns, crime films, films spoofs (e.g., *Bonnie e Clyde all'italiana*, 1982), episode films that are political satires (e.g., *Signore e signori buonanotte*, 1978), and comedies in which he was teamed with Renato Pozetto, such as *Le comiche* (1990) and *Le comiche 2* (1992), proffering a form of low comedy based on physical aggression and bodily functions including excretion. Villaggio and Pozetto together are a comic, often carnivalesque, topsy-turvy scourge of social institutions—the sacrament of marriage, funerary rites, commerce, and the Mafia. Villaggio's popularity has also derived from his character Fantozzi, which he wrote first in books and then created for cinema. Fantozzi is, in Brunetta's terms, an elf, a deformed Hercules, a sacrificial lamb "who pays for the guilt of a society gone bad, an imperfect adult great-grandchild of Lewis Carroll's Alice, the weak link of the evolutionary chain."[105] Pozetto, Villagio, and Celentano are more than a throwback to the earlier *commedia all'italiana*. They are symptoms of a post-postwar society and their comedy borders on the grotesque, if not on horror, and their appeal may reside in the exposure of the dystopian dimensions of late modernity.

In a different vein, Carlo Verdone has earned a reputation for versatility built on his cabaret appearances and his directing and acting in television. He earned a degree in directing from the Centro Sperimentale di Cinematografia. His work in cinema includes films which he has directed and in which he has starred: *Un sacco bello* (A Beautiful Bag, 1980), *Acqua e sapone* (Water and Soap, 1983), *Io e mia sorella* (1987), *Sono pazzo di Iris Blond* (I'm Crazy about Iris Blond, 1996), and *Il mio miglior nemico* (My Best Enemy, 2006). Verdone, who has expressed his admiration for Alberto Sordi, to whom he has been compared, was finally to appear with him on screen in *In viaggio con papa* (Traveling with the Pope, 1982) and *Troppo forte* (Too Strong, 1986). Though his comedy bears a resemblance to the *commedia all'italiana*, it is sensitive to the different landscape of contemporary Italy and speaks to a new generation struggling to survive in the "postmodern" world. Over three decades he has matured as a director and as a comic actor.

In *Acqua e sapone*, as Rolando, Verdone is a down-at-heels educated young man who lives with his grandmother and unfortunately can only find a position as a janitor and as tutor (largely unpaid) to immigrants. However, thanks to a telephone call he erroneously answers at the convent where he works, he impersonates one of the teachers, Father Spinetti, and presents himself in priestly garb, offering his services to a young supermodel, Sandy, who is required by law to have a tutor while she works. His impersonation exposed, young Sandy blackmails him into allowing her the pleasures she is denied because of her career, thus initiating Rolando into the pleasures of food, dancing, sports, and finally sex. With the complicity of his grandmother and a hippie neighbor, Rolando's drab life is momentarily transformed. Verdone, as "heir" of Sordi, is an incarnation of an Italian youth, seeking to find a niche for himself in the changed economic and cultural world of the 1980s, involving immigrants, competition for work, a hedonistic youth culture, and changed sexual patterns.

In *Io e mia sorella*, he stars as Carlo Piergentili, a musician living a sedate life with his wife Serena, a cellist, until his nomadic and free-spirited sister, Silvia, returns home after their mother's death to his and the community's consternation and jars Carlo out of his routine existence. To locate his sister's infant he undertakes a journey through Eastern Europe, where he is further educated into contemporary sexual practices. This film, similar to his others, is not only a journey into a social world previously alien to him, but also an opportunity to travel beyond the borders of Italy, a striking aspect of his films, which often take the form of "road film." His direction and the personas he plays are responsive to the altered world from the 1980s to the present, offering images that hover between traditional landscapes and unsettled portraits of the family, femininity, and masculinity, and the lure and threat of a transgressive sexual lifestyle.

Ornella Muti, who plays Silvia, has appeared in many films since the 1970s. Her performance as a Sicilian young woman in *La moglie più bella* (The Most Beautiful Wife, 1970) has followed Muti throughout her career, and her glamorous appearance has been a dominant aspect of her roles and her publicity. Her films in the 1970s were not particularly well received by critics, though in the 1980s she finally received critical acclaim for her acting, in particular for her role as the nomadic and frenetic Silvia in *Io e mia sorella*. Her personal life has been a subject of gossip and publicity and the parts that she has increasingly played have altered her youthful image but not her reputation for beauty. Her contributions to cinematic and television culture have resulted in her being made a Commendatore of the Italian Republic.[106] However, despite this honor, she has not achieved the international fame accorded Sophia Loren or, more recently for that matter, Monica Bellucci.

Carlo Verdone has continued to capitalize on the plight of the Italian male in a postmodern world with such films as *Sono pazzo di Iris Blond*, a dark comedy that features him as a Roman musician, Romeo, again unfortunate in romance. Rejected by one woman, he goes to a fortune-teller and learns that he will meet a woman who is musical and bears the name of a flower. In Brussels, he meets Marguerite (the "daisy," played by Andréa Ferréol) who can only sing one song, "Ne me quitte pas" by Jacques Brel, and who begins to be a dominatrix, tormenting him with her music, her excessive attachment to her dog, and her attempts to control his life. One day, escaping under pretence of walking the dog, he meets Iris (Claudia Gerini). Iris is a younger version of the sister in *Io e mia sorella*, musically talented, non-monogamous, opportunistic, and disloyal. Romeo grooms her, allows himself to be subjected to her whims, and is finally abandoned by her as she, thanks to his creative work with her, leaves him behind to pursue success in Paris. In this film, Verdone, reminiscent of Sordi's characters, is a middle-class Italian man who has not come to terms with a changing world; he is still trapped in impossible romantic fantasies.

In his more recent *Il mio miglior nemico*, Verdone shares acting honors with Silvio Muccino in a film that focuses on generational conflicts. Orfeo (Muccino), a rootless young man, finally finds a purpose in life: to get revenge on a hotel manager, Achille de Belli, who has fired Orfeo's mother for incompetence. The film depends on a string of episodes designed to humiliate Achille and cause him domestic and economic misfortune. Beginning with the names, the film is ironic. Achille is no epic hero, and the ostensibly fatherless Orfeo is misinformed about his mother's situation. The romance element enters as Orfeo meets a young woman, Cecilia (Ana Caterina Morariu), a variant of Iris Blond, and is smitten. The antagonistic relation between the older man and the younger man is finally overcome in a journey that unites them in the quest to find the missing Cecilia, who, disgusted with them both, has run away.

Not only is the couple united, but Orfeo also finds a surrogate to compensate for his indifferent father. Verdone's comic persona is adjusted to suit his more mature years. He now plays an older man, shorn of romantic fantasies, reconciling himself to another image, that of his superannuation. The star has now aged, but he has not abandoned his "superior gift of treating the most ridiculous aspects of social life."[107] Verdone's character still exposes the dimensions of middle-class existence involving marriage, generational difference, and the chaos they wreak for modern life. The film reinforces how Verdone's image not only accedes to the passage of cinematic time, but also further embodies changing cultural and social perceptions in an ever-changing national and transnational landscape.

Moving from the world of comedy to other forms of popular filmmaking from the 1980s to the present, it is possible to identify actors who might qualify for the tenuous world of stardom. Kim Rossi Stuart, born in Rome, comes from an acting family, and began his work in TV and in cinema in the 1970s. Since that time he has appeared in a variety of historical films, melodramas, crime detection films, and police films. In *Uno bianco* (The White Fiat, 2001), he turned in an adept performance as a cool cop who, despite the infiltration of criminals into the police force and the ineptness of political figures, is able to break the mob. Rossi Stuart's versatility, his good looks, and his understated acting combine to make him a formidable figure. In *Le chiavi di casa* (The Keys to the House, 2004), he offers a muted but tender vision of a young father seeking to develop a relationship with a disabled son that he had rejected many years before. His scenes with Charlotte Rampling, as the mother of a female child stricken with muscular dystrophy, also contribute to the depth and pathos of his performance. The film is representative of the return of family dramas to the screen in the 1990s and its deployment of popular TV and film stars.

In another family melodrama, *Ricordati di me* (2003), the characters live in a world saturated with popular music, movies, TV game shows, theater, and social events, and reminiscent of the Berlusconi era of world media, sex, and consumerism. As its title suggests, memories of youthful aspirations erupt, wreaking havoc with myths of family solidarity, loyalty, and sentiment. The director Gabriele Muccino's cinematic family is the site of conflicting desires that are revealing of the ruptures created by differing generational conceptions of being in the highly televisual postmodern "society of the spectacle." Nonetheless, despite ostensible differences in beliefs and values, the four characters share a fear of failure, of being locked up in their mediocrity: the father Carlo and mother Giulia (Laura Morante) are dissatisfied with their work and feel oppressed by not having lived up to earlier expectations; their son Paolo struggles to find an identity different from his father's; and their daughter Valentina is desperate to make a name for herself in media by becoming, if not a movie star, then at least a TV personality. The father finds temporary solace in a renewed relationship with Alessia (Monica Bellucci), but the melodrama finds a dramatic a way of uniting the fragile and dysfunctional family.

As Giulia, Laura Morante incarnates the nightmare of a woman's failure at being an artist, a wife, and a mother in an acting style that is frantic and designed to appeal to middle-class female discontents. Morante has had a long career in film since the 1970s, having appeared in Carmelo Bene's experimental version of *Hamlet* (1974), Bernardo Bertolucci's *Tragedia di un uomo ridicolo* (Tragedy of a Ridiculous Man, 1981), and Alain Tanner's *La vallée fantôme* (The Phantom Valley, 1987). In the 1990s she appeared in *La famiglia Ricordi* (1993), *L'affaire Dreyfuss* (1995), *L'anniversario* (1999), and, at the turn of the century, in *La stanza del figlio* (2001) and *L'estate del mio prima bacio* (The Summer of My First Kiss, 2006). Her recent TV appearances include *Renzo e Lucia* (2006). Morante's films have tended toward quality productions by established Italian and other European directors. Her long and productive career is another instance of the nomadic careers of actors who move between Italy and Europe.

Monica Bellucci, as Alessia, the other woman, is considered a promising candidate for international stardom. According to her publicity and reviews, her popularity extends beyond Italy to France and the U.S. Her reputation is also built on her role initially as a fashion supermodel and her willingness to be

4.12. "The Most Beautiful Woman in the World," Monica Bellucci in *Malèna*. *Photofest*.

photographed in the nude for magazines. She has garnered publicity through appearances on TV, interviews, films reviews, and reports on her personal life through her unconventional marriage to actor Vincent Cassel, with whom she starred in the French film *L'appartement* (The Apartment, 1996), which won a César Award for Best First Film. Along with her role in *Ricordati di me*, her most notable film role for an Italian director was in Tornatore's *Malèna* (2000), where she plays the wife of a missing soldier during World War II. The photography highlights her beauty in the scenes in which she walks the streets, an object of fantasy for the youths in her Sicilian village and of vengefulness at the hands of women in the community. Befriended by one boy, she becomes a central factor in his initiation into manhood. But it is clear that the exceptional beauty of the feminine face and body remains a prime requisite for stardom along with an aggressive press and ongoing media coverage.

One review describes her physical appearance as casting doubts on the "sincerity [of the film] maybe because the camera lingers on her callipygian beauty."[108] She, however, has described her reputation as the "most beautiful woman in the world" as "a challenge . . . I wanted to see if I could make this part exist just by a body . . . I learned how a body could speak."[109] Her stardom is built on the publicity surrounding her spectacular physical appearance, her courting of controversy, and her oft-expressed desire and prodigious efforts to succeed in media. For her performance as the other woman in *Ricordati di me* she received a David di Donatello Award for Best Supporting Actress. She has appeared on film and television in France, in Hollywood in two of the *Matrix* films, and in Mel Gibson's *The Passion of the Christ* (2004). Bellucci, "the Mediterranean icon," as she has been dubbed, seems poised to emulate her model Sophia Loren, and only time will validate her success.

Like recent aspirants to international stardom, Valeria Golino has shuttled between TV and movies in Italy, Europe, and Hollywood since the early 1980s. Her publicity mentions that she is of mixed Italian and Greek parentage. From her entry into the public eye, she has been praised for her working-class roles and for her "natural expressiveness."[110] She has played Neapolitans, Mexicans, and Sicilians, and her role in *Respiro* (2002) was as a defiant Sicilian wife who struggles against marital and community constraints; the film validates the cinematic fascination with the south of Italy in films of the late 1990s and into the twenty-first century. Like Bellucci's, her popularity (prior to *Respiro*) is greater in the U.S. than in Italy.[111] Golino too has appeared in Hollywood, in French, and increasingly in Italian films, notably in Francesca Comencini's well-publicized and controversial *A casa nostra* (Our House, 2006), and she has won critical acclaim for her acting. These newer stars in Italian cinema are advertisements for a global lifestyle. They lead nomadic lives, are identified with European and Hollywood cinema and with television, and play a determining role in forming their star images. However, as is characteristic of contemporary stardom it is hard to predict the future course of actors such as Bellucci and Golino, given a shrinking and much more competitive film industry and given the shorter memories of audiences bombarded by media images. Despite these constraints, there appear to be more opportunities than in the past for mature women in cinema and TV in Europe, and to a lesser extent in Hollywood, as actors, writers, and directors—but not necessarily as stars. The phenomenon of glamour, hitherto an essential component of cinematic stardom as we have known it, seems nebulous and evanescent in the twenty-first century.

In over a century of stardom, the star has undergone dramatic permutations from the diva of the teens to the arrival of sound, color, wide screen and small, and stardom now confronts the challenges wrought by the globalization of cinema and by digital technology with its special effects, including the coming of the "cyberstar." What changes will the arrival of the cyberstar effect on the future of stardom? Barbara Creed writes,

> Now it is possible to create computer-generated objects, and people that do not have referent to the real world but exist solely in the digital domain of the

computer. In other words, film has been freed from its dependence on history and on the physical world. Central to these changes is the possibility of creating a virtual actor, of replacing the film star, the carbon-based actor who from the first decades of the cinema has been synonymous with cinema itself. In the future, living actors may compete with digital images for the major roles in the recent block buster or romantic comedy.[112]

If the national identity of stars has become blurred in a globally mediated world, succumbing to greater competition and to the speed of technological development, what transformations does the coming of the cyberstar betoken?

5

Starring Directors and Directing Stars: The Cinematic Landscape and Its Changing Bodies

In this chapter I examine the director as star and also as generator of new forms of stardom. The director's elevation to "auteur" through the writings of the *Cahiers du cinéma* and more popularly of Andrew Sarris in the late 1960s, conferred a form of stardom on the director as auteur.[1] On Fellini's star status, Peter

Bondanella writes, "after the international notoriety of *La strada* and *Le notti di Cabiria*, Fellini's international reputation was firmly established as one of Europe's most brilliant young superstar directors who could also deliver at the box office."[2] While the "superstar" directors became famous through their works, their fame brought with it adulation and curiosity about their personal lives, the sources for their creativity, and their opinions on issues beyond cinema (e.g., politics). Their elevation to stardom was a consequence of increased visibility thanks to their own work but also to their images on film, which made them recognizable. They were not only directors; they were also actors. Fellini along with Visconti, De Sica, Rossellini, and Pasolini acted in their own films, were seen in cameo appearances, and acted in fictional roles in other films. They were the subject of numerous news stories, interviews, biographies, television appearances, and even tabloid journalism.

The photographs and the films in which they appear are often quite stylized as they embody anticipated images of what a powerful director looks like. Moreover, cameo appearances often place them in the company of stars. Mastroianni and Fellini appear on the set acting as themselves in *C'eravamo tanto amati*, and Fellini appears with Magnani in *Roma*. Furthermore, the autobiographical elements that directly or indirectly play a role in their works contribute to speculation and inquisitiveness about their lives, their relations with the stars with whom they work, and their personal and critical views on the type of cinema they create. However, these directors both create stars and also are responsible for their transformation in the context of postmodernity.

Another factor that enters into their elevation to stardom is that these directors have explored the power of cinema and impediments to its further development. Their investigations of the cinematic image particularly involve metacinematic considerations that include the character of stardom. Visconti's use of Anna Magnani in *Bellissima* is an instance of using a star to investigate the mechanisms of commercial cinema and, most importantly, to probe the cinematic image "as just an image" misrecognized as real. Pasolini's uses of Magnani in *Mamma Roma* and Silvana Mangano in *Teorema* afford a further opportunity to rethink the impact of contemporary cinema by linking the star's body to the world of commodities and exchange and to a devastated cultural milieu wrought by the new hedonism. Their films further invite investigation on the contemporary character of auteurism and of stardom that implicates both "high" and "low," popular and elite, national and "global" culture. Therefore, this chapter seeks to identify and destabilize the boundaries between commercial and art cinema by bringing the films of Visconti, Antonioni, Fellini, and Pasolini into dialogue with filmmakers such as Sergio Leone and Dario Argento and with forms, such as spaghetti western and horror, that have often been set apart from the intellectually "serious" works of auteurs and their particular uses of stars.

The Cinema of the Time-Image and Stardom

Gilles Deleuze's *Cinema 2: The Time-Image* elaborates on the evolution of the cinematic in the light of philosophical and political transformations that have taken place as a consequence of World War II and concomitant technological changes since the end of that war. Beginning with his assessment of the nature and impact of Italian neorealism, he undertakes with the assistance of Henri Bergson and André Bazin a characterization of cinema that introduces considerations of history, space-time, language, belief, technology, and cerebration into Bazin's question, "What Is Cinema?" Deleuze's technique for exploring the possibilities and problems posed by the cinematic medium relies on the work of key filmmakers who are philosophers, guiding the viewer through fundamental revaluations of perception, affect, and thought. Thus, his writings are informative in considerations of the bodies of stars. They also are important for reflections on the auteur as star and on the evolution of star performance.

The films of Roberto Rossellini, Michelangelo Antonioni, Luchino Visconti, Federico Fellini, and Pier Paolo Pasolini serve Deleuze as guides to both theory and practice concerning concepts of representation. His selection of these directors to discuss is based on the presumption that their films are different from (not necessarily better than) the films of the pre–World War II cinema in which an organic conception of the world prevailed, as exemplified in the works and writings of such filmmakers as D. W. Griffith, John Ford, and Sergei Eisenstein.[3] In their films and in certain commercial films of the 1930s and early 1940s, the cinema was a mass medium predicated on a sensory-motor relation to the cinematic image that elicited profoundly affective perceptions and dynamic conceptions of belief in the potential for action in which the star played a pivotal role. These films either created stars or relied on established stars.

Their emphasis was on situation, space, and action; time was subordinated and often ahistorical, submerged in universal conceptions of truth and justice. Deleuze is not denigrating mainstream forms of filmmaking so much as indicating that at their best and at their height before the coming of fascism, these films expressed a worldview that was identified with a national or international identity, progressive politics, and the power and benevolence of the masses. The filmmaker thus spoke for and with the people, and, correspondingly, the individual (the "star" as hero) was animated by a great mission on behalf of a national community.[4] The romance between the exceptional individual and the masses had solicited fascination with a technology increasingly assimilated to social life. However, fascism and the war offered the spectacle of the masses as automata subjected to the leader as a spiritual automation, and played a critical role in undermining belief in the redemptive powers of cinema for society.[5] By the late 1930s, a "crisis" of the movement-image on an international scale was

becoming apparent, bringing with it conceptions of filmmaking that introduced new forms of thinking into the cinematic image.[6] This "crisis" was to in-
tensify in the postwar era and beyond, becoming evident in film noir, neorealism, the French New Wave, and forms of popular cinema.

Dissatisfaction with the artifice of dominant cinema forms and their stars
was expressed in the writings of many Italian film critics in film journals such
as *Bianco e nero* and *Cinema*, although other magazines such as *Star*, *Foto-
grammi*, *Cinetempo*, *Film*, and *Bis* were more geared to popular Italian and
Hollywood films and continued to focus on American and Italian stars.[7] Increased film production in Italy, coupled to the embargo on Hollywood films,
revealed that the attempts to transform the industry had paid off.[8] By the late
1930s, the Italian cinema could boast technical innovations, greater genre versatility, a growing number of film productions, and the introduction of a host
of new stars through a group of creative directors: Alessandro Blasetti, Mario
Camerini, Raffaello Matarazzo, Renato Castellani, Ferdinando Maria Poggioli,
Mario Soldati, and Vittorio De Sica, all but one of whom would continue to
work in the postwar era (Poggioli died in 1945). The loss of confidence in the
regime and the effects of war saw the introduction of films in the late 1930s and
early 1940s that were highly formal, cryptic, and darker in treatment of character and landscape, and identified by critics as "calligraphic" films. These films,
similarly to film noir, were indicative of a crisis in the movement-image that
injected a different treatment of character and the cinematic body. Acknowledged as a precursor to neorealism, Visconti's 1942 *Ossessione* revealed a critical
engagement with reigning genres and types of narration expressed via its dark
treatment of stars (see below).

Neorealism, its parameters and its character as a dynamic philosophical
and political phenomenon established from its inception, opened the flood-
gates to new possibilities of cinema that could not be contained within familiar
genre categories in the history of cinema. Given its metacritical dimensions,
the role of the director along with scriptwriters and various technicians became
integral to any consideration of the nature and effects of its cinematic character.
When Deleuze in his discussion of the time-image chooses to regard certain
figures in neorealism as producing a new conceptual relation to the cinematic
image, he chooses them not as directors identified with the *politique des auteurs*
so much as philosophers diagnosing the world of technology, information, and
the inhuman in relation to existing and profound transformations in considerations of reality. Their work intersects directly and indirectly with the phenomenon of stardom of the postwar era, since their films were preoccupied with and
influential in calling attention to themselves through direct or indirect assault
on existing cinematic forms. Among the many virtues (or sins) attributed to
neorealism, the star personas of the directors need to be accounted for in the

creation and reception of their works. Furthermore, Italian film "auteurs," identified with neorealism, were part of a growing trend in filmmaking in which
their own personas along with their films were appealing beyond national
borders.

The renewed and growing international character of Italian cinema was
indebted to and sown by neorealism, which affected the treatment of both regional and national mythology as a consequence of the shared transnational
experiences of fascism and a world war. Furthermore, from the late 1950s
through the 1970s, a new mythology identified with Italy came into being, associated with the "economic miracle" and tied to images of affluence, fashion,
consumer commodities, motorcycles and cars, and an association with the "fast
life."[9] The global character of media technology, particularly television, was
further responsible for this cosmopolitanism through its transmission of regional and national images linked to depictions of feminine and masculine
bodies. Equally important to these transformations was "increased prosperity
and greater employment, coupled with expansion of northern industrial centers
and immigration from the south."[10]

The "long march" of Hollywood in Italy had been temporarily halted in
the late 1950s and 1960s due to crises in the American film industry[11] that temporarily afforded opportunities to other film industries. Furthermore, as a consequence of growing industrial development, Italian culture became more decidedly cosmopolitan. Concomitantly, Italian auteurs became identified with
the landscape of the "sweet life" in Italy and abroad. As a consequence, the
Italian film industry found new audiences in the U.S., Europe, and also in other
parts of the world. Along with the growing popularity of Italian comedy, peplum epics, and spaghetti westerns, audiences witnessed the emergence of an
"art cinema" that traveled transnationally. While the art cinema in its explorations of space, the human body, mobility, history, and sexuality may seem eccentric to dominant forms of filmmaking, there are many point of convergence
with this popular cinema, not the least of which resides in the phenomenon of
stardom[12] as the carrier of new and unsettling images. Stardom in the films of
these auteurs loses its cohesive contours, voided of its affective grounding in
experience, becoming a fragmented and free-floating avatar of time. More remote than ever from realism, the star gradually underwent a further metamorphosis, and this chapter seeks to trace the nature and effects of that transformation. This form of filmmaking introduced a direct presentation of time by
means of its idle moments and its characters (somnambulists, counterfeiters,
visionaries), who are "'actor mediums' capable of seeing and showing rather
than acting," placed in situations where the everyday and ceremonial are
blurred, where clichés are put under pressure, and where the cinema (through
the particular uses of stars) "becomes an analytic of the image."[13]

The Case of Visconti

During the fascist era, Luchino Visconti, along with Michelangelo Antonioni, Giuseppe De Santis, and Carlo Lizzani, among other cineastes, had been part of the group who wrote for the journal *Cinema* and who participated in making documentary films for LUCE (L'unione cinematografica educativa). Directors, writers, and technicians within existing political constraints were active in discussing, analyzing, and projecting different practices for the cinema as a cultural force. Their writings were influential in charting new directions, and Visconti's film *Ossessione* (1942) was to become identified with neorealism. The film is an indirect exploration of earlier literary and cinematic styles (e.g., verismo and melodrama), and a harbinger of things to come in the cinema. It was also to become attached to the star lore of its director.

Visconti's stardom has been nourished by critics who identify his works with his aristocratic background, his involvement with La Scala Opera, his left-leaning politics, and the erudition and precision of his cinematic style. The resources at Cinecittà contributed to the lavish painterly style of his films, the reproductions of famous artworks, the opulent *mise-en-scènes*, and the lavish costuming of his stars. The mythological status of his stardom was enhanced by such later films as *La caduta degli dei* (The Damned, 1969), *Ludwig* (1972), and the D'Annunzian *L'innocente* (1976) that tempt critics to excoriate them as "decadent" or "nostalgic," and to acknowledge, if not apologize for, their autobiographical character. As is the case with many of the star directors of the 1960s and 1970s, Visconti was celebrated in critical reviews, scholarly books, festival series dedicated to him, biographies and biographical films (e.g., Lizzani's *Luchino Visconti* [1999]), TV appearances, documentaries on Italian cinema, such as *Bellissimo* (1985), that celebrate his style of filming, and his presence in documentaries about other celebrities (e.g., *Io sono Anna Magnani* [1979] and *Maria Callas: La Divina: A Portrait* [1987]).

Beginning with *Ossessione*, an unrelenting attention to the role of art and of the cinematic medium in his own films will be characteristic of Visconti's auteurist concerns and contribute to his star status and that of the stars created through his films. *Ossessione* bears resemblance to the style of the calligraphers in its pictorialism, its stylization of character, its noir-like use of lighting, its framing, and its refusal of narrative reconciliation in the death of Giovanna, held in Gino's arms as an ironic Pietà. However, the film's dependence on a popular American novel, a contemporary setting, and stars of the fascist era suggests different and metacinematic concerns. Using two stars of the time—glamorous Clara Calamai of *Addio Giovanezza* (Goodbye Youth, 1940), *Luci nel tenebre* (Light in Darkness, 1941), and *Le Sorelle Materassi* (The Materassi Sisters, 1943) and romantic adventurer, swashbuckler, and Tarzan-figure Massimo Girotti of *I pirati della Malesia*

5.1. Transforming stars: Clara Calamai and Massimo Girotti in Visconti's *Ossessione*. *Photofest*.

(The Malay Pirates, 1941) and *La corona di ferro* (The Iron Crown, 1941)—Visconti altered their roles, their physical appearance, and their acting. Not a minor star in the fascist era, Calamai had been identified largely with costume dramas, where she had played seducers and courtesans and had been, at one point, the subject of the censor's scissors for a scene in which her nude body was exposed. Under Visconti's direction Calamai's star persona was invoked and then transformed, its glamour stripped away, exposing a materialist and sordid side of eroticism as well as linking this to opera with its penchant for melodrama. Girotti the virile protagonist of historical films became for Visconti, as he did for Pasolini later, a cryptic figure of masculinity.

While subject to the censor's scalpel in its references to the war in Spain against fascism and to implied homosocial relations between Gino and Lo Spagnolo (Elio Marcuzzo, also an actor popular in 1940s films), *Ossessione* was a prism reflecting many of the concerns of a later generation of filmmakers identified with neorealism. The film offers different conceptions of adaptation from literature into film, an oblique critique of contemporary cinema, an exploration of melodrama in relation to realism, and an investigation of the potential of cinematic language to offer an alternative to purely political discourse.[14] In "Sex in the Cinema," David Forgacs is critical of a reading that narrowly situates *Ossessione* within the rubric of fascism and anti-fascism, claiming that the film has more "in common with many of the French and American films noir of the 1940s which it resembles, its narrative centers on a fatal desire for a powerful woman which leads to both the man's downfall and the death of the woman, and that *as a narrative* there is nothing intrinsically anti-fascist about this."[15] Forgacs puts to rest a film analysis that equates narrative with a specific polemical position. While Forgacs is correct in saying that the film "intrinsically" as a narrative does not address fascism, having more in common with familiar scenarios of melodrama and film noir, nonetheless an examination of the film's allusive style, its form of acting, and its treatment of the cinematic image leads elsewhere, back to the cinema under fascism, to the fantasies which it nourished, and to the crisis of the image in the 1930s and 1940s. *Ossessione* may indeed be reminiscent of French and American film noir, but in its figuration of its stars and landscape, and its invocation of cultural and social cliché, it creates a milieu that is redolent of memories of the dominant culture via the cinema and also the popular uses of lyric opera. Though adapting a popular American novel and drawing on the conventions and codes of melodrama and film noir to stylistically investigate existing cinematic practices, *Ossessione* "is not merely one of the versions of the American thriller, or the transposition of the novel to the plain of the Po. In Visconti's film, we witness a subtle change, the beginnings of a mutation of the general notion of situation. In the old realism or on the model of the action-image, objects and settings already had a reality of their own, but it was a functional reality already determined by the demands of the situation."[16]

The narrative of *Ossessione* involves a journey, a *femme fatale*, triangulation (Gino, Bragana, and Giovanna; Giovanna, Gino, and Spagnolo; Anita, Giovanna, and Gino, each of the triads invoking familial, heterosexual, and homosocial forms of bonding), obsession, crime, guilt, and punishment. What is different in this film from mainstream classical realism is how character and situation are visualized. They are "diverting clichés" whereby the "melodrama" has to be qualified in the light of the film's emphasis on the cinematic properties of sight and sound by means of the lighting, framing, tracking shots, *mise-en-scène*, and on-screen and off-screen sound (such as that of the cat). The film's "realism" does not merely reiterate critical or "transgressive" dimensions of melodrama: it questions their existence, attributing to them an operatic mode infected with what Antonio Gramsci called "the disease of pompousness, stylistic hypocrisy, and oratorical style."[17]

Ossessione invokes forms of entertainment in its allusions to opera and dance, and forms of street entertainment through the characters of Bragana, Anita, and Spagnolo. However, these allusions are more than intertextual embellishment; they provide insight into the protagonists' appearance and behavior and their connections to the cultural milieu. In the reunion of Giovanna and Gino at the singing contest, their dialogue is ironically juxtaposed to the music and lyrics of *La traviata*, calling attention to the banal, even grotesque character of the operatic contestants and their performance. The film's treatment of the road is juxtaposed to the cramped milieu of the trattoria, highlighting a tension between closed and open space, the closed space linked to the contained and seemingly fated world of melodrama, the open leading to another world beyond the frame and associated with freedom and a horizontal view of collectivity against hierarchized, constraining myths of femininity and masculinity. The final scenes on the road with Gina and Gino involve their inability to see the road that leads to her death and his arrest. The characters are somnambulistic, looking but not seeing, trapped in their mirror images, framed by windows and doors, swallowed up in darkness as further testimony to the film's shift from an affectively charged melodrama to another mode of cinematic expression whereby familiar bodies and behaviors of stars are scrutinized not in the interests of emulation so much as for challenging identification.

Visconti's use of stars furthers the film's metacinematic strategies. His choice of them conforms to their theatricality, presenting them as performers and deflecting attention away from authenticity to the indeterminacy of their presences. In the case of Calamai, her popularity in the cinema of the fascist years enriches the metacinematic dimensions of the film. Unlike in her other roles, she is ultimately filmed without makeup, with unkempt hair, and in simple frocks, with her death becoming a moment not of transfiguration of her star image but of its ultimate destruction. The film also refashions Girotti's image from a handsome leading man to a dirty, disheveled, childlike nomad, a somnambulist trapped in a dark and claustrophobic world. The star is thus a key not only to the "meaning" of the film but also to its designs on the medium and on its audiences.

Girotti was an ideal figure for the role of the inarticulate and nomadic Gino, since his cinematic persona was protean enough to be able to mould to the needs of the film. Girotti serves the director as both a protagonist in a melodrama and as a means of shifting focus from a real landscape to an imaginary or dreamlike one that resembles popular cinema and a culture of theatricality. The film focuses on the bodies of the characters, on Giovanna's legs, her shapely body, the hairy and muscular body of Gino, the obese Bragana, and the lithe body of Lo Spagnolo (played by Elio Marcuzzo, an actor identified with the films of Poggioli). These bodies are indicative of the film's investment in the stylized and highly choreographed world of noir and melodrama that focuses on the imprisoned body and on a claustrophobic treatment of space.

Calamai's role in this film evokes memories of her starring image as glamorous, erotic, Hollywood-ized transgressive female in other films of the fascist era (e.g., *Addio Giovinezza* and *Le Sorelle Materassi*), but then her filming exposes a significant difference from the previous cinema. While Calamai may have had a greater claim to stardom than Girotti, the film reverses the conventional star treatment of femininity to focus on Gino as object of desire by means of camera angle, close-ups, framing, and lighting. She is introduced by the siren sound of her singing and then with an image of her dangling legs from Gino's perspective as he enters the trattoria. The viewer is also provided a sustained look at Gino's body. As the film develops, Giovanna and Gino's images undergo a visual meta-morphosis, she from a seductive *femme fatale*, to a calculating business woman, and finally to a maternal figure in relation to a recalcitrant and then repentant Gino. In stripping away the beauty and seductiveness of Calamai's femininity, the film prefigures the metamorphosis of Visconti's other women characters, namely Alida Valli as Livia in *Senso* (1954) and Ingrid Thulin as Sophie *in La caduta degli dei* (The Damned, 1969). Girotti's masculine persona was further altered by Pa-solini in *Teorema* and later by Ferzan Ozpetek in *La finestra di fronte* (Facing Windows, 2003), where homosexuality becomes explicit.

Visconti's selection and treatment of stars for *Ossessione* was determined in part by the state of the film industry in the early 1940s, but in the early postwar cinema he made use of non-professional actors, as in *La terra trema* (The Earth Trembles, 1948). His fame as a director relies in part on the prestige he gained for this film in relation to his use of landscape and effective employment of non-pro-fessional actors. In his filming of the characters in the southern Italian context, he beautifies their appearance, filming them as one would film stars. *Rocco e suoi fratelli* (Rocco and His Brothers, 1960) mingles professionals and non-profession-als as its rural characters journey from the south of Italy to the urban north of Milan: the film features international actors such as Alain Delon, Katina Paxinou, and Annie Girardot along with veteran Italian actor Renato Salvatori. Visconti's effective and acclaimed uses of non-professional actors notwithstanding, his fame rests on his use of literary texts and major stars as well as on his own penchant for aristocratic landscapes. In *Bellissima* (1951), Visconti critically probes the illusory world of commercial cinema in contrast to a cinema identified with the neorealist aesthetic[18] (see chapter 3), offering in the process a metacritical treatment of star-dom via the figure of Anna Magnani.

In *Senso* (1954), Alida Valli stars as Countess Lidia Serpieri, a decadent noblewoman obsessed with romantic, operatic, novelistic conceptions of love. Her role again invokes the memory of the many films of the 1930s that estab-lished her as a major star; she had appeared in costume films such as *Il feroce Saladino* (Ferocious Saladin, 1937), the successful Hungarian-style comedy *Mille lire al mese* (A Thousands Liras per Month, 1938), the romantic melo-drama *Assenza ingiustifacta* (Unjustified Absence, 1939), in which she starred with the major Italian star of the era, Amedeo Nazzari, and the patriotic Risor-

gimento melodrama *Piccolo mondo antico* (1941). On the set Valli had the reputation of being an "anti-diva" (unlike Calamai), not given to histrionics and
pliable in the hands of directors and technicians. Her popularity was at its peak
between 1939 and 1942, when she made four or five films a year, appearing in
a variety of genres: costume dramas, contemporary melodramas, and comedies.
She and Isa Miranda "were the two true queens of the fascist cinema."[19] Valli's
role in *Senso* offered an ironic contrast, in particular, to her suffering and submissive role in *Piccolo mondo antico* and her consistency of commitment to
anti-communism in *Noi vivi* (1942). Her rejection at the end of *Senso* by her
Austrian lover Franz Mahler, played by the American star Farley Granger, is an
unmasking of her operatic excess and her image as an operatic diva. Her glamorous image is drastically transformed during the course of the film. Arriving
dusty and disheveled from the journey she was enjoined by Franz not to make,
she is set in stark contrast to a young prostitute and made to appear old, hag-
gard, ugly, and vengeful alongside the younger woman. Valli's position as a star
enables Visconti further to undermine the glamour and spectacle of stardom,
reducing it to squalor and moral degradation by utilizing it while diminishing
its power (as he did with Calamai in *Ossessione*). This exposure of masquerade
through his treatment of stars and *mise-en-scène* is intrinsic to the style of his
works and helped to consolidate his image as a consummate craftsman, an au-
tocrat, a dandy, and a connoisseur dedicated to every detail of the films.

In *Il gattopardo* (The Leopard, 1963), Visconti also draws on the phenomenon of stardom, utilizing international as well as Italian stars in a cast that includes Burt Lancaster, Alain Delon, Claudia Cardinale, and supporting actors
Rina Morelli, Paolo Stoppa, and Romolo Valli. Once again through its use of
glamorous stars, the film directs attention to connections between spectacle,
historicizing, and masquerade. Similarly to *Senso*, the film utilizes spectacle
via makeup, costuming, and lavish sets, but the spectacle is subtler as are the
techniques employed for its unmasking. The spectacle is not undermined by
destroying the beauty of Claudia Cardinale and Alain Delon, but the vision of
their youth and glamour underscores the manipulative and deceptive world
that they embody, a world that is beautiful but ultimately deadly and subject to
decay. Their filming emphasizes their exquisite appearance in the lengthy ball
scene that concludes the film. The viewer is drawn into their orbit, viewing
them through the eyes of Don Fabrizio as the renewal of the old order in a more
modern and aesthetically appealing appearance.

However, the film also dramatizes, if not in the same grotesque terms as
the ending of *Senso*, the lies, machinations, economic self-interest, and tempo-
ral, not immortal, character of this privileged world in the throes of change.
The Greuze painting "The Death of the Just Man" and the ubiquitous mirror
shots call attention to the prince's illness and impending death and the fragility

of the images of beauty. Visconti's use of landscape, exquisitely developed in *Il gattopardo*, becomes a meditation on time: "One of *The Leopard's* delights is the rich visual poetry of the dusty, the earthly and the sun-burnt—making palpable the shimmering heat, blinding light and stifling power of the island. Visconti does not seek to explain anything: the incandescence of the day is not a painful metaphor for the immobility of Sicily; it is merely an impression that the brightness of the screen is able to translate."[20] The particular aristocratic milieu in *Senso* and *Il gattopardo* has led critics to regard Visconti's characters and their relation to a determinate landscape as personal exploration, thus enhancing his identification with auterism.

Four elements characterize Visconti's films from *Senso* to *Ludwig* or *L'innocente* and are related to the aesthetics of stardom: (1) the focus on the aristocratic world, which is "outside divine creation where freedom is demanded but as an empty privilege"; (2) the invocation of a world that is "inseparable from the decomposition that eats it from within"; (3) an awareness of history "which growls at the door," which is never scenery, and "to which Visconti sometimes dedicates marvelous images, and sometimes grants a presence which is all the more intense for being elliptical and out-of-field"; and (4) "the revelation, that *something* arrives too late . . . [but] it is history, and nature itself, the structure of the crystal that makes it impossible . . . to arrive in time."[21] The sense of forking time and of the ways in which it inflects visual and auditory perception is communicated through a complex treatment of spectacle that animates figures and objects from the past but, at the same time, punctures their appeal.

The cinematic image is an incitement to memory, to thought, and to another less reductive sense of the past as this involves the use of stars. Stars are aligned to other aesthetic objects in Visconti's films and are subject to the same reflection on decay and mortality. From Clara Calamai, Alida Valli, and Anna Magnani to Burt Lancaster, Dirk Bogarde, Ingrid Thulin, and Giancarlo Giannini, among others, these stars play a significant role in initially establishing their beauty and desirability and then gradually registering their disintegration or, at best, their entrapment in the cinematic apparatus. His stars become further instruments for exposing the virtual character of the cinematic image and, hence, for undermining classic expectations of beauty and desire.

Sempre De Sica

Vittorio De Sica was another director elevated to stardom, first due to his starring roles in the comedies of Mario Camerini (see chapter 2), then through his taking on the directorial mantle with such fascist-era films as *Teresa Venerdì*, *Un garibaldino in convento*, and *I bambini ci guardano*, and finally for the canonical status granted him for his "neorealist" works, *Ladri di biciclette*, *Sciuscià*, and *Umberto D.* His collaboration with Cesare Zavattini was critical to his later career, as was his earlier work as actor for Camerini. Moreover, his career was to be a dual one, as actor and as director in both Italian and European cinema. Graduating from his image as matinee idol, singing star, romantic lead, and icon of the working class, De Sica's on-screen persona altered with age: as an older man he could play sophisticated and upper-class figures, as in Ophüls's *La ronde*, and a hen-pecked aristocrat and gambler in his own directed *L'oro di Napoli*, or the rakish, uxorious, and often thwarted chief of police, Maresciallo Carotenuto, in *Pane, amore e fantasia* (Bread, Love and Fantasy, 1953), in *Pane, amore e Gelosia* (1954) with the popular Gina Lollobrigida, and with Sophia Loren in *Pane, amore e . . .* (1955). In these rural comedies De Sica takes a back seat to the women who manage to outwit him and get what they want. The image of a barefoot Lollobrigida in a peasant blouse that exposes her shoulders and shapely bosom, astride her donkey, singing, crooning, uttering invectives, and inflaming men's desires, was evidence of the heyday of the "supermaggiorata," the new embodiment of feminine stardom associated largely with the landscape of the south and with rural and urban contexts.

His now-aging and somewhat heavy body, and his subordination to these animated women, renders him a paternal rather than romantic figure. His direction of Sophia Loren in such films as *L'oro di Napoli*, *La Ciociara*, and *Ieri, oggi, domani* served to enhance and extend the parameters of Loren's stardom, if not his own as director and as actor. De Sica as director capitalized on Loren's image as an Italian "sex goddess," but Carlo Ponti also aided in the transformation of Loren into a serious actress who won an Academy Award for her role as Cesira in *La Ciociara*. More associated with the popular cinema than were Rossellini and Antonioni, and with comedy as well as melodrama, De Sica's star image by the late 1950s was consolidated through the numerous films he directed and in which he acted, through his acting for other directors, through documentaries about him, through cameo appearances in films of other directors (e.g., *C'eravamo tanto amati*), and through publicity about his life. His work straddled art and commercial cinema, and is often undervalued for the contributions it makes to an understanding of stardom.

A major dimension of De Sica's image was of a poseur adept at impersonation (see chapter 2). Rossellini's *Il Generale della Rovere* (1959) captured De Sica's protean, elusive, and intriguing star persona in a dual role. Despite Rossellini's dismissal of this film as a piece of hackwork, it is a critical text focusing not only on the war and fascist collaboration but on the nature and uses of stardom. De Sica's star image not only makes connections with De Sica's origins, his cinematic identification with Naples through his biography and through the setting for many of his films, but also reinforces the union of his character with the lore surrounding the star. De Sica's character becomes a self-conscious instrument with which to investigate the connections between realism and theatricality. De Sica's own explorations of the cinematic image are evident in *Ladri di biciclette* with the poster of Rita Hayworth as Gilda that Antonio is employed to paste on city walls, and the references to cinema in *I bambini ci guardano* and *Umberto D*, and are most developed in the visual journey through cinema in *Oggi, ieri, domani*. In consistent fashion, De Sica's persona was intimately tied to directly and obliquely exploring the world of the cinematic image in a manner consistent with the tendency of neorealism to investigate the conditions of its production.

Rossellini's film uses De Sica's stardom as a pretext to explore a motif central to stardom, namely the illusion of authenticity. De Sica's on-screen and off-screen persona becomes the instrument for investigating the nature of belief in and identification with the star. The film draws on the spectator's memory of De Sica's biography and career in relation to his womanizing, his gambling and indebtedness, and the memory of his other film performances. In public life, De Sica, despite his divorce from his first wife, was considered a distinguished citizen, honored for his cultural contributions, especially the creation of postwar classics identified with neorealism, and his contributions to liberal politics and to the cinema of auteurs. De Sica's appearance in the Rossellini film is another powerful instance of the multiple considerations inherent to stardom that include the director as both creator of and created by the phenomenon of stardom.

The subject of authenticity remains ambiguous in relation to De Sica's role in the film. Is Bardone's conversion to hero/martyr to be regarded as "genuine" or "real"? Or is authenticity the proper criterion with which to assess performance? The film leaves the answer to the first of these questions open. De Sica's impersonation shifts from the "real meaning" or the "realism" of performance to a consideration of its theatricality and ethical effects. By extension, the film's focus is transferred from commonsense interpretation to a philosophical inquiry about image making and meaning. The film becomes an investigation involving misperceptions concerning the cinematic image. The star, in this case De Sica as a quintessential creation of cinema, becomes the film's instrument for examining its construction and reception.

Rossellini and His Stars

Roberto Rossellini's career is considerably more dramatic than De Sica's, a target for journalists, tabloids, and gossip. His reputation as a playboy, his friendship with Vittorio Mussolini, his relationship with Anna Magnani as well as other Italian stars (including Assia Noris), the ban in the U.S. on *Il miracolo*, and the international scandal of his affair with and marriage to Ingrid Bergman guaranteed him the notoriety of a star. His championing by the *Cahiers du cinéma* as an auteur further enhanced his legend, inspiring French cineastes and critics, and filmmakers such as Jean-Luc Godard (who inserted references to Rossellini and his work desk in *Forever Mozart*).

From the earliest documentaries to the wartime trilogy, Rossellini's connections to the regime and to Vittorio Mussolini remain ambiguous. However, *Roma, città aperta* and *Paisà* established his reputation. The films are regarded as foundational texts of neorealism and the extensive critical work on his films and biography from the 1970s to the present has reconsidered the contributions of his wartime films to the shape of postwar cinema. His films and the later television texts—*L'età de ferro* (The Age of Iron, 1964), *La prise du pouvoir de Louis XIV* (The Rise to Power of Louis XIV, 1966), and *Socrate* (1970)—reveal a different stylistic trajectory from those of De Sica and De Santis. Working much less in a genre mode, Rossellini adopts a different treatment of the Italian landscape, of social history, and of his actors. *Roma, città aperta, Paisà, La macchina ammazzacattivi*, and *Una voce umana* incorporate issues of surveillance, photography, and telephony.

Not averse to using popular actors and stars, Rossellini not only cast Anna Magnani, with whom he had an intimate relationship and who was well known for her work in theatre and increasingly in cinema; he also played a determining role in Ingrid Bergman's personal life and career. His work with both Bergman and Magnani reveals the ways in which he shaped or re-shaped their stardom according to his own predilections. Magnani's star image can be said to come together through the roles she played for him, most particularly through her role as Pina in *Roma, città aperta* (see chapter 3). Magnani's role in this film was emblematic of the changed and changing conceptions of the feminine body and its relation to the Italian and international imaginary, and she became for many an icon of Italian-ness associated with organic forms of representation. Her image as a tough working-class woman carried over to her Hollywood roles in such films as *The Rose Tattoo*, for which she won an Academy Award. In *Il miracolo* (1948), directed by Rossellini, she enacts an illiterate and wild peasant woman's fantasy of sexual encounter with a saint (St. Joseph, played by Federico Fellini). As in other Rossellini films her role challenges reductive conceptions of "normality" and religious belief. The films Rossellini created with Magnani consolidated her star persona.

In *Una voce umana* (The Human Voice, 1948) she is the only character on screen, a distraught and enraged woman abandoned by her lover and speaking to him via the telephone. Her role again invokes the Rossellinian preoccupation with "the nature of linguistic, and, by extension, cinematic representation and its adequacy to the real world. . . . [I]f artifice cannot be avoided in one's pursuit of 'reality,' then perhaps one had best embrace it openly."[22] Magnani's image in this film testifies to her star persona as an instrument *par excellence* with which to explore connections between the illusory character of femininity (and of stardom) and its intimate dependence on Rossellini's insistent probing of cinematic illusion through his use of stars, particularly female stars.

If Magnani's role in Rossellini's films was a further exploration of the director's ongoing cinematic quarrel with simplistic notions of the real, his films with Ingrid Bergman further develop this concern. Among the elements contributing to his stardom are his use of his female stars and his own and the stars' publicizing of their relationships with the director. There was nothing scandalous initially when superstar Bergman left Hollywood for Italy to work with Rossellini, but the situation changed dramatically. The international proportions of the saga of her "adulterous" relationship with Rossellini and her bearing his child became a cause célèbre. The scandal reached the halls of the U.S. Congress, with Senator Edwin Johnson (Colorado) calling for Bergman to be barred from returning to the U.S. As Stephen Gundle points out, the "Bergman-Rossellini affair was by any definition a global scandal. It involved three countries—the United States, Italy, and Bergman's home country, Sweden—and it excited the interest of the world's media."[23]

At first, their romance was greeted with enthusiasm by the Italian media. Only later did the Bergman-Rossellini relationship become sordid.[24] More germane to the Italians were the charges leveled at the director, who was criticized by the left for abandoning the political character of neorealism and for "'selling out' through his use of a Hollywood star."[25] Thus, the affair served to implicate not only the actress but the director as well. Furthermore Rossellini's public image involved "expansive gestures and flamboyant lifestyle."[26]

Prior to the "scandal" of her relationship with Rossellini, Bergman's Hollywood star persona, based on Hollywood studio publicity, was circulated as wholesome and spiritual. This publicity was especially pertinent to her role as Joan of Arc. However, a careful overview of her Hollywood roles reveals otherwise: she had played disreputable roles as a sexually seductive promiscuous woman in *Dr. Jekyll and Mr. Hyde* (1941), *Saratoga Trunk* (1945), and *Notorious* (1946), and an abject woman driven to the brink of madness in *Gaslight* (1944).[27] The films in which Bergman acted for Rossellini became an instrument for scanning the mechanisms of stardom and of the director privileging certain of her traits for his own ends. In contrast to Rossellini's use of Magnani as a personification of Italian life and values, Bergman was not an embodiment of working-class femininity; she was an alien, a displaced person. In *Stromboli, terra di dio* (Stromboli, God's Country, 1949), the director creates visual and auditory disjunctions between the Sicilian landscape and the European woman. She is stripped of glamour in makeup and costuming, and subject to a loose script and improvisational directing. She is doubly displaced: from national identification and from Hollywood filmmaking. Bergman as Karin is no "terra madre": she is too worldly; despite her uses of sex for survival, earthiness frightens her and causes her to seek escape from this alien world, the earth being associated with volcanic eruption, violence, carnal sexuality, birth, and death.

The camera pursues her relentlessly. Because she is deprived of the verbal means to express herself, her means of communication are ultimately non-verbal, revealing her inability to reconcile her needs with the inhabitants (husband, priest, villagers). She ultimately is identified with the dark volcanic forces that initiate her into a different, spiritual relationship with the world that removes her from the prison of self and her judgments about others. Karin has confronted her isolation and established contact with her body, life, and belief. Rossellini has once again appropriated not only Bergman's star image but also that of an archetypal form of femininity to explore a different relation to the cinema by way of interrogating clichés and inviting a relation to images that are ambiguous and situations that are inconclusive.

Bergman's stardom in Rossellini's films relies heavily on an "alien" national identity. Consistently, films she made for Rossellini present her as *heimatlos*, a middle-class woman displaced, a nomad, and a star removed from Hollywood. In *Europa 51* (1952), she is a mother grieving for her dead son and consumed with guilt (perhaps as Rossellini himself was at the death earlier in his life of his own son). From the outset of the film, Bergman is a somnambulist, at first going through the motions of a proper and sterile life. With the death of her son, her somnambulistic journey in search of life involves her confrontation with poverty and death. While she becomes an enigma, later a madwoman to her family and friends in her peregrinations, assuming various social positions that were earlier unknown to her, she passes through the images of a world that had earlier constituted the parameters of her life.

If ever the meaning of the image of the woman at the window carried a profound cultural resonance in relation to the iconography of femininity, the image of Bergman framed in the window of the hospital room where she is imprisoned captures the uncertain character of femininity. This shot further enhances the reflexive dimensions of Rossellini's uses of her star image to convey her isolation and separateness, and the cinematic apparatus as a mechanism that conceals and potentially reveals the contours of thought. Increasingly, she is removed from the familiar landmarks of cinema, culminating in her becoming a cipher through the film robbing her of speech, erasing the images of a conventional landscape, and thereby dissolving boundaries between normal and pathological vision. Whatever identification exists between this image of her and her Hollywood star image merely serves to underscore the film's and Rossellini's engagement with and critique of realism (though not of reality).

The filmmaker and his star are fused in a fascinating exploration of what Deleuze has described as the potential and tendency of certain forms of cinema to unite body and brain in search of thinking through images.

Similar to *Europa 51*, *Viaggio in Italia* (1954) is a multi-layered exploration of the potential of cinema to become philosophy that interrogates language at its most clichéd, and an exercise in exposing romantic fantasies derived from literature and cinema. The director's thinly concealed investment in his own position is portrayed through his uses of Hollywood star George Sanders and Rossellini's then-wife and star Bergman. The scaffolding of the narrative is spare, narrating the journey of an English-speaking couple to Italy to sell the house of "Uncle Horace," a wealthy man who had become enamored of Italy and whose history is tied to the presence of Americans and British in Italy during World War II. The Joyces are themselves apparently unsentimental about the commercial transaction, particularly the husband, but it appears that the selling of the house begins to assume critical importance for their relationship and their individual connections to their contemporary world and to each other.

The film takes its stars on a journey into marriage, memories of World War II, homelessness, history, and meditation of time. A ghost stands between Katherine and Alex in the memory of a dead young poet whose poems she continues to recollect and recite, to Alex's consternation. The allusion to Joyce's "The Dead" extends beyond the couple's surname to the evocation of Greta Conroy's memory of the young Michael Furey, whose ghost stands between her and her husband Gabriel. And the film's use of Bergman is hardly contained in this allusion to James Joyce. In her journeys through the Neapolitan landscape by car and on foot, Katherine encounters a world of difference[28] through the women that she sees on the streets as she sits enclosed and isolated in her car, talking to herself and complaining of her husband. Through Katherine's perspective, the viewer sees unglamorous women, pregnant or pushing prams. In contrast to images of life, she views a funeral cortege. Moving through time, armed with her camera, she confronts the world of the early Romans and of the Christian martyrs. She confronts natural catastrophes in the form of volcanic springs as well as humanly created disasters. The incremental engagements with time and death involve a visit to a church that houses human skulls from the classical past and present (shots that are reiterated in Lina Wertmüller's *Sette Bellezze* in the later film's invocation of the Mafia and of the Holocaust). *Viaggio* has an equally ambitious trajectory reaching farther back in time and inviting the viewer into the cinematic uses of the past and of the camera as a time machine, with its Hollywood stars as guides to that journey.

The linking of the scenes at Pompei and the scenes of the couple's rupture and then reunion at a religious festival, as well as the framing of the film beginning with the two driving on the road and ending with the two out of their car

5.2. Transnational stars: Ingrid Bergman and George Sanders in *Viaggio in Italia*. Photofest.

and standing on the street in the midst of a crowd, have consequences for an understanding of Rossellini's conception of character. The characters are voided of their individuality in much the same manner as the entwined excavated bodies exhumed at Pompei have no specific identity. The film stars are also ultimately robbed of their familiar cinematic identities, though paradoxically, the film has invoked the specificity of their star personas throughout their appearance: Sanders as a cynical, bored, and passive figure and Bergman as a seeker in search of passion. Peter Brunette describes how the film might be considered as a "road film,"[29] an indication of the functioning of the time-image by means of the voyage form in which "any-space-what-evers proliferate . . . which are opposed to the determined spaces of the old realism."[30] And Katherine and Alex, rather than being instigators of action, again in Brunette's language "represent opposing sets of abstractions" and are not "complete human beings, but parts of a whole." Or, in Deleuze's terms, they are "actor mediums" where objects and settings (*milieux*) take on an autonomous material reality. Bergman's Hollywood persona is invoked and then tampered with in the film, primarily through the film's engagement with the character's romantic fantasies, her *ressentiment*. If she remains inscrutable and enigmatic to the end, this may be accounted for by the film's use of its stars/actors as somnambulists who reinforce the film's investigative mode rather than conventions of escapist or sociological treatments of narrative that rely on cinematic style to generate an affective bridge between the characters, the events, and the spectator's expectations. Katherine's journey moves her (and the spectator) into different registers of time and memory. *Viaggio* is not merely a "Bergman film"; it is a "Rossellini film" that enables him, as director, to exploit his stars in philosophical and unsettling fashion.

In *Siamo donne* (1953, see chapter 3) he directed Bergman in a documentary-like sketch supposedly, according to both of them, just as a joke; however, the segment is revealing for Rossellini's uses of this star. In the other sketches, featuring Alida Valli, Isa Miranda, and Anna Magnani, the stars enact familiar dimensions of their personas derived from films in which they starred and from assumed quasi-biographical items about their personal lives. By contrast, Rossellini's treatment of Bergman is improvisational. The episode is an anecdote about Bergman's troubles with managing her home, gardening, neighbors, animals, and her son by Rossellini. Featuring Bergman speaking directly into the camera, this episode seems to provide an element of "authenticity." It has an improvisational quality that is missing from the others, but, on closer inspection, the "joke" turns out to be that the anecdote is fictional despite Bergman's direct address, the use of Rossellini and Bergman's home and garden, and the presence of their child.[31]

The humor, if it can be called that, of the sketch is that Rossellini in this short film has again played with the spectator's conceptions of realism via his handling of Bergman. He has sacrificed his "star" to his philosophic preoccupation with the fictional character of reality and the reality of fiction through the female star. He uses Bergman as one might unprofessional actors, concerned more with the cinematic image that suits his investment in experimenting with narration than with one consistent with the star's prior cinematic reputation. In Peter Brunette's terms, this segment, like Magnani's monologue in *Una voce umana*, "problematizes the difference between actress and role, inevitably raising questions concerning the boundaries between such dualities."[32] An indirect free discourse troubles a neat alignment of image and interpretation, spectator and text, star and person. The star fuses with her ironic creator.

Fellini: The Director and His Stars in a Dream World

There is no blueprint for the treatment of stars by different auteurist directors. Fellini is a director about whom volumes have been written and numerous films made (e.g., *Mémoire: Federico Fellini, Io sono un gran buggiardo* [I Am a Great Liar, 2002] and *Cinecittà: La casa di Fellini* [The House of Fellini, 2004]); and he has also appeared in films for other directors (e.g., *C'eravamo tanto amati* [We All Loved Each Other So Much, 1974] and *Il tassinaro* [The Taxi Driver, 1983]). These books, films, and essays recount his rise to international popularity, his biography, his seminal role in defining the Italian cinema of the postwar era, and influences on his films. Perhaps Douglas Sirk had Fellini in mind when he has Lana Turner, as Lora Meredith in *Imitation of Life* (1959), accept an invitation to make a film in Italy with a prominent director named "Felluci."

From *Luci di varietà* (Variety Lights, 1950) and beyond, Fellini's films are preoccupied with entertainment, spectacle, creativity, media, and theatricality. They are eclectic histories of popular culture, cinema, and television in his portraits of silent cinema, *Divismo, commedia dell'arte, fumetti, fotoromanzi,* and musical hall and variety forms of entertainment. His films, reliant on Freudian and Jungian psychoanalysis, are historical, offering versions of the past involving Roman times, the fascist era, World War II, the "Economic Miracle," and spectacular vignettes of contemporary culture and society.[33] Fellini had a predilection for certain actors and had no problem with using stars in his films or, for that matter, creating stars. In this respect, he shares with Rossellini an indifference to prescriptions, neorealist and otherwise. However, his work, like that of Rossellini, is further testimony to the cinematic questions and styles set in motion by neorealism, leading in their works to conceptual explorations of realism and, in others, to more socially engaged forms of representation.

Fellini's uses of Giulietta Masina, his wife of long standing, in *Luci del varietà* (1950), *Lo sceicco bianco* (The White Sheik, 1952), *La strada* (The Road, 1954), *Il bidone* (The Swindle, 1955), *Le notti di Cabiria* (Nights of Cabiria, 1957), *Giulietta degli spiriti* (Juliet of the Spirits, 1965), and *Ginger e Fred* (1986) run counter to the uses of other stars in Fellini's works as well as Rossellini's. Masina's roles do not appear as fused to Fellini's persona as do those of Mastroianni. While she is associated with important Fellini films, she is never discussed as part of a star/director duo. In fact, "it would be difficult to say whether it was Giulietta who resembled Fellini's characters or, on the contrary, they who were inspired by her."[34] She played character parts for Fellini and for other directors, and "While the majority of Italian actresses banked on their attractiveness, Giulietta built her career on dramatic talent."[35] In Fellini and Lattuada's *Luci del varietà*, as in Fellini's *La strada*, the focus is on popular entertainment, and the strolling players are reminiscent of the *commedia dell'arte* world with its rich and strange character types. As is evident from most of Fellini's films and from his popularity as a personality and incarnation of the flamboyant director, his works are personal documents: they are not confessional, though they do contain anecdotal moments (albeit transformed) from his own biography. Their structures are as much a journey as are the journeys of the characters within the narratives, and the spectator's journey through the changing landscapes. If in films such as *La strada*, the strolling theater of Zampanò and Gelsomina captures the world of entertainment, it functions beyond a mere reflexive device, to stray into questions of metaphysics by means of allegory, not so much national but metaphysical or spiritual allegory in the sense that landscape, characters, and events offer a collage that portrays colliding, often disparate, images of worlds that do not neatly connect to one another. In *La strada* the uses of Anthony Quinn and Giulietta Masina do not offer the viewer comfortable and accessible analogues to contemporary reality. Instead, adopting the journey framework of the *Divine Comedy* as one of enlightenment, the film's treatment of character and landscape (the sea, earth, and sky) invokes the familiar opposition between body and spirit. These oppositions are not signs of irrevocable difference in need of reconciliation so much as creative elements in Fellini's metamorphosis of life into art. As so many critics have commented in affirmative or negative terms, Fellini is not a political film-maker—that is, not in the conventional sense of the term. His films are political insofar as they are dense reflections on forms of belief, on the nature of life and death, on memory and history, and on their cultural expression in art, particularly in cinema as the medium *par excellence* to communicate insights about these concepts.

Hence Fellini's use of actors and of those who qualify as stars is subject to his idiosyncratic uses of the cinematic image, which are a further permutation of earlier views on neorealism. Fellini's "realism" often appears akin to surrealism in its predilection for fantastic images that rely on dream memory but are often more accessible to the viewer than to the characters. Fellini's is a landscape where images of space are disconnected and where, as in memory, they jostle with each other, conveying a dislocation from crude materiality but yet vividly linked to nature and to the body. For example, in *La dolce vita* (1960), the spectator is assailed by images of the sea, the beach, the famous scenes at the Fountain of Trevi with Ekberg, traffic, crowded bar locales, upper-class parties, street life, paparazzi, religious imposters, and the overwhelming presence of commodities both on and around the protagonist. The film was a scandalous success, decried by critics and Churchmen, but at the same time irresistible to both Italian and international audiences, to fans of both art and popular cinema, and Mastroianni's role consolidated his popularity not only with Italian audiences but internationally. He became an international star, if not the erroneous epitome or the undermining of the "Latin Lover." As Gundle recites the events leading to the selection of Mastroianni for the role, he states: "Marcello was in fact chosen because he was familiar and reliable, a respectable and unexciting everyman with whom spectators could easily identify. His cordial and unexceptional features were the ideal vehicle for transporting audiences on a journey through a world of temptation and corruption."[36] This sociological and historical reading relies heavily on the film as a critique of contemporary Italian society, exemplifying (as was also the case with Schlesinger's *Darling* that starred Julie Christie), the fast and nomadic lives of the upper classes and youth in the "swinging sixties."

However, *La dolce vita* did much more than provide cultural and social commentary: it reinforced for popular audiences the self-conscious uses of cinema as a major arbiter of contemporary life. Not that cinema had not been reflexive about its properties, but in this film as in others of the decades from the 1960s, the equation was strengthened between cinema and other cultural artifacts—dress fashions, architecture, paintings, urban life, music—within a context that leapt over national boundaries. In *La dolce vita*, as in Fellini's later *Roma*, Rome becomes again an international center, a place of convergence for the wealthy, famous, titled, and notorious (and even the Church does not escape). Rome became the leading European centre for American location films, so a substantial movie colony sprang up that included both former stars at the end of their careers, such as Stan Laurel and Oliver Hardy, and established names such as Kirk Douglas, Deborah Kerr, and Ava Gardner.

Thanks to the stars, Rome became "an outpost of international café society, a gathering point of exiled foreign royalty, speculators, playboys, socialites, and artists."[37] Fellini made use of these international celebrities and stars, among whom can be counted Anthony Quinn as Zampanò in *La strada*, a role that enhanced Quinn's career, Anouk Aimee and Anita Ekberg in *La dolce vita*, and Donald Sutherland in *Casanova*, exemplary of his creative and critical treatment of stars. Ekberg became immortalized as the quintessence of a feminine Hollywood star whose unconventional behavior, exoticism, mammary abundance, and blondeness captured the excessive images of Marilyn Monroe and Jayne Mansfield. Ekberg's image, identified with the Roman landscape, is neither an endorsement of the fast, sexualized, and commodified life of the 1960s nor, by the same token, a moral diatribe against decadence. This Amazonian female image, like an exotic full-breasted fertility figure, reaches deep into cultural fantasies about femininity. And Mastroianni's persona was received as corroboration of the Italian male as "Latin Lover" rather than as an exploration of fantasies of masculinity through media.[38]

Consonant with Fellini's style generally, the characters, events, and uses of place convey a distant, bemused, anti-sentimental treatment that offers its images for a different form of meditation on history and media, one that differs from Juvenalian satire. The film is an exploration of the "sweet life": social success, fashion, money, mobility, and media. The initial helicopter views of the

Christ statue are a source of curiosity and bemusement rather than overt judgment about a world in which Christ's image can be transported aerially and filmed. The film is reminiscent of Bolognini's (with the aid of Pasolini's writing) use of Mastroianni in comic and satiric fashion in *Il bell'Antonio* (1960), a film in which male sexuality exposes fissures in the cultural and social façade of the heterosexual (and southern Italian) investment in marriage, reproduction, and family.

It is tempting to regard Mastroianni as Fellini's puppet; however, as Fellini observed in an interview: "Marcello Mastroianni is many things to many people. For me, he is not my alter ego. He is Marcello, an actor who conforms perfectly to what I want from him like a contortionist who can do anything."[39] This comment validates the view that Fellini's conception of filmmaking entails the plastic uses of actors, and further that this form of star making is closely allied to the director's capacity for working with and even producing cultural icons. As Peter Bondanella has written: "Fellini treated his actors as faces and potential images rather than performers, creating his own form of typage. His casting was always based on the actor's image on the screen rather than any special dramatic talent."[40] This comment goes some way to explaining Fellini's relationship to his actors. Foremost in Fellini's work, that which has merited the appellation of "Fellini-esque," is that the director identified his stars with a cinematic milieu resistant to conventional realism or melodrama.

Fellini's films blatantly announce their creator's signature: his use of memories from his past, persistent images that are polysemic involving dancing bodies, oversized female figures, inviting and threatening prostitutes. The grotesque and carnivalesque are made quotidian and the quotidian made grotesque, as in *La strada*, *8½* (1963), *Roma* (1972), *Amarcord* (1973), and *Prova d'orchestra* (Orchestra Rehearsal, 1978). Central to his films, including *Ginger e Fred* (1986) and *Intervista* (1987), is a philosophic, theoretical, and personal exploration that transforms life into a dynamic, expanding spectacle, identifying the cinema as the medium that has the power to mystify, performing its delusive magic while also communicating its sleight of hand for those who are watching and listening.

Amarcord, for example, is a film that conveys its mistrust of history even while offering its own version of the past as fragments of memory to the spectator. The film introduces its investments in the cinematic past and the role of stars through Gradisca (Magali Noël), the town's Greta Garbo, and the movie house owner, the town's Ronald Colman. The images of the Grand Hotel that were part of the cinematic landscape of the 1930s bring Hollywood and Italy into closer contact and link movie theater and cinema-going to the world of fascism. The film also portrays another dimension of stardom through the visit of Il Duce, parodying the numerous newsreels that filmed Mussolini's triumphal visits to various Italian towns and the orgiastic responses of its citizens. Gradisca's meeting with her "prince" at the Grand Hotel invokes the Orientalist aspects of popular cinema in the 1930s and its connections to masculine and feminine star lore. However, this film, in contrast to *La dolce vita*, 8½, and, to a lesser extent, *La città delle donne* (The City of Women, 1980), does not use major stars. In fact, Fellini's engagement with stardom is a matter of suitability of an actor or star for a particular role via their acting and physical characteristics, so that his work is a balance between familiar stars and his own repertoire of actors as well as new ones that suit the artistic occasion.

Fellini's fascination with the cinema as entertainment is reiterated in his *Intervista* (1987), a biographical, quasi-documentary film that the director made at Cinecittà. The film explores changes that have transpired in cinema (particularly through the episode with the aging and disheveled Ekberg and Mastroianni). Rather than an exercise in nostalgia, the film acknowledges changes in filmmaking toward the end of the millennium, injecting the director's profound acknowledgment of passing time, of mortality, and of the vital role of cinematic memory as a measure of that change. Similarly in *Ginger e Fred*, Fellini continues his engagement as in *Amarcord* and *Intervista* with cinematic (and televisual) history and its various expressions and reception in the popular culture of Italy, again through the lens of stardom, particularly of the 1940s, implicating Hollywood and Italy. The film is also "autobiographical," drawing on Fellini's own prior films and on the spectacle of earlier Astaire and Rogers musicals re-animated by Masina and Mastroianni, and invoking the director's professional and personal relationship to his wife, Masina.[41]

The film introduces Amelia Bonetti (Masina) and Pippo Botticella (Mastroianni) as aging vaudeville performers who had made a career in the forties through imitating the style of Ginger Rogers and Fred Astaire. They are invited to appear on television to perform for contemporary audiences in a show entitled *Ed Eco a Voi* (We Are Proud to Present). The filming of the "show" satirizes contemporary TV, its mélange of other forms—quiz shows, standup comedy, news, and exploitation of the past. Television is exposed as a machine to fill the seemingly endless spots of time, a postmodern machine that is always on and always in the service of "information," and that has no regard for context or time for reflection. Through Mastroianni and Masina and their objects of emulation, Ginger Rogers and Fred Astaire, the film marks the passing of stardom, of Astaire and Rogers, Masina and Mastroianni, and perhaps of Fellini as well. Masina and Mastroianni's aging images are tropes not merely for their now unglamorous and awkward images in the present but for the passing of cinematic stardom in the age of TV and electronic media. If the couple were never successful, famous, and talented performers of the ilk of Rogers and Astaire, they were, however, emblematic of the power of images of Hollywood genres

5.3. "Memories are made of this": Giulietta Masina and Marcello Mastroianni in *Ginger e Fred. Photofest.*

and stars and also of the assimilative, vital character of Italian cinematic culture. Fellini's most familiar stars as aging, frail, and situated in a shabby and unattractive milieu contrast to the glamorous world that the names of Astaire and Rogers conjure up in the imagination of past cinema. Fred appears to resemble the aging Fellini,[42] and once again Fellini strikes the familiar personal chord by using himself to investigate the fate of the auteur/star image.

Michelangelo Antonioni: A Cinematic Adventurer

No director has been so acutely sensitive to cinematic questions of the body, space, and time as Michelangelo Antonioni, or to images of the human and the cinematic body conveyed through the use of Italian stars such as Monica Vitti, Marcello Mastroianni, and Massimo Girotti, French stars such as Jeanne Moreau and Alain Delon, British stars such as Vanessa Redgrave and David Hemmings, and American stars such as Jack Nicholson. Antonioni, like Rossellini, was identified with making films outside of Italy, in Britain, France, and in the United States. Antonioni's position as "an icon of cinema's aspiration to art status" has derived from his "composition of forms and colours," his resis-

tance to commercial narrative styles, and his undermining of clichés concerning social class, media, landscape, and individual behavior.[43] For example, the
negative, if not virulent, reception of *Zabriskie Point* (1970), especially within
the American context during the turbulent 1960s, was indicative of misrecognition on the part of reviewers of this form of filmmaking, since this film was
consonant with the style and philosophic preoccupations of his earlier films.
The negative response to this film and to recent ones belongs to a mythology
of stardom that positions the star within a narrative of initial anonymity, success, waning power, and transfiguration or obscurity. Antonioni's career in cinema, however, reveals a cineaste who was adventurous in his approach to filmmaking narration.

Initially part of the *Cinema* group in the early 1940s along with Giuseppe
De Santis, Carlo Lizzani, Francesco Pasinetti, Luchino Visconti, and Mario
Alicata, Antonioni shared in the critical investigation and articulation of new
directions for the cinema that were to be identified with the broad lines of neorealism. Working with these critics and filmmakers, his early nonfiction (*Il
gente del Po* [People of the Po, 1943–1947]) and fiction films, such as *Caccia
tragica* (Tragic Pursuit, 1948, with De Santis), were explorations of a landscape
and culture different stylistically from the spectacles identified with the cinema
of the 1930s. In the vein of conceptual, not sociological, neorealism, his films
focused on quotidian life, the contradictory nature of cinematic images in unfamiliar landscapes, and ambiguous and complex personal relationships. Antonioni's adventures in cinematic form were extended beyond docudrama and
melodrama to modernist experimentation with visual and sound images, forms
of narration, and uses of actors.

Amore in città (Love in the City, 1952) and *Il grido* (The Cry, 1957) reveal
the director working broadly within the parameters of neorealist experimentation and genre, in these films of melodrama. Antonioni had also undertaken a
cinematic exploration of stardom in *La signora senza camelie* (1953), a film that
along with Blasetti's *La fortuna d'essere donna* (The Fortune of Being a Woman,
1956) makes visible a self-reflexive preoccupation with cinema culture, both
high and low, and with the role of acting and stardom within that culture.[44]
However, it became clear that Antonioni's theories of cinema as evidenced by
his practice were moving in more idiosyncratic directions. *L'avventura* (1960)
demonstrated how the physical, philosophic, and cinematic landscape was
being steadily transformed in the cinema of the late 1950s and 1960s, becoming
attuned to the economic and political implications of popular culture and also
to the more radical explorations of cinematic forms.

When *L'avventura* (1960) appeared, Antonioni was criticized by some of his
earlier colleagues such as De Santis for focusing on middle-class protagonists
and "dealing with a limited dimension of Italian reality."[45] But it was also evi-

dent that the director was now assuming different directions in his work as well as gaining international acclaim. Among the distinctive features of his films, most evident in *Il deserto rosso* (1964), is a different treatment of his actors: camera focus, color, and sound work to de-familiarize character.[46] The visual and aural images invite contemplation of an exterior world that displaces the ennui, the tedium, and the over-personalization of behavioral interpretation. In this respect, Antonioni has played a critical role in altering the agency of the star and affective identification with her.

The director's uses of Monica Vitti enabled her to become an icon of international stardom in the 1960s, though she was also known later for her comedic abilities, particularly in her parodies of commercial genres. In Antonioni's film, her lithe physical appearance was aided by her wearing extremely fashionable, elegant, but not ostentatious outfits of the time, particularly sheaths, flats, bouffant hairdos, and arty costumes slightly off the mainstream. She exemplifies Deleuze's description of the actor in the regime of the time-image—as a sleepwalker, moving apparently aimlessly through the world, a spectator more than a verbal commentator or "actant" (active agent) in a landscape that is often barren of populace—a scrubby, rocky landscape, an island, a sandy beach, or an open road. Her movements appear either random, or static as in a still life. Her facial expressions are bland rather than animated but have the effect of increasing ambiguity and inciting curiosity about her affect or thoughts.[47] But the cumulative effect is to shift attention onto the events, thus rendering her less of an erotic object of desire while corroborating the often-made equation between the camera and the feminine body as object of investigation. In the case of *L'avventura* as well as *La notte* (1961) and *Il deserto rosso*, Antonioni's feminine figures are guides to help the spectator to meditate on an unfamiliar landscape. While Vitti's image (like that of Jeanne Moreau in *La notte*) evokes images of elegant middle-class femininity trapped in an arid world of social conventions, bored, frustrated, in quest of sensation, her role and appearance in these films invite scrutiny for other ends. She is conduit to the films' meditation on the sights and sounds of modernity. Vitti is instrumental in realizing this journey not as a familiar star image but as Antonioni's interrogation of visuality.

Antonioni's use and creation of female stars shift emphasis and interest from the body of the woman to the body of cinema, as embodying the intellectual and investigative concerns of the filmmaker. What appears critical in *L'avventura* is the missing body of a woman, Anna (Lea Massari), that Claudia (Vitti) undertakes to locate. Claudia is not the only clue to the film's preoccupation with the connections between the female, the missing body, painting, cinema, and stardom. The presence of Gloria Perkins (Dorothy De Poliolo) further assists in the process of allegorizing cinema.[48] A common denominator in the films of Fellini, Antonioni, and Pasolini (see below) resides in their metacinematic explorations, not merely as reflexive technique, but as a critical inquiry into the virtual properties of cinema and by indirection into the character of stardom.

In the case of *Il deserto rosso*, the spectator is provided with an elaborate treatment of vision and sound. The film makes reference not merely to color but to the ways in which Technicolor comes to express the texture of cinema. Color and its absence convey a world constantly in motion, making evident the passage of time, the minutes, seasons, months, years, etc. In *Il deserto rosso* this movement is evident also in the images of smoke, fog, and gaseous emanations that call attention to the often largely unseen world. In *Il deserto rosso*, color is not a simple issue of realism via tinting; it challenges "information" and "facts" about how cinematic perception can supplant outworn values and beliefs. Character becomes flattened, linked as Giuliana is to blue walls, yellow noxious smoke, and colorless fog. The world is reduced to its molecular dimensions (an effect achieved by Fellini in *Amarcord* through puff balls, rain, snowflakes, and dust motes) in a diversion from the conventional ways of regarding subjectivity (and stardom).

As Pasolini commented in his *Heretical Empiricism*,

> In *Red Desert* Antonioni no longer superimposes his own formalistic vision of the world on a generally committed content (the problem of neurosis caused by alienation). . . . Instead he looks at the world by immersing himself in his neurotic protagonist, reanimating the facts through her eyes. . . . [H]e has been able to represent the world seen through his eyes, because he has substituted for the world-view of a neurotic his own delirious view of aesthetics. . . . [I]n Antonioni we find the wholesale substitution of a filmmaker's feverish formalism for the view of a neurotic woman.[49]

Pasolini's critical observations are indicative too of his contentious relationship to other directors. The image of the star/personality when emptied becomes a receptacle for the filmmaker (and for the spectator) to enter a different world. In this sense, the director uses and alters the star's image.

Antonioni's uses of Italian and international stars enhance this auto-critique of contemporary culture and of the potential of cinema to offer a visual and aural language to account for cinematic culture of the 1960s. However, what starts out as a critical, even oppositional, position often ends up as fashion. Antonioni's treatment of Vitti is parodied in Scola's *C'eravamo tanti amati*. The character of Elide is transformed from a garrulous and awkward figure to a fashionable icon who mimes Vitti's persona in enigmatic behavior, resistance to verbal speech, and futile quest for meaningful love. In the case of the Scola film, the cinema is not only imitable but also expressive of a particular moment in the history of cinema and of the culture it reveals and disseminates. However, the director does not have control over the film once it moves into the national and international world where, subject to varying readings, to imitation, to the burdens of its success, it becomes appropriated in ways that it has interrogated and criticized. It connects to the world of fashion, beauty culture, tourism, and design. It makes stars of the directors as well as of their actors and in the case of Antonioni's films not merely national but also international stars. These star directors are thus not removed from the world of popular culture and commerce but are, in more complicated fashion, its avatars and its victims.

Pier Paolo Pasolini: A Star among Stars

Pier Paolo Pasolini is another instance of a star/director who did not disdain working with stars, though transforming them for his own ends, and enhancing their careers by their novel use his films. He was a star in his own right, gaining notoriety for his lifestyle, his homosexuality, his physical attractiveness, his literary and cinematic experimentation, his rocky relations with the Italian Communist Party, his violent death, the publicity that surrounded it, the criminal trials that followed, and the films that have been made about him. He is also known for acting in his own films, including *Edipo re* (1967), *Il Decameron* (1971), and *Racconti di Canterbury* (Canterbury Tales, 1972), and in Carlo Lizzani's *Requiescant* (Kill and Pray, 1967). Not only his life but his films too were considered notorious, for their focus on sexuality, their contradictory treatment of religion, their focus on the "Third World," and their uses of spectacle, myths, and prominent stars for Pasolini's own critical ends. Among the Italian and international stars who appear in his films are Silvana Mangano, Massimo Girotti, Terence Stamp, the opera singer Maria Callas, Totò, and Anna Magnani.

In his treatment of female stars—Mangano, Magnani, and Callas (a diva in opera and in film)—Pasolini exploited their star images but not in the direction of enhancing and reinforcing them. His treatment of their bodies, their uses of gestural and verbal language, their identification with conventional signifying practices as fashion icons, their expressive qualities as divas and as maternal forces, capitalized on the legendary cultural power of these figures who were not "real" people but poetic and mythic. They were part of his critical effort to redefine what Viano has described as "a certain realism," one that shifts attention away from the naturalized, hence so-called realism of the commercial cinema.[50] By using myths of Oedipus, Medea, and Mamma Roma as well as those identified with stars who reincarnate these myths, Pasolini could underscore the heretical potential of cinema initiated in the post–World War II era to destabilize ways of seeing and thinking about cinema and its stars.

In his choice of Anna Magnani to play the title role in *Mamma Roma* (1962), Pier Paolo Pasolini defused organic connections between the female

5.4. Glamorous publicity shot of Pier Paolo Pasolini. *Photofest*.

body and the nation, exploiting her star image in the interests of de-territorializing and dislocating it from its prior associations. Over the years, Magnani became for many an icon of Italian-ness. In *Roma, città aperta*, in the role that consolidated this image, she is identified with the working class, with Rome, and with a maternal role, one that she was to repeat in numerous films both in Italy and the U.S. By casting her as "Mamma Roma," Pasolini did not appropriate her as an "uncomplicated earthy, joyous, and sensuous creature" but as a prostitute: "Far from representing the glory of Italy, the word 'Roma' is at first uplifted by the association with 'mother'—indeed one of the sacred signifiers in Italian culture—and then degraded as the nickname of the prostitute."[51] If, in Giuliana Bruno's terms, *Mamma Roma* conveys how "the borders of the home and the world become disorientingly confused,"[52] similarly, the boundaries of stardom are destabilized. In Pasolini's film, stardom via Magnani's image becomes a composite of a number of polysemic positions, including motherhood, prostitution, femininity, national identity, and the fascist past, that unsettle any stable contours of stardom. Pasolini's treatment of Magnani's role evokes memories of Pina if rather to create "a harsh commentary on the idealism of *Rome, Open City* which had portrayed the lower classes as basically immune from greed."[53] Magnani's maternal concerns in *Mamma Roma* are tainted, dramatized in her treatment of her son, Ettore, her attempts to buy his affection, her scheming to find him respectable work, her berating him about his thieving and his relationship with a young woman of easy morals: her hankering after bourgeois values is exposed as calculating, angry, materialistic, and tragic.

As Pina, Magnani was identified with the Roman streets in the vandalizing of the bakery and its aftermath, in her walk with Don Pietro, and in her death also on the street. *Mamma Roma* also highlights the streets of Rome, where Magnani repeatedly seeks to follow Ettore, who eludes her, where she works as an outdoor fruit vendor, and where, as a prostitute in the two striking night scenes, she is joined on the streets by would-be clients and homosexuals. The streets, like Magnani's persona, are radically estranged, associated with unfamiliar characters and places: "*Mamma Roma* denies viewers any familiar sight of Rome."[54] The final moments of the film, after Ettore's death, as she gazes in agony out of her window at the dome in the distance (also reminiscent of the last shots of *Roma, città aperta*), are also indicative of an "open city," but one which leaves the spectator with a different set of questions about this "openness." Maternal and national values appear uncertain, and the persona of Magnani who had embodied these values is also subject to indeterminacy.

The landscapes, like the actors in his films, are indicative of Pasolini's overleaping national borders. Geography is non-localizable. His films are often set outside of Italy, in North Africa or Greece, or are made to conjure up mythic places even though they are set in Italy (as in *Il vangelo*). In *Medea*, Maria Callas, a prima donna of grand opera and an international diva, is used in contradictory fashion. She does not sing, and she barely speaks. If the film is indeed operatic, its musical dimensions come from its soundtrack and from the treatment of the African landscape, the physical movement of the characters, the minimizing of verbal language, and the silence of a woman who is identified with expressive sounds. In Pasolini's treatment of *Medea*, as in his *Edipo re* (Oedipus the King, 1967), the camera and editing serve as free indirect discourse to shift the conventional as well as scholarly interpretations of the Greek myths and of contemporary myths of cinema and the body to another register. He employs the polysemic dimensions of myth to use the myth against itself, or perhaps to use it as a weapon against both forms of historicizing that are too narrowly tied to facts and forms of myth that are unmindful of history and indifferent to time and change.

Pasolini's use of Silvana Mangano in *Edipo re* and in *Teorema* (Theorem, 1968) remotely evokes, but in a radically different fashion, her image in *Riso amaro* as a sexually transgressive and erotic figure of desire. *Teorema* transforms the star from the reflexive image of a popular female pin-up of the 1950s to a critical, even philosophic, image of threatening maternity with its disruptive sexuality often concealed and pacified in cultural mythology. In *Teorema*, the mysterious visitor played by Terence Stamp, an icon of Swinging London, might be construed as a surrogate for the director, who has entered uninvited into a bourgeois domestic scenario that is usually accorded a more conventional treatment. Yet the guest is never named, his identity remains ambiguous, and he disappears as mysteriously as he arrives. He transforms the tidy and predictable lives of this upper-class family, creating a scandalous scenario, wreaking havoc with social conventions, decorum, and religious belief until what remains is an assault on inherited forms of seeing and hearing and particularly on classical forms of realism that rely on scenarios of romance, conflict, resolution, and affirmation. The film employs another familiar star, Massimo Girotti, no longer a romantic hero but a paternal figure identified with ambiguous sexuality. The barren volcanic landscape and his ambiguous character function finally to communicate a degree zero of meaning in relation to the politics of class, national, and sexual identity.

Pasolini tampered with the star persona of Totò, whose appearance in films spanned the 1930s through the 1960s and the heyday of the movement-image to the uncertainties of the time-image (see chapter 4). Over his long and prominent career he was able to cross over from the popular theater to commercial cinema as well as to art cinema, and to European from Italian cinema. In the 1950s and 1960s, international audiences became acquainted with him through *L'oro di Napoli* and *Uccellacci e Uccellini* (1966). Associated with the *commedia dell'arte* and with Neapolitan comedy, he was a consummate mime. Often described as a clown, his comic persona relied heavily on the use of his body and on his facial expression in the tradition of the great comedic film stars, Chaplin, Keaton, and Fernandel, to whom he has been compared. Gaunt, angular, with large sad eyes and a crooked nose, he is, like other comic stars, associated with physicality, with characteristics and gestures that link stardom to earlier cinematic images that I have identified with the movement-image. While Totò's face is bony, his expressions are not deadpan but express, like a range of comic masks, a variety of affects. Through his body movement, he assumes different poses—subservient, ingratiating, expansive, and even aggressive—in protean fashion, and these movements call attention to the theater and to the cinematic apparatus. As an incarnation of the oppressed little man, heir of the *commedia all'italiana*, he manages to triumph over adversity. His movements are often spastic like those of a marionette. Thus, it is no coincidence that he has played Pinocchio (a role more recently undertaken by Roberto Benigni [2002]).

Totò's stardom relies on a form of pantomime that is more then posturing but a form of gesturing that allows the viewer to perceive the comedian's careful discrimination. Of Totò's stardom, Sorlin writes, "Caught between two worlds, past and future, unable to master events, he gave his spectators a sense of the suspension of time."[55] His stardom was a throwback to earlier cinema, particularly to the silent cinema, in the style and types of situations. His body, his face, and his gestures were, in the strong sense of the movement-image, geared to exposing the inequities and hypocrisies of social life, contaminating the sacred and the profane, the pure and the impure through the masks he assumes. Totò was, in De Sica's words, "a great clown in the most exalted sense of the term that today no longer exists."[56]

While in most of his films, Totò's stardom remained constant, it changed course (as did Magnani's) under Pasolini's direction. Once again, Pasolini was able to characterize significant transformations that had transpired in the cinema through stardom. In *Uccellacci e Uccellini* (1966), he refashioned Totò's stardom to unsettle cultural values. If stardom embodied a benevolent image of humankind in films for other directors, in Pasolini's film, Totò's face and body movement offer a "permutation of the trivial and the noble."[57] Pasolini's ambition was to "decodify him," and the code that Pasolini wanted to break was of the figure of "the basest Italian bourgeois carried to the extreme of vulgarity, expressiveness, inertia and cultural indifference."[58] In *Uccellacci e Uccellini* Pasolini exploited Totò's stardom against itself, using the star's consummate and familiar use of faciality and gesture to enact a postmodern rendition of St. Francis of Assisi, recalling Rossellini's film *Francesco, giullare di Dio* (St. Francis, God's Jester, 1950). Consistently, the film undermines received cinematic forms and the expectation of resolution through "a happy outcome" and "a gaze fulfilled."[59] In other words, through Totò, stardom was transformed so as to expose through gestures how the all-too-human body creates the "powers of the false," and, therefore, puts truth in crisis. Pasolini's putting stardom in crisis becomes another critical instrument in the director's arsenal of tools to reveal further the virtuality of the image and to explore its potential for unsettling normalized and automatic responses. Pasolini's star image and his uses of stars consolidated the various and contradictory dimensions of his personal life, politics, and career, and his appropriation of stars was an extension of his intellectual and political concerns, functioning paradoxically to reinforce stardom, his own and his actors'.

Female Directors: Lina Wertmüller in Another Firmament

While there have been instances in the past of women stars in Italian films (e.g., Elvira Notari and to some extent Francesca Bertini) who have assumed an active role in production in relation to their characters and possibly to directorial decisions, examples of female directors who wield the same authority as male directors and who have achieved the same status and fame are more rare (though this situation is meliorating, albeit modestly). Two major exceptions in the late twentieth century are Liliana Cavani and Lina Wertmüller, with the latter achieving the greater publicity, notoriety, and recognition. More recently, one can add the names of Cristina, Francesca, and Paola Comencini, Roberta Torre, and Asia Argento; however, these more recent directors function in a different economic and cultural milieu that makes national and international stardom more tenuous and more evanescent.

By contrast, Cavani's best-known film, *Il portiere di notte* (1974), received international acclaim and stands as one of the seminal and contentious films on Nazism. Starring British actors Charlotte Rampling and Dirk Bogarde, *Il portiere di notte* in memorable and prototypic roles visualizes and enacts the complex erotic relationship between Nazi "master" and Jewish female slave. While Cavani's other films are deeply philosophical, they are not as widely disseminated and discussed as Wertmüller's. Wertmüller became identified with feminism through such films as *Mimì metallurgico ferito nel' onore* (The Seduction of Mimi, 1972), *Film d'amore e d'anarchia* (Love and Anarchy, 1973), and *Travolti da un insolito destino nell' azzurro mare d'agosto* (Swept Away, 1974). But the film that catapulted her into the echelon of international auteurs was *Pasqualino Sette Bellezze* (Seven Beauties, 1975), which earned her numerous awards. Photos of her dressed in white with her large-framed glasses appeared everywhere and interviews allowed scope for her to talk about her eccentric upbringing and her contacts with such prominent cinema personalities/stars as Federico Fellini (with whom she had worked, and whose work exerted an influence on her own films). Her earlier acclaimed works, which challenge prevailing conceptions of femininity, sexuality, and empowerment, belong to an era of attention to women artists due to the rise of feminism in the 1970s, a time that witnessed the First International Women's Festival in New York City in 1977. In Italy by the 1980s, the women's movement had grown to include not only historical research on women but also an exploration of theoretical and practical concerns relating to cinematic representation, to cine-feminism.

Wertmüller's rise to stardom followed the trajectory of a spectacular rise to fame and then a descent into an indifferent if not negative critical response internationally. Along with her outspoken and flamboyant personality (notably expressed in the large white frames of her eyeglasses), her films challenged conventional sexual politics in their satiric treatment of gendered and class taboos. *Film d'amore e d'anarchia*, which stars Mariangela Melato and Giancarlo Giannini, alters the images of its stars by presenting them in highly stylized terms, he as the freckle-faced and vulnerable anarchist under the sway of romance and politics, and she as the garrulous, heavily madeup, overdressed (according to the style of the era), and politically committed prostitute. In the spirit of *commedia all'italiana* with its distinctive style, the two stars assume roles that exceed realism and in their artifice contribute to making their characters allegorical types rather than individuals. Like many other auteurs, Wertmüller employed her own team of actors who became distinctive in her films but who also carved out careers apart from her. Hardly filmed in glamorous terms, the most well-known of her stars, Melato and Giannini, became popular with art house audiences internationally. They were reminiscent of Fellini's cartoon-like and surreal character portraits, highly theatrical emanations of the auteur's sensibility and political/historical predilections.

Sette Bellezze, starring Giancarlo Giannini, essays a historical portrayal of fascism in which satiric comedy and tragedy again unite, and in which the role of the star is even more grotesque and harshly judgmental than in *Film d'amore e d'anarchia*. Undertaking, as did Benigni in *La vita è bella* (Life Is Beautiful, 1997), a treatment of Nazism including life in the concentration camps, Wertmüller initially casts Giannini as a narcissistic and slick tyrant over his family, a killer, and then reduces him in appearance and behavior to a squirming, opportunistic, and obsequious survivor, an incarnation of the cost of surviving without an awareness of the consequences of his behavior and moral choices. Giannini's image finally becomes emblematic of the loss of an ability to act and is reduced to reacting passively to events.

While some critics regard the film as a "masterpiece,"[60] there are others who are more critical of it (and of other Wertmüller films). Wertmüller's persona produces strong positive and negative reactions. For example, in Nanni Moretti's *Io sono un autarchico* (I Am a Self-Sufficient Man, 1976), he characterized her as "the most oppressive of generic 'mothers,'"[61] another indication of the conflicting responses to her persona, her form of Italian comedy, and her treatment of politics.

However, her waning international popularity and the adverse criticism of her films has not halted her productivity and she continues to make films that focus on contemporary political subjects:[62] lesbianism in *Sotto . . . Sotto* (1984); class, gendered, and sexual warfare in *In una notte d'estate con profilo greco, occhi a mandorla e odore di basilico* (Summer Night, with Greek Profile, Almond Eyes and Scent of Basil, 1986); AIDS, starring Rutger Hauer and Nastassia Kinski, in *Una notte di chiaro di luna* (On a Moonlit Night, 1989); the southern question in *Io speriamo che me la cavo* (Ciao, Professore! 1992). Wertmüller, like Cristina Comencini in such films as *Il più bel giorno della mia vita* (The Best Day of My Life, 2002) and *La bestia nel cuore* (The Beast in the Heart, 2005), dramatizes familial and generational conflicts, exploring femininity and masculinity, homosexuality, and heterosexuality. However, Comencini's style is psychosocial, involving memory and trauma, while Wertmüller's continues to be theatrical and comedic, often satirical, and reliant on older stars.

Roberto Benigni: The "Clown Prince"

An instance of a star initially created by television, Roberto Benigni's star persona relies on the heterogeneity of the televisual format with its sensitivity to current events, its dependence on personality, and its never-ending flow in time. Benigni has been a popular figure in television and later in cinema and has been compared to Italian and Hollywood stars such as Totò, Buster Keaton, Charlie Chaplin, Woody Allen, and Jim Carrey. Prior to his work in cinema, Benigni was associated with theater, cabaret, and television, and specifically with an invented character, Cioni, that had gained currency with theater, film, and television audiences. In a prodigious career in all these media, he has produced, directed, written, and acted in such popular films such as *Johnny Stecchino* (1991) and *Il mostro*. *Pinocchio* (2002) was less well received than his other films. He has also gained star status through his acting roles, which include *Chiedo asilo* (Seeking Asylum, 1979), *Down by Law* (1986), *Son of the Pink Panther* (1983), and *Night on Earth* (1991). He is also familiar to audiences as the husband of Nicoletta Braschi, and the two have appeared together in many Benigni-directed films; however, she has also worked independently from him, having appeared in Francesca Comencini's *Mi piace lavorare—Mobbing 2004* (I Like to Work). His films have garnered larger international attention than Maurizio Nichetti's *Ladri di saponette* or Nanni Moretti's *Caro diario*, though both men are, like Benigni, directors, writers of, and actors in their films and align themselves with oppositional politics.

In appearance, Benigni is small and light with "disconnected movements like a puppet."[63] He is an uncontrollable force in his display of bodily movement, his childlike exuberance, and even more in the torrent of his verbal language. In this respect, he has been compared to Jerry Lewis, also a comic actor, director, and writer. Benigni is the reincarnation of the image of the little man battling forces far greater than he. The characters he chooses to play are naïve, altruistic, romantic, but clever. His appearance has been described as "unprepossessing," with his "unkempt black hair that juts out in different directions" and his big teeth that "form a donkey grin."[64] Often the victim of accident, mistiming, or misrecognition on the part of others, he overcomes his adversaries through clowning, through gestures that disorient his opponents, and through a seemingly endless flow of words that create confusion.

In *Life Is Beautiful* the comedy relies heavily on Benigni's ability to enact a "slippage between the roles of adult and child,"[65] a fantasy world that is obviously incommensurate with a grim reality. Benigni's childlike persona wages a struggle to survive in a world that threatens the individual and collective body with annihilation. A mixture of history, personal memory, fable, and fantasy, the film situates its reflexivity in a conception of storytelling as a game of will to overcome deadly forces. Here gesture is liberated from verbal language. In mimicking the Nazi when he "translates" the incomprehensible speech of the torturer, Benigni dramatizes how the gesture is "essentially always a gesture of not being able to figure something out in language: it is always a gag in the proper meaning of the term, indicating first of all something that could be put into your mouth to hinder speech, as well as in the sense of the actor's improvisation meant to compensate a loss of memory or an inability to speak."[66] Through gesture, Benigni destroys the speaker's identity and, along with it, "the identity of the actor."[67] His "clown prince" offers the audience consolation in the face of an insuperable reality. As in his other films, Benigni maintains a role for the comic star as highlighting rather than mitigating the horror of the events. Perhaps this "clown prince" will maintain his position as national media "royalty," but certainly his international image has begun to fade, and time will tell if the big screen can sustain his particular form of stardom.

A Belated Star: Dario Argento

Dario Argento is a controversial director who has been regarded with disdain as well as adulation. His films are identified with the international production of horror, an interesting illustration of the crossover between popular and auteurist cinema by the likes of David Cronenberg. Despite negative, even hostile, critical reviews describing him as a madman, a pervert, and a criminal, he has pursued his conception of cinema supported by such international filmmakers as John Carpenter and George Romero (with whom he has worked). As noted in chapter

4, the horror film was not a major genre in Italian cinema of the pre–World War II era. Nor did it seem to be in the immediate years succeeding the end of the war. However, its appearance in the 1950s and its growing popularity became part of the post-Holocaust and post-atomic culture of the 1950s in Asia, Hollywood, the UK, and areas in Europe.[68] Horror was linked to the greater focus in the 1960s on Freudian and Lacanian psychology as well as on popular journalistic expressions of trauma and stress and more overt concerns with sexuality and gender. The genre, while generally aligned in the past with expressionism and surrealism as well as Hollywood Gothic and monster genres, branched out into fantasy, science fiction, and hair-raising dramas of the unreliability, insidiousness, and even malevolence of social institutions and professional authorities—lawyers, writers, judges, teachers, physicians, and psychologists.

Argento's career in cinema has undergone various permutations. As the son of prominent producer Salvatore Argento and brother of Claudio Argento, he was familiar with Italian and international filmmaking. In addition to directing films, he has worked as writer on his own films but also for other directors of westerns and horror (e.g., Sergio Leone and actor/director/writer Michele Soavi). Initially regarded as just another popular genre filmmaker for his films in the 1960s and 1970s, Dario Argento's reputation has grown steadily, aided by French critical writings. In the 1990s his cult status was augmented through a sustained critical evaluation of his work. He has also been involved in a number of documentaries on horror cinema, on his own and on the films of others, such as those by Mario Bava. In addition, Argento has appeared in his films mainly as a voice or through images of his hands. He has also been the subject of numerous interviews.

In talking about his development as a filmmaker, Argento pays homage to the Nouvelle Vague, describing it as "a new form of expression, a new way of looking at and of moving the camera,"[69] acknowledging that this type of cinema changed his views on his own work. With the exception of *Le cinque giornate* (Five Days in Milan, 1973), his films have been urban crime detection films (the *giallo*) and also psychological thrillers that he describes as involving "the metaphysics of horror."[70] Argento is particularly interested in seeing how traditional stories undergo transmutation, becoming tales of horror that transform the everyday world through different perceptual relations to image making, particularly of the body. In *Suspiria* (1977), Argento began to experiment with heavy metal music and with other aural and visual effects that could deliver "a punch in the stomach."[71] His fascination with insects (à la Luis Bunuel) is most consummately explored visually in *Phenomena* (Creepers, 1985).

In many ways, his vision of cinema is reminiscent of Antonioni: *Il deserto rosso* is invoked in Argento's *Profondo rosso* (Deep Red, 1975). The works share in their experimentation with color, sound, and a visionary landscape, the exploration of mental states, and their challenge to visual and verbal clichés. Most significantly, both directors share in a concern to probe the the fascinating and threatening properties of optical and sound images. *Profondo rosso* is self-reflexive and metacinematic. In its allusions to other filmmakers (Hitchcock and Michael Powell), in its use of David Hemmings, a star associated with British cinema of the "Swinging London" era, and in its naming the key character Mark as an homage to Powell's *Peeping Tom* (1960), though making him a musician and not a filmmaker, *Profondo rosso* resembles many of Argento's films, which not only acknowledge precursors to the horror cinema but are also replete with allusions to the other arts, opera, dance, popular and electronic music, painting and architecture, and even entomology. His use of landscape has been attributed to his fascination with Antonioni's filming of Roman landscapes.[72] Further, Argento's films indeed explore the mechanisms of vision by invoking paintings, mirrors, and windows to produce a disjunction between exterior and interior, nearness and proximity. Also in *Profondo rosso* with Clara Calamai, and *Suspiria* with Alida Valli and Joan Bennett, Argento adopts the practice of using international stars much as Antonioni did in his trilogy, but rendering them distorted and grotesque, emphasizing their aging and monstrous bodies. Most distinctively, this against-the-grain use of these stars unsettles any comfortable relation to their prevailing star images. The experience of horror in his films is obsessively tied to their engagement with the dangers, uncertainty, and violent character of vision.

In *Profondo rosso*, the issue of parapsychology is tied to the seen, the unseen, and inevitable failures of perception in relation to vision, a central motif in Antonioni as well and another indication of the metacinematic bent of Argento's cinema. Macha Méril, as the figure of the psychic, was familiar to members of the audience as Godard's actress and also wife at the time. Her role is restricted to the early moments of the film, where she becomes a double victim (of the mysterious killer and the legacy of the Holocaust). But her limited presence is nonetheless meaningful. It signals further connections between Argento's reflexive uses of stars and forms of filmmaking, in this case of the New Wave, that concern themselves with the nature and function of cinematic images and their role in the history of cinema. A further prod to memory relies on the use of star Clara Calamai, identified with the cinema of the fascist years and also with *Ossessione* (through photos and verbal allusions), now portrayed as an agent of brutality and destruction.

Argento's casting of Italian and international stars such as Calamai, Méril, and David Hemmings in *Profondo rosso*, Anthony Franciosa in *Tenebre* (1982), Alida Valli and Joan Bennett in *Suspiria* (1977), and Donald Pleasance in *Phenomena* (1985) provides further insights into how films play on social history and memory via the faces and personas of various star images, European and American, earlier and contemporary, successful or no longer prominent, popular icons or museum figures. The spectator is drawn to the former image of the

5.5. Horror of aging stars in Dario Argento's *Suspiria*. *Photofest*.

star, if memory permits, but any expectation of recognition, pleasure, and reassurance of familiarity is violently disrupted. Instead there is disorientation, and grotesque metamorphosis. The stars enhance the films' probing of visual and auditory perception and misperception, and of the cinematic image as one of aggression enacted on a fragile body. However, a significant dimension of Argento's use of familiar stars is that they rarely assume the starring role in the films: usually these are assigned to new actors and to young women, including Jessica Harper in *Suspiria*, Jennifer Connelly in *Phenomena*, Spanish actress Cristina Marsillach in *Opera* (1987), and daughter Asia in *Trauma* (1993), *La sintome di Stendahl* (The Stendahl Syndrome, 1996), and *Il fantasma dell opera* (The Phantom of the Opera, 1998). Through these films and through those she has acted in for other directors and has directed, Asia Argento has been regarded by some as an international star; however, she denies this status, identifying it with undesired socializing, scandal, and unwonted publicity.

In *Opera*, an opera singer, Betty (Marsillach), is understudy to older tempestuous diva Mara Czeckova in a performance of Verdi's *Macbeth*, and is called upon to perform after an attack on the diva. Her success makes her the target of a psychopathic killer. Betty is tormented by her own superstitions, nightmares from her childhood, and a killer whose pleasure is to force her to observe his acts of killing and mutilating his victims. The numerous close-ups of her with mouth gagged and eyes held open by pins that could blind her if she blinks are tropes that underscore the pleasure and the punishment attendant on viewing obscene acts of destruction.[73] She becomes both a spectator and nearly a victim in a film that plumbs, as do all of Argento's films, the sensory dimensions of sight and sound to reveal a dark, threatening world that implicates aggressor and victim, challenging conventional assumptions about what is portrayed in terms of normality and pathology.

Opera connects Argento not merely to Hitchcock but also to Luchino Visconti in his uses of grand opera, of spectacle, to strip away the veneer of beauty to expose its dark and sensual underside. Featuring familiar stars such as Ian Charleson, remembered for his roles as a religious figure in *Gandhi* (1982) and *Chariots of Fire* (1981), and Daria Nicolodi, a former partner of Argento who made five films with him, and less familiar ones such as Cristina Marsillach, Argento once again reveals that his primary focus is not on the personality of an established star but on an exploration of the effects of horror and violence on a younger, presumably naïve young woman who is a surrogate for the spectator. Betty's encounters with the murderer are the film's strategy for investigating the bonds between aggressor and victim, acts of violence and their effects on a viewer. Betty and Inspector Santini share a buried past: he as the perpetrator of brutal crimes, and she as the viewer of them (and both as surrogates for the external viewer). The restless camera, the uses of color, sound effects, and music, and the special effects create the beauty and sensuality of the unsettling obsessional and demonic image as articulated by Santini, who connects Betty's "frigidity" to her (and the spectator's) fascination with, connection to, and revulsion toward violence.

Opera is a film that exploits autobiographical, intertextual references to the other arts (theater, poetry, grand opera, painting, allusions to other filmmakers and to other Argento films) in the process of "an investigation and analysis of the image."[74] The miracle of his filmmaking resides in Argento's skill in drawing on the visual and auditory images of mass media while also incorporating canonical texts, though adapted to the philosophical, psychological, and aesthetic concerns that animate his films. Furthermore, *Opera*, in its reliance on grand opera and through the role of Betty as diva, provides further evidence of Argento's interests in investigating the feminine body and the myths that surround it. Marsillach in this film and Jennifer Connelly in *Phenomena*, like other feminine leads in Argento's films, are young, and hence their images are not laden with associations with prior work, but they are also the director's instruments for investigating the threats to physical and psychic integrity that arise from a world of forgotten memories and dreams, inevitably calling into question a commonsense view of sensory perception. In *Opera* as in *Phenomena*, these young female figures function as somnambulists and visionaries

5.6. The painful pleasures of vision: Cristina Marsillach in *Opera*. *Photofest*.

(reminiscent of Deleuze's description of character in the time-image), guides to another world of perception that is conjured through the increasing disruption of normal vision and the unsettling music and sound. Argento's work is an assault on conventional and sentimental images so as to elicit a vision of a landscape that is not only threatening but also surrealistic, involving often the animal and insect world and supernaturalism via the paranormal, focusing on the unlikeliest characters as the producers of cruelty, mayhem, and murder and also salvation.

Betty's forced viewing of the murders is akin to the experience of viewing the film, which doubles with the spectator's role in looking while also recoiling from the signs of decomposition and death. The use of the opera *Macbeth* and allusions to other horror films serve as a pedagogy, an introduction to Argento's contamination of received forms and how they are conventionally received, whether of Shakespeare and Verdi or of heavy metal. This contamination is not sensationalism but a major strategy for challenging so-called "normal" perception. The dominant leitmotif resides in the relentless insistence on the multifarious and obsessive uses of the camera to disturb the spectator's view of events, creating a dramatic reversal of expectations of what is seen and how, and endowing the director with an extraordinary magical power that links his work to a baroque vision where reality metamorphoses and "disappears little by little in the field of vision."[75] Similarly, *The Stendahl Syndrome* is a complex exploration of the fetishization of vision in art and cinema. Akin to Godard's "It's not blood, it's red," Argento regards the cinematic image as fake though potentially deadly for those who do not understand the power of fantasy.

Argento chose Asia for the starring role rather than Bridget Fonda or Jennifer Jason Leigh, since she, like Marsillach in *Opera*, could communicate (without prejudice from her prior roles) the slipperiness of boundaries between the "normal" and the fantastic without reducing this dilemma to the common sense of popular psychology. The ambiguity of her relationship to her father, the director, is an additional element that contributes to the appeal of her image in this and other Argento films. Asia's star image is not merely due to her being born into a family of cineastes. An examination of her career reveals that aside from her writing short stories and novels, she has undertaken a wide range of roles for major directors in films and TV from 1985 to the present, including Sergio Citti, Michele Soavi, Nanni Moretti, Michael Radford, Amos Gitai, Gus Van Sant, Abel Ferrara, Sofia Coppola, Lamberto Bava, and Dario Argento. Since 1994, she has directed a number of films in which she has also starred, the most striking being *Scarlet Diva* (2000), for which she won awards as Best Actress and Best New Director. While the film is autobiographical, it takes on more than a personal tone, becoming a critical excursion into the film industry and the struggles and vicissitudes of international stardom. Through her films, the abundant publicity about her, her collaboration with Dario Argento, and her numerous prestigious personal contacts in the Italian and international world of cinema, she has established a glamorous, free-spirited, daring and un-conventional (on-screen and off), and talented and troubled image of feminin-ity that has earned her wide popularity, if at times also controversy.

She has further enhanced Argento's status as a maker of stars and as a star in his own right. In his public appearances and in publicity shots, Argento has the aura of a modern star, shorn of the glamour normally associated with main-stream figures but not of the fascination derived from the controversial charac-ter of his work in horror. The experimental character of his cinematic work in crime detection and horror exceeds conventional genre analysis. In them, the viewer moves between surface and depth, works of art (opera and painting) that lose their familiar shapes, boundaries between the real and the imaginary, and, like the characters, become prey to the terrors of a constantly altering visible world. Publicity images of the director and TV appearances are unlike the the-atrical and posed portraits of Fellini or Pasolini. Instead, photographs reveal his thin, lanky body and his bony face framed by moderately long hair; he is dressed casually in wash-and-wear trousers, tie-less and often jacket-less. His fame has been spread by his films and imitations of them; his identification with the filmmaking of Riccardo Freda, Lucio Fulci, Mario Bava, Asia Argento, Aristide Massacessi (Joe D'Amato), and Michele Soavi; the growth of retrospectives due to the renewed interest in horror films; the Internet; reissues of his films on DVD; and growing numbers of commentaries on his films. His persona and his films are indicative of the altering state of media forms and are an invitation to rethink the current preoccupation with the "death of cinema" and hence the fate of stardom.[76] Are we witnesses to a death or to inevitable transmutations inherent to the history of cinema?

Epilogue: An End to Stardom?

From the 1960s to the present, television and what have come to be known as "new media" have increasingly altered the contemporary landscape of Italian stardom in contradictory fashion, as exemplified by Maurizio Nichetti's *Ladri di saponette* (The Icicle Thief, 1989) and Gabriele Muccino's *Ricordati di me* (Remember Me, 2003). The characters live in a media world saturated with popular music, movies, TV game shows, and advertisements. TV has created new types of stars through quiz, variety, and game shows--e.g., such personalities as announcers and game show hosts Mike Bongiorno and Pippo Baudo, among other male hosts. Television has sponsored the production of films, and continues to be an outlet for the screening of earlier and recent Italian films. For example, media mogul Silvio Berlusconi has purchased old films, telefilms, and cartoons.

Through talk shows and biographical films, television has also evoked history and cultural memory by showcasing Italian stars from an earlier era (e.g.,

Francesca Bertini in *The Last Diva* as well as conversations with fading stars such as Gina Lollobrigida). It has also strengthened the star system of the small screen, "demonstrated by the extraordinary interest that is displayed in the family and love lives of personalities."[1] The effects of television have not been monolithic. On the one hand, TV has been responsible for building a greater linguistic community in Italy.[2] For good or ill, it has sought to play a role in "developing a shared sense of belonging and a shared collective [national] identity."[3] On the other, it has reined in more innovative and critically exploratory aspects of Italian social and cultural life.

While the all-encompassing and repetitive output of television might be responsible for further domesticating and destroying the distinctive character of cinematic stardom and perhaps shortening the life span of the movie star, it has not impeded the growth of some director/stars, as in the case of Nanni Moretti, known also for his writing and for appearing in his own films (e.g., *Ecce bomba* [1978], *Caro diario* [Dear Diary, 1994], *Aprile* [1998], *La stanza del figlio* [The Son's Room, 2001], and *Il caimano* [The Crocodile, 2006], a satire on TV tycoon Silvio Berlusconi). An outspoken public figure on political issues, Moretti is not as indebted to TV as is Roberto Benigni, but he has appeared on TV in interviews, has been financed through TV, and in certain films has included the medium of television as symptomatic of contemporary culture and politics.

Film directors have explored the "death of cinema," the most internationally successful being Giuseppe Tornatore, director of *Nuovo Cinema Paradiso* (1989). *L'uomo delle stelle* (The Starmaker, 1995) is another foray into cinema's demise featuring the small screen prominently, and *Malèna* (2000) taps into memories of fascism and the war. But directors have also been sustained and creative through a merging of television and cinema. Gianni Amelio is known for his work on television through such films as *La fine del gioco* (The End of the Game, 1970), *Effetti speciali* (Special Effects, 1978) (TV), and *La morte al lavoro* (Death at Work, 1978). He is known for films including the documentary *Bertolucci secondo il cinema* (1975) and the dramas *Ladro di Bambini* (The Stolen Children, 1992), *Lamerica* (1994), *Cosi ridevano* (The Way They Laughed, 1998), and *Le chiavi di casa* (The Keys to the House, 2004), and for bringing such actors as Michele Placido and Enrico Lo Verso to international attention. Marco Tullio Giordana has gained a reputation for his TV work and for such films as *Pasolini: un delitto italiano* (Pasolini: An Italian Crime, 1995), *I cento passi* (The Hundred Steps, 2000), and *Lo meglio gioventù* (The Best of Youth, 2003); Emanuele Crialese garnered a number of national and international awards for *Respiro* (2002) and *Nuovomondo* (Golden Door, 2006), as has Cristina Comencini for *Il più bel giorno della mia vita* (The Most Beautiful Day of My Life, 2002) and *La bestia nel cuore* (Beast in the Heart, 2005, released in English as *Don't Talk*).

Nonetheless, Italian filmmaking since the 1980s has undergone a steep decline in production.[4] The number of Italian films and co-productions has considerably declined from the 1980s to the present thanks to the preeminence of Hollywood, international competition, the subsequent reduction of movie theaters in
Italy, television, and the increasing exploitation of new digital technologies. Quality films continue to emerge, though the fate of directors and stars becomes increasingly uncertain, given the commitment to quick, often astounding, profits
for some films. The picture of filmmaking in Italy is hardly rosy, characterized as
a marriage between the poverty of financial and organizational means and a
poverty of ideas.[5] No one has reproduced the coup carried off by Tornatore in
Nuovo cinema paradiso and Roberto Benigni for *La vita è bella*, which garnered
numerous Italian and international awards. Benigni's comic persona reveals a
further permutation of stardom. As director, writer, actor, television personality,
and public intellectual, he maintains high visibility. These qualities not only ensure his celebrity status but also carry the threat of premature superannuation.

National and international celebrity reveals the ways visual and auditory
images have permutated through the increased global speed and mobility of
people, capital, and value, effecting biological and political representations of
the cinematic body, the human body, and with them conceptions of stardom.
An examination of Italian cinema over the course of a century reveals how
stardom has never been "a unified or closed whole, but rather . . . an ensemble
or set of logical relations that are in a state of continual transformation,"[6] unsettling "all the comforts and stabilities of meaning."[7] Stardom now exhibits the
nervous symptoms of "post-modernity": sensitivity to the power of media and to
controversies over relations between official history and memory, and self-con-
sciousness about the politics of the body and the body politic. It is in a contest
with time and with the changing dimensions of media forms involving different
forms of affect, attention, and also forgetfulness.

A Postscript

The political figure of Silvio Berlusconi is instructive about the vicissitudes of politics, stardom, and media in the twentieth and twenty-first centuries. In accounting for the Berlusconi phenomenon, Paul Ginsborg writes that he was "not just the President of the Council of Ministers, he also presides over the imagination of a consistent segment of the nation; not just those who already enjoy considerable wealth, but also those who would like to. . . . Perhaps it is his charisma that is forged, in the sense of being constructed within the confines, practices and symbols of modern communication and consumption, carefully *manufactured*."[1] Berlusconi's putative "charisma" has relied on his being a "master of evasion," an "unrivalled salesman of escapist dreams," a "self-made tycoon," and a personification of a "part-Dallas, part Mediterranean chic."[2]

Berlusconi's figure has been disseminated by the media and by his own prodigious efforts, and built on his voracious and successful economic acquisitiveness, his affluent lifestyle, his initially hidden affair with and later marriage to actress Veronica Lario, his fanaticism for football, his acquisition of political power, and his clashes with and disregard for the law. Berlusconi is a mirror with which Italians can regard themselves as "opulent and powerful."[3] He embodies the social, economic, and cultural transformation of the 1990s and the turn of the century. In keeping with the rhetoric and politics of neo-liberalism, Berlusconi is associated with anti-communism, the Catholic Church, privatization, the free market, and individual initiative, positions that unite him to other European and American leaders from Thatcher to George W. Bush as well as such powerful media magnates as Rupert Murdoch.

While comparisons have been made between Berlusconi and Mussolini and while media technology is fundamental in the rise of both, Berlusconi's persona differs in context and performance from that of Il Duce. As portrayed in newsreels of the 1930s and in Fellini's *Amarcord*, responses to Mussolini were orgiastic from the 1920s to the late 1930s, reminiscent of Rudolph Valentino's effect on spectators. The admiration and adulation of him by the masses depended on the illusion that he was one with people, that he "lived a life like other people, shares their hopes and fears." Yet at the same time, like a star, he was "also removed from the life of mere mortals,"[4] his image hovering between the promise of gratification and its impossibility. He appeared both common and remote. Though it has been argued that stars are different from political figures in having no access to political power, "there is clearly some correspondence between political and star charisma."[5]

Berlusconi is "not an able orator, nor physically particularly compelling, renowned for his heroism, or endowed with any other naturally compelling qualities."[6] His ostensible appeal may lie in the absence of these qualities. Comparisons of Berlusconi to J. R. Ewing of the TV drama series *Dallas* (1978–1991) suggest that their exceptionality resides less in their magnetism and more in the images of these tycoons' extravagant lifestyles, economic power, and self-promotion in tandem with the vicissitudes in their personal lives, their scheming, failures and triumphs, and physical vulnerability. As the scion of televisuality, Berlusconi differs from the cinema star that relies on a human pose and solicits affective engagement. He is more akin to the stars of television.

The effects of the televisual image still remain to be determined, for, in TV, "the screen itself, even if it keeps a vertical position, no longer seems to refer to the human posture, like a window or a painting, but rather constitutes a table of information, an opaque surface on which are inscribed 'data,' information replacing nature."[7] Viewing relies on a "continuous and competing flow of programming and rapid changes of images, advertising, takes place in either domestic or places of transit, and demands a lower state of concentration."[8] Berlusconi's image belongs to the protean and fleeting character of television, to the empty desires generated by an "opaque surface" that resists materiality, but in its hyper-reality and evanescence may lie the seeds of his vulnerable cultural and political position or also a portent of new forms of control. For better or worse, we are in a different realm of media performance and personality.

The phenomenon of stardom as we have known it would seem to be in crisis, its future tentative. The durability of stars like Sophia Loren and Marcello Mastroianni is exceptional, while the fate of newer stars is uncertain. Cinematic stardom has had to compete with television, video, and digital media as well as profound cultural transformations in conceptions of national, gender, and sexual identity. Major challenges to historical and material conceptions of stardom are mounted by computer animation. At the same time that "fictional" stars are being created, actual ones (once living but now dead) are being revivified through TV, videocassettes, re-animation, and morphing, refashioning images culled and transformed from their cinematic sources.

This development must lead the media critic to ask: What is the work of the star in the Age of Digital Reproduction? If stardom lives on, what are the ways in which we recognize its new status as reliant on new modes of production, circulation, and reception, its increasingly protean dimensions in the now-global character of media? What can we learn about the cultural character and impact of the star phenomenon at a time when television and the Internet, through their emphasis on history, docudrama, biography, tabloids, and the news itself, have reduced the celestial horizon of the star? The constellations of stars are now as vast as the universe, and their once-consensual aspect, having been rooted in specific historical moments, may be doomed to disappear amid the quantity of competing and ambiguous news reportage, advertisements, tabloids, endless generation of new personalities, and recycled genres that indiscriminately bombard the spectator. Equally challenging in this scenario is the portent of the triumph of the virtual human subject, the synthespian. No longer on celluloid, now created through digital images and their computer-generated special effects, how will this technological development transform not only stardom but the spectator's sense of history, memory, and cultural imperatives?

Notes

Unless otherwise indicated, translations from Italian and French are mine.

Introduction

1. Among the numerous books and articles on the subject of stardom, I have consulted Parker Tyler, *Magic and Myth of the Movies* (New York: Simon and Schuster, 1970); Alexander Walker, *Stardom: The Hollywood Phenomenon* (New York: Stein and Day, 1970); Richard Dyer, *Stars* (London: BFI, 1979) and *Heavenly Bodies: Film Stars and Society* (London: British Film Institute, 1986); Christine Gledhill, *Stardom: Industry of Desire* (London: Routledge, 1991); Ginette Vincendeau, *Stars and Stardom in French Cinema* (London: Continuum, 2000); Gian Piero Brunetta, "Divismo, misticismo, e spettacolo della politica," in *Storia del cinema mondiale*, Vol. 1 (Venice: Giulio Einaudi, 1999), 527–559; Stefan Masi and Enrico Lancia, *Stelle d'Italia: piccole e grandi dive del cinema italiano* (Rome: Gremese, 1994); Stefano Masi, *Silvana Mangano: Il teorema della bellezza* (Rome: Gremese, 1994); and Elena Mosconi, ed., *Light from a Star* (Cremona: Persico, 2003).

2. Walter Benjamin, "The Work of Art in the Age of Mechanical Reproduction," in *Illuminations* (New York: Schocken Books, 1976), 229.

3. Stanley Cavell, *The World Viewed: Reflections on the Ontology of Film* (New York: Viking, 1974), xii–xiii.

4. Steven Shaviro, *The Cinematic Body* (Minneapolis: University of Minnesota Press, 1993), 25–26.

5. André Bazin, *What Is Cinema?* Vol. 1 (Berkeley: University of California Press, 1967), 15.

6. Gilles Deleuze, *Cinema 1: The Movement-Image*, trans. Hugh Tomlinson and Barbara Habberjam (Minneapolis: University of Minnesota Press, 1986), and *Cinema 2: The Time-Image*, trans. Hugh Tomlinson and Robert Galeta (Minneapolis: University of Minnesota Press, 1989).

7. Deleuze, *Cinema 2*, 171.

8. Ibid., 20.

9. Ibid., 22.

10. Alan Lovell and Peter Krämer, *Screen Acting* (London: Routledge, 1999), 4.

11. For a fascinating phenomenological discussion of "the cinematic body," see Vivian Sobchack, *Carnal Thoughts: Embodiment and Moving Image Culture* (Berkeley: University of California Press, 2004).

12. Pierre Sorlin, *European National Cinema 1896–1996* (London: Routledge, 1996), 48.

13. Sorlin asks, "Was there not an unconscious association, in the minds of lots of Italians, between the shielding hero and the vigilant leader? Did not Mussolini borrow a few features from the favorite actor?" Ibid., 50.

14. For two recent studies of Mussolini, see R. W. B. Bosworth, *Mussolini* (London: Arnold, 2002), and Sergio Luzzatto, *The Body of Il Duce: Mussolini's Corpse and the Fortunes of Italy*, trans. Frederika Randall (New York: Henry Holt, 2005).

15. On the subject of cinema's relationship to fascism see Gian Piero Brunetta, *Storia del cinema italiano: Il cinema del regime 1929–1945* (Rome; Riuniti, 2001); James Hay, *Popular Film Culture in Fascist Italy: The Passing of the Rex* (Bloomington: Indiana University Press, 1987); Elaine Mancini, *Struggles of the Italian Film Industry during Fascism, 1930–1935* (Ann Arbor, Mich.: UMI Research Press, 1985); Marcia Landy, *Fascism in Film: The Italian Commercial Cinema 1929–1943* (Princeton, N.J.: Princeton University Press, 1986); Ruth Ben-Ghiat, *Fascist Modernities: Italy 1922–1945* (Berkeley: University of California Press, 2004); Vito Zagarrio, *Cinema e fascismo: Film, modelli, immaginari* (Venice, Marsilio, 2004).

16. On various views of neorealism and its permutations, see André Bazin, *What Is Cinema?* Vol. 1 (Berkeley: University of California Press, 1967); Gian Piero Brunetta, *Storia del cinema italiano: dal neorealismo al miracolo economico*, Vol. 3 (Rome: Riuniti, 2001); Millicent Marcus, *Italian Cinema in the Light of Neorealism* (Princeton, N.J.: Princeton University Press, 1986); Peter Bondanella, *Italian Cinema: From Neorealism to the Present* (New York: Continuum, 2002); Antonio Vitti, *Giuseppe De Santis and Postwar Italian Cinema* (Toronto: University of Toronto Press, 1996); Callisto Cosulich, "Neorealisti al guado," *Storia del cinema italiano*, Vol. 9, ed. Sandro Bernardi (Turin: Marsilio, 2004), 197–215; Angelo Restivo, *The Cinema of Economic Miracles* (Durham, N.C.: Duke University Press, 2002); and Mark Sheil, *Italian Neorealism: Rebuilding the Cinematic City* (London: Wallflower, 2006).

17. Marco Pistoia, "Il melodrama e l'eredità del neorealismo," *Storia del cinema italiano*, Vol. 9, ed. Sandro Bernardi (Turin: Marsilio, 2004), 163–175.

18. See Jacqueline Reich, *Beyond the Latin Lover: Marcello Mastroianni, Masculinity, and Italian Cinema* (Bloomington: Indiana University Press, 2004).

19. I am indebted, as are many general readers and critics, to Christopher Frayling's *Spaghetti Westerns: Cowboys and Europeans from Karl May to Sergio Leone* (London: I. B. Tauris, 1998).

20. Stefano Della Casa's *Storia e stories del cinema popolare italiano* (Turin: La Stampa, 2001) is an important book for reevaluating popular cinema and its relations to Italian cinema generally.

21. For analytic treatments of horror films, see Maggie Günsberg, *Italian Cinema, Gender and Genre* (Houndsmills, Basingstoke, Hants.: Palgrave, 2005), 133–173. See also Adam Lowenstein, *Shocking Representations: Historical Trauma, National Cinema, and the Modern Horror Film* (New York: Columbia University Press, 2002).

22. For examples of critical and theoretical discussions of Argento's work, see Colette Balmain, "Mario Bava's Evil Eye: Realism and the Horror Film," *Post Script* 21, no. 3 (Summer 2002): 20–31; Maitland McDonagh, "Broken Mirrors/Broken Minds: The Dark Dreams of Dario Argento," *Film Quarterly* 41, no. 2 (Winter 1987–1988): 2–13, and "The Elegant Brutality of Dario Argento," *Film Comment* 29, no. 1 (Jan./Feb. 1993): 55–58; and Jean-Baptiste Thoret, *Dario Argento: Magicien de la peur* (Paris: Cahiers du Cinéma, 2002).

1. Eloquent Bodies

1. Antonio Gramsci, *Selections from the Cultural Writings*, ed. David Forgacs and Geoffrey Nowell-Smith, trans. William Boelhower (Cambridge: Harvard University Press, 1985), 123. See also *Quaderni del carcere*, ed. Valentino Gerratana (Turin: Giulio Einaudi, 1975), 4:2194–2195.

2. Gramsci, *Selections from the Cultural Writings*, 56.

3. Ibid., 56, 203–204.

4. Michele Canosa, "Febo Mari: Vigilò l'esecuzione," in *A nuova luce*, ed. Michele and Antonio Costa, Bologna: *Fotogenia* 4/5 (1999): 274.

5. James Naremore, *Acting in the Cinema* (Berkeley: University of California Press, 1988), 64.

6. Gramsci, *Selections from the Cultural Writings*, 377.

7. Lucia Re, "Il mostro della memoria di Gabriele D'Annunzio: Il Vittoriale degli Italiani," *The Journal of Decorative and Propaganda Arts 1875–1945*, no. 3 (Winter 1987): 8.

8. See Michael A. Ledeen, *The First Duce: D'Annunzio at Fiume* (Baltimore: Johns Hopkins University Press, 1977).

9. Re, "Il mostro," 28.

10. Gian Piero Brunetta, *Storia del cinema italiano: Il cinema muto 1895–1929* (Rome: Editori Riuniti, 2001), 90.

11. Re, "Il mostro," 10.

12. Brunetta, *Storia del cinema mondiale* (Venice: Giulio Einaudi, 1999), 1:216.

13. Gramsci, *Selections from the Cultural Writings*, 253.

14. Barbara Spackman, *Fascist Virilities: Rhetoric, Ideology, and Social Fantasy in Italy* (Minneapolis: University of Minnesota Press, 1996), 80.

15. Ibid., p. 91.

16. Brunetta, *Storia del cinema italiano: Il cinema muto 1895–1929*, 538.

17. Ibid., 154.

18. Spackman, *Fascist Virilities*, 126.

19. Elaine Mancini, *Struggles of the Italian Film Industry during Fascism, 1930–1935* (Ann Arbor, Mich.: UMI Research Press, 1985), 121.

20. Ibid., 128.

21. Marco Palla, *Mussolini and Fascism*, trans. Arthur Figliola and Claudia Rattazzi Papka (New York: Interlink Books, 2000), 21.

22. Ibid., 29.

23. R. J. B. Bosworth, *Mussolini* (London: Arnold, 2002), 211.

24. Ibid., 212.

25. On various representations of the "strong man," see Alberto Farassino and Tatti Sanguinetti, eds., *Gli uomini forti* (Milan: Mazzotta, 1983).

26. Pierre Sorlin, *Italian National Cinema 1896–1996* (London: Routledge, 1996), 48.

27. Michele Canosa, "Muto di luce," in *A nuova luce*, ed. Michele Canosa and Antonio Costa, Bologna: Fotogenia 4/5 (1999): 22–23.

28. Monica Dall' Asta, "La diffusione del film a episodi in Europa," in *Storia del cinema mondiale*, ed. Gian Piero Brunetta (Venice: Einaudi, 1999), 277–315.

29. Canosa, "Muto di luce," 22–23.

30. Dall' Asta, "La diffusione," 312.

31. Ibid., 313.

32. Vittorio Martinelli, "Nascita del *Divismo*," in *Storia del cinema mondiale*, ed. Gian Piero Brunetta (Venice: Einaudi, 1999), 238.

33. Sorlin, *Italian National Cinema*, 35.

34. Silvio Alovisio, "The 'Pastrone System': Itala Film from the Origins to World War 1," *Film History* 12, no. 3 (2000): 259.

35. Angela Dalle Vacche, *The Body and the Mirror: The Shapes of History in Italian Cinema* (Princeton, N.J.: Princeton University Press, 1992), 30.

36. Ibid., 36–37.

37. Farassino and Sanguinetti, eds., *Gli uomini forti*, 41.

38. Canosa, "Muto di luce," 20.

39. Martinelli, "Nascita del *Divismo*," 237.

40. Ibid., 222.

41. Ibid., 222.

42. Astrid Söderberg Widding, "Denmark," in *Nordic National Cinemas*, by Tytti Soila, Astrid Söderberg Widding, and Gunnar Iversen (London: Routledge, 1998), 8.

43. Lotte Eisner, *The Haunted Screen* (Berkeley: University of California Press, 1977), 262.

44. Barbara Spackman, *Decadent Genealogies: The Rhetoric of Sickness from Baudelaire to D'Annunzio* (Ithaca, N.Y.: Cornell University Press, 1989), 129.

45. Angela Dalle Vacche and Gian Luca Farinelli, *Passion and Defiance: Silent Divas of Italian Cinema* (Milan: Olivares, 2000), 11.

46. Massimo Moretti, "Febo Mari vigilò l'esecuzione," in *A nuova luce*, ed. Michele Canosa and Antonio Costa, Bologna: Fotogenia 4/5 (1999): 149–165.

47. Ibid., 151.

48. Ibid., 155.

49. For further discussion of the diva Menichelli, see Vittorio Martinelli, *Pina Menichelli: Le sfumature del fascino* (Rome: Bulzoni, 2002).

50. Dalle Vacche, *Silent Divas*, 12–28.

51. Brunetta, *Storia del cinema italiano: Il cinema muto 1895–1929*, 78.

52. Dalle Vacche, *Silent Divas*, 38.

53. Giulio Cesare Castello, *Il Divismo: Mitologia del cinema* (Italy: Edizione Radio Italiana, 1957), 14.

54. Brunetta, *Storia del cinema italiano: Il cinema muto 1895–1929*, 108.

55. Victoria de Grazia, *How Fascism Ruled Women: Italy, 1922–1945* (Berkeley: University of California Press, 1992), 211.

56. Antonina Campisciano, "Body As Text: Lyda Borelli in *Malombra*," in *Pagina, Pellicola, Pratica: Studi sul cinema italiano*, ed. Rebecca West (Ravenna: Longo, 2000), 58.

57. Dalle Vacche, *Silent Divas*, 12.

58. Brunetta, *Storia del cinema italiano: Il cinema muto 1895–1929*, 81.

59. Ibid., 82.

60. Antonio Gramsci, *Letteratura e vita nazionale* (Turin: Einaudi, 1972), 272.

61. Ibid., 273.

62. Antonio Fogazzaro, *Malombra* (Milan: Mondadori, 1978), 114.

63. Campisciano, "Body As Text," 67.

64. Valerie Mendes and Amy de la Haye, *20th Century Fashion* (London: Thames and Hudson, 1999), 24.

65. Gianfranco Mingozzi, *Francesca Bertini* (Genoa: Le Mani, 2003), 183–216.

66. Giuliana Bruno, *Streetwalking on a Ruined Map: Cultural Theory and the Films of Elvira Notari* (Princeton, N.J.: Princeton University Press, 1993), 30.

67. Francesca Bertini, *Il resto non conta* (Pisa: Guardini, 1969). See also Mingozzi's film *L'ultima diva* (The Last Diva, 1982).

68. Brunetta, *Storia del cinema italiano: Il cinema muto 1895–1929*, 84.

69. Bruno, *Streetwalking*, 212; see also Adriano Aprà and Jean Gili, *Naples et le cinéma* (Paris: Fabbri, 1994).

70. Bruno, *Streetwalking*, 176.

71. Ibid., 30.

72. Helen Sheehy, *Eleanora Duse: A Biography* (New York: Alfred A. Knopf, 2003), 170.

73. Ibid., 47.

74. Giorgio Agamben, *Means without End: Notes on Politics*, trans. Vincenzo Binetti and Cesare Casarino (Minneapolis: University of Minnesota Press, 2000), 58.

75. Dalle Vacche, *Silent Divas*, 34.

76. Walter Benjamin, *Illuminations* (New York: Schocken Books, 1976), 233.

77. Gilles Deleuze, *Cinema 1: The Movement-Image*, trans. Hugh Tomlinson and Barbara Habberjam (Minneapolis: University of Minnesota, 1986), 71–73.

78. Ibid., 71–72.

79. Ibid., 60.

80. Ibid., 64.

81. Ibid., 64.

82. Ibid., 66.

83. D. N. Rodowick, *Gilles Deleuze's Time Machine* (Durham, N.C.: Duke University Press, 1997), 67.

84. Ibid., 64.

85. Sorlin, *Italian National Cinema*, 29.

86. Ibid., 40.

87. Antonio Gramsci, *Selections from the Cultural Writings,* 190.

88. Marcia Landy, *The Folklore of Consensus: Theatricality in the Italian Cinema, 1930–1943* (Albany: SUNY University Press, 1998), xi–xiii.

2. The Stars Talk

1. Gian Piero Brunetta, *Cinema italiano tra le due guerre: Fascismo e politica cinematografica* (Milan: Mursia, 1975), 1–28.

2. Pierre Leprohon, *Italian Cinema* (New York: Praeger, 1972), 47–61.

3. Elaine Mancini, *Struggles of the Italian Film Industry during Fascism, 1930–1935* (Ann Arbor, Mich.: UMI Research Press, 1985), 33; Pierre Sorlin, *Italian National Cinema 1896–1996* (London: Routledge, 1996), 54.

4. Gian Piero Brunetta, "The Long March of American Cinema in Italy: From Fascism to the Cold War," in David E. Ellwood and Rob Kroes, eds., *Hollywood in Europe: Experiences of a Cultural Hegemony* (Amsterdam: VU University Press, 1994), 139–155.

5. Sorlin, *Italian National Cinema,* 53.

6. Leprohon, *Italian Cinema,* 50.

7. Jasper Ridley, *Mussolini* (New York, St. Martin's Press, 1997), 103–104.

8. Victoria de Grazia, *The Culture of Consent: Mass Organization of Leisure in Fascist Italy* (Cambridge: Cambridge University Press, 1981), 155.

9. Jonathan Dunnage, *Twentieth Century Italy: A Social History* (London: Longman, 2002), 92.

10. Toll, Robert C., *The Entertainment Machine: American Show Business in the Twentieth Century* (Oxford: Oxford University Press, 1982), 52–56.

11. Michael Chion, *The Voice in Cinema,* ed. and trans. Claudia Gorbman (New York: Columbia University Press, 1999), 18, 21.

12. Ibid., 126.

13. James Lastra, *Sound Technology and the American Cinema: Perception, Reception, Modernity* (New York: Columbia University Press, 2000), 192.

14. James Hay, "Placing the Cinema, Fascism, the Nation in a Diagram of Italian Modernity," in *Re-viewing Fascism: Italian Cinema, 1922–1943,* ed. Jacqueline Reich and Piero Garofalo (Bloomington: Indiana University Press, 2002), 122.

15. For an analysis of these directors in the stylistic context of Cines production, see Vincenzo Buccheri, *Stile Cines: Studi sul cinema italiano 1930–1934* (Milan: Vita e Pensiero, 2004).

16. Sorlin, *Italian National Cinema,* 59–61.

17. Buccheri, *Stile Cines,* 157.

18. Raffaele De Berti, "La Signora di tutti e l'avvento del divismo italiano," in *Light from a Star,* ed. Elena Mosconi (Cremona: Persico, 2003), 33–38.

19. Sorlin, *Italian National Cinema,* 61–63.

20. For discussions of the forms and context of these calligraphic films, consult Andrea Martini, ed., *La bella forma: Poggioli, I calligrafici, e dintorni* (Venice: Marsilio, 1992).

21. Antonio Costa, "Risotto con i tartufi: Soldati, Fogazzaro e il calligrafismo," in *La bella forma: Poggioli, I calligrafici, e dintorni* (Venice: Marsilio, 1992): 95–105.

22. Marcia Landy, *The Folklore of Consensus: Theatricality in the Italian Cinema, 1930–1943* (Albany: SUNY Press, 1998), 169–236.

23. Sorlin, *Italian National Cinema*, 65.

24. Buccheri, *Stile Cines*, 39.

25. Mancini, *Struggles of the Italian Film Industry*, 73; Buccheri, *Stile Cines*, 22–26.

26. Buccheri, *Stile Cines*, 18.

27. Sorlin attributes the success of *Gli uomini che mascalzoni* largely to De Sica, as follows: "Handsome, tall, slim, elegant, Vittorio De Sica bore a physical likeness to the kind of ideal man one would have expected to find in film magazines. His dress and manner were appealingly smart and formal, his attractive, well-spoken, inviting voice sounded at once promising and elusive. Although exceptionally gifted, he was not pretentious." *Italian National Cinema*, 65.

28. G. Casadio, E. G. Laura, and F. Cristiano, *Telefoni bianchi: Realtà e finzione nella società e nel cinema degli anni quaranta* (Ravenna: Longo, 1991), 17.

29. Francesco Savio, *Cinecittà anni trenta: Parlano 116 protagonisti del secondo cinema italiano 1930–1943*, 4 vols. (Roma: Bulzoni, 1979), 912.

30. Adriano Aprà and Patrizia Pistagnesi, *I favolosi anni trenta: Cinema italiano 1929–1944* (Milan: Electa, 1979), 56.

31. Buccheri, *Stile Cines*, 106–117.

32. Ibid., 117.

33. James Hay, *Popular Film Culture in Fascist Italy: The Passing of the Rex* (Bloomington: Indiana University Press, 1987), 113.

34. Stephen Gundle, "Film Stars and Society in Fascist Italy," in *Re-viewing Fascism: Italian Cinema, 1922–1943*, ed. Jacqueline Reich and Piero Garofalo (Bloomington: Indiana University Press, 2002), 324.

35. Ermanno Comuzio, "De Sica o della doppia costante: Il sorriso e il tarlo segreto," *Cineforum* 15, no. 140 (1975): 31.

36. Aprà and Pistagnesi, *I favolosi anni trenta*, 82.

37. Mancini, *Struggles of the Italian Film Industry*, 94.

38. Paola Valentini, "Il cinema e gli altri media," in *Storia del cinema italiano*, Vol. 8, ed. Luciano de Gusti (Venice; Marsilio 2003), 115.

39. Stefano Masi and Enrico Lancia, *Stelle d'Italia: piccole e grandi dive del cinema italiano* (Rome: Gremese, 1994), 18–19.

40. Ibid., 146.

41. Ibid., 64.

42. Aprà and Pistagnesi, *I favolosi anni trenta*, 77.

43. Valentini, "Il cinema e gli altri media," 115.

44. Aprà and Pistagnesi, *I favolosi anni trenta*, 76.

45. For a sympathetic biography of Amedeo Nazzari, see Giuseppe Gubitosi, *Amedeo Nazzari* (Bologna: Mulino, 1998).

46. Ibid., 28.

47. Savio, *Cinecittà anni trenta*, 579.

48. Stephen Gundle, "Film Stars and Society," 334.

49. Savio, *Cinecittà anni trenta*, 587.

50. Raffaele De Berti, "La signora di tutti e l'avvento del divismo italiano," in Elena Mosconi, ed., *Light from a Star* (Cremona: Persico, 2003), 34.

51. Ibid., 35.

52. Masi and Lancia, *Stelle d'Italia*, 14.

53. Mary Ann Doane, *Femmes Fatales: Feminism, Film Theory, Psychoanalysis* (New York: Routledge, 1991), 123.

54. Ibid., 125.

55. Parker Tyler, *Magic and Myth of the Movies* (New York: Simon and Schuster, 1970), 82.

56. De Berti, "La signora di tutti," 48–49.

57. Giorgio Bacchiega, "I fotografi e Isa Miranda," in Elena Mosconi, ed., *Light from a Star* (Cremona: Persico, 2003): 47.

58. Angela Dalle Vacche, *The Body and the Mirror: The Shapes of History in Italian Cinema* (Princeton, N.J.: Princeton University Press, 1992), 45.

59. Leprohon, *Italian Cinema*, 242.

60. Savio, *Cinecittà anni trenta*, 1045.

61. Antonio Costa, "Risotto con i tartufi: Soldati, Fogazzaro e il calligrafismo," in *La bella forma: Poggioli, I calligrafici, e dintorni* (Venice: Marsilio, 1992), 100.

62. Leprohon, *Italian Cinema*, 39.

63. Ibid., 37.

64. Davide Papotti, "Amate sponde: L'imagine lacuale in due adattamenti cine-matografici di *Malombra* di Antonio Fogazzaro," in *Pagina, Pellicola, Pratica: Studia sul cinema italiano*, ed. Rebecca West (Ravenna; Longo, 2000), 30–55.

65. Victoria De Grazia, *How Fascism Ruled Women: Italy, 1922–1945* (Berkeley: University of California Press, 1992), 211.

66. R. J. B. Bosworth, *Mussolini* (London: Arnold, 2002), 385.

67. Sergio Luzzatto, *The Body of Il Duce: Mussolini's Corpse and the Fortunes of Italy*, trans. Frederika Randall (Henry Holt, 2005), 116–172.

3. Stars amidst the Ruins

1. Roberto Rossellini, *My Method: Writings and Interviews* (New York: Marsilio, 1992), 44.

2. Gian Piero Brunetta, *Storia del cinema italiano*, Vol. 3 (Rome: Riuniti, 2001), 3–12.

3. Ibid., 18–34.

4. David Forgacs, *Italian Culture in the Industrial Era 1880–1980: Cultural Indus-tries, Politics, and the Public* (Manchester: Manchester University Press, 1990), 117.

5. Ibid., 124.

6. Mary P. Wood, *Italian Cinema* (Oxford: Berg, 2005), 83.

7. Gilles Deleuze, *Cinema 1: The Movement-Image*, trans. Hugh Tomlinson and Barbara Habberjam (Minneapolis: University of Minnesota Press, 1986), 211–212.

8. For a discussion of the relation of Italian cinema to romances, photo-romances, cartoons, illustrated magazines, etc., see Raffaele De Berti, *Dallo schermo alla carta: Romanzo, Fotoromanzi, rotocalchi, cinematografici, il film e suo paratesti* (Milan: Vita e Pensiero, 2000).

9. Brunetta, "Italian Cinema and the Hard Road to Democracy, 1945," *Historical Journal of Film, Radio, and Television* 15, no. 3 (1995): 343.

10. Ibid., 343.

11. Angelo Restivo, *The Cinema of Economic Miracles: Visuality and Modernization in the Italian Art Film* (Durham, N.C.: Duke University Press), 25.

12. Brunetta, "The Long March of American Cinema in Italy: From Fascism to the Cold War," in *Hollywood in Europe: Experiences of a Cultural Hegemony*, ed. David E. Ellwood and Rob Kroes (Amsterdam: VU University Press, 1994), 145.

13. Ibid., 147.

14. Restivo, *Cinema of Economic Miracles*, 25.

15. Pierre Sorlin, *Italian National Cinema 1896–1996* (London: Routledge, 1996), 83.

16. Cesare Zavattini, "Some Ideas on the Cinema," in *Film: A Montage of Theories*, ed. Richard Dyer MacCann (New York: E. P. Dutton, 1966), 219.

17. André Bazin, *What Is Cinema?* Vol. 1 (Berkeley: University of California Press, 1967), 37.

18. Dudley Andrew, "André Bazin's Evolution," in *Defining Cinema*, ed. Peter Lehman (New Brunswick, N.J.: Rutgers University Press, 1997), 82.

19. Millicent Marcus, *Italian Cinema in the Light of Neorealism* (Princeton, N.J.: Princeton University Press, 1986), 34.

20. Ibid., 23.

21. Wood, *Italian Cinema*, 89.

22. Alberto Farassino, "Margini, attraversamenti, contaminazioni," *Storia del cinema italiano: 1945–1948*, Vol. 7, ed. Callisto Cosulich (Venice: Marsilio, 2003), 156–171.

23. Giovanna Grignaffini, "Female Identity and the Italian Cinema of the 1950s," *Off Screen: Women and Film in Italy*, ed. Giuliana Bruno and Maria Nadotti (London: Routledge, 1988), 120.

24. Ibid., 120.

25. Ibid., 121.

26. Stefano Masi and Enrico Lancia, *Italian Movie Goddesses: Over Eighty of the Greatest Women in Italian Cinema* (Rome: Gremese, 1992), 67.

27. Tony Mitchell, "The Construction and Reception of Anna Magnani in Italy and the English-Speaking World," *Film Criticism* 14, no. 1 (Fall 1989): 7.

28. Marcus, *Italian Cinema in the Light of Neorealism*, 39.

29. Grignaffini, 123.

30. David Forgacs, "Space, Rhetoric and the Divided City," in *Roberto Rossellini's Rome Open City*, ed. Sidney Gottlieb (Cambridge: Cambridge University Press, 2004), 106–107.

31. Tag Gallagher, *The Adventures of Roberto Rossellini* (New York: Da Capo Press, 1998), 118–158. See also David Forgacs, *Rome Open City* (London: BFI Publishing, 2000), 11.

32. Pierre Leprohon, *Italian Cinema* (New York: Praeger, 1972), 93.

33. David Forgacs, *Rome Open City*, 11–12.

34. Gallagher, *Adventures*, 25–29.

35. Forgacs, *Rome Open City*, 13–19.

36. Peter Brunette, *Roberto Rossellini* (New York: Oxford University Press, 1987), 41–60.

37. Forgacs, *Rome Open City*, 44.

38. Ibid., 36.

39. Ibid., 36.

40. Marcus, *Italian Cinema in the Light of Neorealism*, 46.

41. Ibid., 39.

42. Peter Bondanella, *Italian Cinema: From Neorealism to the Present* (New York: Continuum, 2002), 38–39; Peter Brunette, *Roberto Rossellini*, 44–45; Restivo, *The Cinema of Economic Miracles*, 23–24.

43. Deleuze, *Cinema 1*, 208.

44. Victoria de Grazia, *How Fascism Ruled Women: Italy, 1922–1945* (Berkeley: University of California Press, 1992), 78.

45. Roberto Rossellini, "Interviews with Roberto Rossellini," in *Cahiers du cinéma: The 1950s, Neo-Realism, New Wave*, ed. Jim Hillier (Cambridge, Mass.: Harvard University Press, 1985), 210.

46. Mitchell, "Construction," 8.

47. Francesco Casetti, "Cinema in the Cinema in Italian Films of the 1950s: *Bellissima* and *La signora senza camelie*," *Screen* 33, no. 4 (1992): 375.

48. Geoffrey Nowell-Smith, *Luchino Visconti* (Garden City, N.Y.: Doubleday, 1968), 55.

49. Anna Maria Torriglia, *Broken Time, Fragmented Space: A Cultural Map for Postwar Italy* (Toronto: University of Toronto Press, 2002), 71.

50. Deleuze, *Cinema 2*, 20–22.

51. Casetti, "Cinema in the Cinema," 384.

52. Maurizio Viano, *A Certain Realism: Making Use of Pasolini's Film Theory and Practice* (Berkeley: University of California Press, 1993), 90.

53. Ibid., 93.

54. Patrizia Carrano, *La Magnani* (Milan: Rizzoli, 1982), 252.

55. Stephen Gundle, "Sophia Loren, Italian Icon," *Historical Journal of Film, Radio, and Television* 15, no. 3 (1995): 367–385.

56. For a review of Mangano's life, career, public and professional reception, and appreciation by representatives of the film industry, see Giovanni Cimmino and Stefano Masi, *Silvana Mangano: Il teorema della bellezza* (Rome: Gremese, 1994).

57. Réka C. V. Buckley, "National Body: Gina Lollobrigida and the Cult of the Star in the 1950s," *Historical Journal of Film, Radio, and Television* 20, no.4 (2000): 527–528.

58. Antonio Vitti, *Giuseppe De Santis and Postwar Italian Cinema* (Toronto: University of Toronto Press, 1996), 51.

59. Ibid., 51.

60. Masi and Lancia, *Italian Movie Goddesses*, 74.

61. Vitti, *Giuseppe De Santis*, 51.

62. Jacqueline Reich, *Beyond the Latin Lover: Marcello Mastroianni, Masculinity, and Italian Cinema* (Bloomington: Indiana University Press, 2004), 112.

63. Masi and Lancia, *Italian Movie Goddesses*, 75, 192.

64. Brunette, *Rossellini*, 88.

65. Ibid., 103.

66. Ibid., 97.

67. Deleuze, *Cinema 2*, 126–155.

68. Reich, *Beyond the Latin Lover*, 105–129.

69. Ibid., 21.

70. Ibid., 22.

71. Ibid., 209–221.

72. Ibid.

73. Deleuze, *Cinema 2*, 3.

74. Adriano Aprà and Patrizia Pistagnesi, *Comedy, Italian Style, 1950–1980* (Turin: Edizione Radiotelevisione Italiana, 1986), 260.

75. Gundle, "Sophia Loren," 367–385.

76. Reich, *Beyond the Latin Lover*, 113.

77. Millicent Marcus, *Filmmaking by the Book: Italian Cinema and Literary Adaptation* (Baltimore: The Johns Hopkins University Press, 1993), 84.

78. Paul Ginsborg, *A History of Contemporary Italy, Society and Politics, 1943–1988* (London: Penguin, 1990), 248.

4. Popular Genres and Stars

1. Mark Sheil, *Italian Neorealism: Rebuilding the Cinematic City* (London: Wallflower, 2006), 86.

2. Gundle, "Sophia Loren: Italian Icon," *Historical Journal of Film, Radio, and Television* 15, no. 3 (1995): 367–385.

3. Gian Piero Brunetta, "Italian Cinema and the Hard Road to Democracy, 1945," *Historical Journal of Film, Radio, and Television* 15, no. 3 (1995): 345.

4. Mary P. Wood, *Italian Cinema* (Oxford: Berg, 2005), 16.

5. Paola Valentini, "Il cinema e gli altri media," in *Storia del cinema italiano*, Vol. 8, ed. Luciano de Gusti (Venice; Marsilio 2003): 110.

6. Stephen Gundle, "Feminine Beauty, National Identity, and Political Conflict in Postwar Italy," *Contemporary European History* 8, no. 3 (1999): 360.

7. Tim Bergfelder, "The Nation Vanishes: European Co-Productions and Popular Genre Formulae in the 1950s and 1960s," in *Cinema and Nation*, ed. Mette Hjort and Scott Mackenzie (London: Routledge, 2000): 139–152.

8. Vito Zagarrio, *L'anello mancante: storia e teoria del rapporto cinema-television* (Turin: Lindau, 2004), 149–161.

9. Bergfelder, "The Nation Vanishes," 140, 150.

10. Wood, *Italian Cinema*, 36.

11. Giuseppe Gubitosi, *Amedeo Nazzari* (Bologna: Mulino, 1998), 95.

12. Maggie Günsberg, *Italian Cinema, Gender and Genre* (Houndsmills, Basingstoke, Hants.: Palgrave, 2005), 1–60.

13. Christine Gledhill, ed., *Home Is Where the Heart Is: Studies in Melodrama and the Woman's Film* (London: BFI, 1987).

14. Chuck Kleinhans, "Notes on Melodrama and the Family under Capitalism," in *Imitations of Life: A Reader on Film and Television Melodrama*, ed. Marcia Landy (Detroit: Wayne State University Press, 1990), 203.

15. Wood, *Italian Cinema*, 106.

16. Ibid., 106.,

17. Günsberg, *Italian Cinema*, 27.

18. Pierre Sorlin, *Italian National Cinema, 1896–1996* (London: Routledge, 1996), 87.

19. Günsberg, *Italian Cinema*, 25.

20. Gundle, "Feminine Beauty, National Identity," 366.

21. Günsberg, *Italian Cinema*, 28.

22. Sergio Tofetti, "Dai telefoni bianchi alle bandiere rosse: genre, filoni, luoghi narrativi," in *Storia del cinema italiano, 1945–1948*, Vol. 7, ed. Callisto Cosulich (Venice: Marsilio, 2003), 285.

23. Gubitosi, *Amedeo Nazzari*, 11.

24. Ibid., 11.

25. Stephen Gundle, "Fame, Fashion, and Style," *Italian Cultural Studies: An In-*

troduction, ed. David Forgacs and Robert Lumley (Oxford: Oxford University Press, 1996), 315.

26. Alberto Farassino, "Viaggi del neorealismo: Rosa e altri colori," *Storia del cinema italiano: 1949–1952,* Vol. 8, ed. Luciano de Gusti (Venice: Marsilio, 2003): 213.

27. Wood, *Italian Cinema,* 161; see also Gubitosi, *Amedeo Nazzari,* 9.

28. Jacqueline Reich, *Beyond the Latin Lover: Marcello Mastroianni, Masculinity, and Italian Cinema* (Bloomington: Indiana University Press, 2004), 22.

29. Aldo Viganò, "La commedia all'italiana," in *Storia del cinema italiano: 1960–1964,* Vol. 10, ed. Giorgio Vincenti (Venice: Marsilio, 2001), 237.

30. David W. Ellwood, ed., *The Movies as History: Visions of the Twentieth Century* (Trowbridge, Wilts.: Sutton, 2000), 114.

31. Ibid., 114.

32. Valerio Caprara, "L'evoluzione del cinema comico; dal cinema autarchico alle parodie," in *Storia del cinema italiano: 1945–1948,* Vol. 7, ed. Callisto Cosulich (Venice: Marsilio, 2003), 295.

33. Ibid., 298.

34. Dario Fo, *Totò: Manuale dell' attor comico* (Florence: Vallecchi, 1995), 125.

35. Orio Caldiron, *Totò a colori di Steno: Il film, il personaggio, il mito* (Rome: Edizione Intercultural, 2003), 152.

36. David W. Ellwood, "Un Americano a Roma," *History Today* 46, no. 5 (May 1996): 46.

37. Reich, *Beyond the Latin Lover,* 22.

38. Ellwood, "Un americano," 44–49.

39. Enrico Giacovelli, *Un Italiano a Roma: La vita, i successi, le passioni di Alberto Sordi* (Turin: Lindau, 2003), 53.

40. Stephen Gundle, "From Neo-Realism to *Luci Rosse:* Cinema, Politics, and Society, 1945–85," in *Culture and Conflict in Postwar Italy: Essays on Mass and Popular Culture,* ed. Zygmunt G. Baránski and Robert Lumley (New York: St. Martin's, 1990), 216.

41. Jean A. Gili, "Alberto Sordi: J'ai toujours cherché à représenter la vie," *Positif* (June 2003), 59.

42. Ibid., 59.

43. Goffredo Fofi, *Alberto Sordi: L'Italia in bianco e nero* (Milan: Mondadori. 2004), 23.

44. Giacovelli, "Un italiano," 33.

45. Stefano Della Casa, *Storia e storie del cinema popolare* (Turin: La Stampa, 2001), 115.

46. Marco Chieffa, "Plebeo Impostore e inabilie: Da *I soliti ignoti* a *Brancaleone,*" in *Vittorio Gassman: L'ultimo mattatore,* ed. Fabrizio Deriu (Venice: Marsilio, 1999), 148.

47. Della Casa, *Storia e storie,* 67–68.

48. André Tournès, "Profession: Acteur, Vittorio Gassman," *Jeune Cinéma* no. 90 (Nov. 1975): 17.

49. Reich, *Beyond the Latin Lover,* 9.

50. Giacomo Gambetti, *Vittorio Gassman* (Rome: Gremese, 1999), 107.

51. Reich, *Beyond the Latin Lover,* 30–31.

52. Fabrizio Deriu, *Vittorio Gassman: L'ultimo mattatore* (Venice: Marsilio Press, 1999), 149.

53. Restivo, *The Cinema of Economic Miracles*, 57.

54. Della Casa, *Storia e storie*, 70–71.

55. Gambetti, *Vittorio Gassman*, 166.

56. Vitti, *Giuseppe de Santis*, 120.

57. Marcia Landy, *Italian Film* (Cambridge: Cambridge University Press, 2000), 331–334.

58. Bert Cardullo, Harry Geduld, Ronald Gottesman, and Leigh Woods, eds., *Playing to the Camera: Film Actors Discuss Their Craft* (New Haven: Yale University Press, 1998), 156.

59. Reich, *Beyond the Latin Lover*, 209–221.

60. Christopher Wagstaff, "Marcello Mastroianni," *Sight and Sound* 7, no. 3 (March 1997): 39.

61. Donald Dewey, *Marcello Mastroianni: His Life and Art* (New York: Birch Lane Press, 1993), 74.

62. Gilles Deleuze, *Cinema 2: The Time-Image*, trans. Hugh Tomlinson and Robert Galeta (Minneapolis: University of Minnesota Press, 1989), 3.

63. Peter Bondanella, *Italian Cinema: From Neorealism to the Present* (New York: Continuum, 2002), 243.

64. Adriano Aprà and Patrizia Pistagnesi, *Comedy, Italian Style, 1950–1980* (Turin: Edizione Radiotelevisione Italiana, 1986), 94.

65. In the changing portraits of sexual and gendered identity in Italian cinema, according to Reich, the male "inetto" is the complement to "the unruly woman"; *Beyond the Latin Lover*, 112.

66. Ibid., 112.

67. Of her reception in Italy, Vitti has commented that "the Italian comedies are more respected in France than in Italy"; Emmanuel Decaux and Bruno Villien, "Entretien avec Monica Vitti," *Cinématographe* no. 84 (Dec. 1982): 22–26.

68. Laura Delli Colli, *Monica Vitti* (Rome: Gremese, 1987), 25–26,

69. Stefano Masi and Enrico Lancia, *Italian Movie Goddesses: Over Eighty of the Greatest Women in Italian Cinema* (Rome: Gremese, 1992), 194.

70. See Delli Colli for a sample of reviews of Vitti's performance and comic persona in *Polvere di stele*; *Monica Vitti*, 115.

71. Restivo emphasizes that "the South [and femininity] becomes for the nation a site of displacement, the site upon which its own anxieties about the transformations wrought by modernization can be displaced"; *The Cinema of Economic Miracles*, 47.

72. Masi and Lancia, *Italian Movie Goddesses*, 83.

73. Ibid., 83.

74. Moya Luckett, "Travel and Mobility: Femininity and National Identity in Swinging London Films," *British Cinema: Past and Present*, ed. Justine Ashby and Andrew Higson (London: Routledge, 2000): 235–245.

75. Della Casa, *Storia e storie*, 42.

76. Christopher Frayling, *Spaghetti Westerns: Cowboys and Europeans from Karl May to Sergio Leone* (London: I. B. Tauris, 1998), 73.

77. Günsberg, *Italian Cinema*, 97–132.

78. Ibid., 100.

79. Arthur Marwick, *The Sixties: Cultural Revolution in Britain, France, Italy, and the United States, c. 1958–1974* (Oxford: Oxford University Press, 1998), 93–95, 173–177.

80. Frayling, *Spaghetti Westerns*, 70.

81. He directed Bertini in *La donna nuda* (The Nude Woman, 1918), *Eugenia Grandet* (1918), *Conquistador del mondo* (Conqueror of the World, 1919), Marion (1919), *La Contessa Sara* (1920), and La fanciulla d'Amalfi (Young Girl of Amalfi, 1921), among others, and Bartolomeo Pagano in *Polizziotto* (Policeman, 1917).

82. Della Casa, *Storia e storie*, 63–64.

83. Landy, *Italian Film*, 200–204.

84. Della Casa, *Storia e storie*, 59.

85. Fabio Piccione, *Due cialtroni alla rovescia: Studio sulla comicità* (Genoa: Fratelli, 2004), 56–62.

86. Della Casa, *Storia e storie*, 73.

87. Ibid., 75.

88. Adam Lowenstein, *Shocking Representations: Historical Trauma, National Cinema, and the Modern Horror Film* (New York: Columbia University Press, 2002).

89. David Pirie, *A Heritage of Horror, 1946–1972* (New York: Avon, 1973).

90. For a productive discussion of Italian horror as it connects to neorealism, the cinema books of Deleuze, and the films of Mario Bava, see Colette Balmain, "Mario Bava's Evil Eye: Realism and the Horror Film," *Post Script* 21, no. 3 (Summer 2002): 20–31.

91. Deleuze, *Cinema 2*, 3.

92. Della Casa, *Storia e storie*, 79.

93. Ibid., 80.

94. Ibid., 81.

95. Ibid., 81.

96. Ibid., 82.

97. Ibid., 82.

98. Günsberg, *Italian Cinema*, 172.

99. Mark A. Miller, "Barbara Steele: 'Diva of Dark Drama,'" *Filmfax* no. 51 (July/Aug. 1995): 38.

100. Christopher Duggan, *A Concise History of Italy* (Cambridge: Cambridge University Press, 1994), 286–289.

101. Milly Buonanno, "Recombinant Stories: Italian Television Fiction in 1996," in *Imaginary Dreamspaces: Television in Europe*, ed. Milly Buonanno (Luton, Beds.: University of Luton Press, 1998), 51–80.

102. Wood, *Italian Cinema*, 43–44.

103. Gian Piero Brunetta, *Storia del cinema italiano: Dal miracolo economico agli anni novanta 1960–1993*, vol. 4 (Rome: Riuniti, 2001), 164.

104. Ibid., 165.

105. Ibid., 166.

106. Masi and Lancia, *Italian Movie Goddesses*, 169; see also Stefano Reggiani, *Dizionario del postdivismo: Centuno attori italiani del cinema e della TV* (Turin: ERI, 1985), 149.

107. Zagarrio, *L'anello mancante*, 100.

108. Roger Ebert, "*Malèna*," *Chicago Sun Times*, 23 December 2000.

109. See Marcus Stiglegger, "Der Zauber von Monica: Anmerkungen von Phänomen Monica Belluccci," *Film-dienst* 48, no. 20 (2005): 6; and "Monica Bellucci," *Current Biography International Yearbook*, ed. Clifford Thompson and Miriam Helbok (New York: The Wilson Company, 2003–2004).

110. Masi and Lancia, *Italian Movie Goddesses*, 202.

111. Ibid., 202.

112. Barbara Creed, "The Cyberstar: Digital Pleasures and the End of the Unconscious," *Screen* 41, no. 1 (Spring 2000): 80.

5. Starring Directors and Directing Stars

1. Andrew Sarris, "Notes on the Auteur Theory in 1962," in *Film Theory and Criticism: Introductory Readings*, ed. Leo Braudy and Marshall Cohen (New York: Oxford University Press, 1999): 515–519.

2. Peter Bondanella, *Italian Cinema: From Neorealism to the Present* (New York: Continuum, 2002), 66.

3. Gilles Deleuze, *Cinema 1: The Movement-Image*, trans. Hugh Tomlinson and Barbara Habberjam (Minneapolis: University of Minnesota Press, 1986), 31–33.

4. Ibid., 157.

5. Deleuze, *Cinema 2: The Time-Image*, trans. Hugh Tomlinson and Robert Galeta (Minneapolis: University of Minnesota Press, 1989), 264.

6. Deleuze, *Cinema 1*, 197–215.

7. Lorenzo Pellizzari, "Il cinema pensato: tra liberazione e colonizzazione," in *Storia del cinema italiano: 1945–1948*, Vol. 7, ed. Callisto Cosulich (Venice: Marsilio, 2003), 471–476.

8. Barbara Corsi, *Con qualque dollaro in meno: Storia economica del cinema italiano* (Rome: Riuniti, 2001), 32–35.

9. Tony Judt, *Postwar: A History of Europe since 1945* (London: Penguin, 2005), 344–352.

10. Mary P. Wood, *Italian Cinema* (Oxford: Berg, 2005), 16.

11. Bondanella, *Italian Cinema*, 142.

12. Stefano Della Casa, *Storia e storie del cinema popolare* (Turin: La Stampa, 2001), 67–72.

13. Deleuze, *Cinema 2*, 20, 22.

14. For an analysis of the critical context for the creation of *Ossessione*, its connections to neorealism, its divergences from the James M. Cain novel, and a close examination of the text, see Lino Miccichè, *Visconti e il neorealismo: Ossessione, La terra trema, Bellissima* (Venice: Marsilio, 1998): 27–72.

15. David Forgacs, "Sex in the Cinema," in *Re-viewing Fascism: Italian Cinema 1922–1943*, ed. Jacqueline Reich and Piero Garofolo (Bloomington: Indiana University Press, 2002), 166.

16. Deleuze, *Cinema 2*, 4.

17. Antonio Gramsci, *Selections from the Cultural Writings*, ed. David Forgacs and Geoffrey Nowell-Smith, trans. William Boelhower (Cambridge: Harvard University Press, 1985), 203.

18. Miccichè, *Visconti e il neorealismo*, 200, 205–206.

19. Stefano Masi and Enrico Lancia, *Stelle d'Italia: piccole e grandi dive del cinema italiano* (Rome: Gremese, 1994), 38.

20. David W. Ellwood, *The Movies as History: Visions of the Twentieth Century* (Trowbridge, Wilts.: Sutton, 2000), 175–176.

21. Deleuze, *Cinema 2*, 96.

22. Peter Brunette, *Roberto Rossellini* (New York: Oxford University Press, 1987), 88.

23. Stephen Gundle, "Saint Ingrid at the Stake: Stardom and Scandal in the Bergman-Rossellini Collaboration," in *Roberto Rossellini: Magician of the Real,* ed. David Forgacs, Sarah Lutton, and Geoffrey Nowell-Smith (London: BFI, 2000), 71.

24. Ibid., 72.

25. Ibid., 73.

26. Ibid., 74.

27. James Damico, "Ingrid from Lorraine to Stromboli: Analyzing the Public's Perception of a Film Star," in *Star Texts: Image and Performance in Film and Television,* ed. Jeremy Butler (Detroit: Wayne State University Press, 1991), 249.

28. Giuliana Bruno, *Atlas of Emotion: Journeys in Art, Architecture, and Film* (New York: Verso, 2002), 384–385.

29. Brunette, *Rossellini,* 164.

30. Deleuze, *Cinema* 1, 212.

31. Brunette, *Rossellini,* 162.

32. Ibid., 175.

33. Peter Bondanella, *The Films of Federico Fellini* (Cambridge: Cambridge University Press, 2002).

34. Masi and Lancia, *Stelle d'Italia,* 73.

35. Ibid., 72.

36. Stephen Gundle, "La dolce vita," in *The Movies as History: Visions of the Twentieth Century,* ed. David W. Elwood (Trowbridge, Wilts.: Sutton, 2000), 132–140.

37. Ibid., 134.

38. Reich, *Beyond the Latin Lover: Marcello Mastroianni, Masculinity, and Italian Cinema* (Bloomington: Indiana University Press, 2004), 45.

39. Landy, *Italian Film,* 332.

40. Bondanella, *The Cinema of Federico Fellini,* 142.

41. Millicent Marcus writes that "The collaboration between the two characters in the narrative enables Fellini at once to reflect on his life with Giulietta Masina and to unify the elements of his filmography." See *After Fellini: National Cinema in the Postmodern Age* (Baltimore: Johns Hopkins University Press, 2002), 184.

42. Reich, *Beyond the Latin Lover,* 152.

43. Peter Brunette, *The Films of Michelangelo Antonioni* (Cambridge: Cambridge University Press, 1998), 14–19; see recent critical discussion of his work by Mark Le Fanu in "No Place Like the Present," *Sight and Sound,* July 2006, 36.

44. Francesco Casetti, "Cinema in the Cinema in Italian Films of the Fifties: *Bellissima* and *La signora senza camelie,*" *Screen* 33, no. 4 (Winter 1992): 375–393.

45. Antonio Vitti, *Giuseppe De Santis and Postwar Italian Cinema* (Toronto: University of Toronto Press, 1996), 105.

46. For a discussion of the formal elements of this film, see Peter Brunette, "*Deserto rosso/ Red Desert,*" in Giorgio Bertellini, ed., *The Cinema of Italy* (London: Wallflower, 2004), 153–162.

47. Laura Delli Colli, *Monica Vitti* (Rome: Gremese, 1987), 27.

48. Landy, *Italian Film,* 299.

49. Deleuze, *Cinema* 2, 49. Also see Pier Paolo Pasolini, *Heretical Empiricism,* trans. Ben Lawton and Louise Barnett (Bloomington: Indiana University Press, 1988), 179–180.

50. Maurizio Viano, *A Certain Realism: Making Use of Pasolini's Film Theory and Practice* (Berkeley: University of California Press, 1993).

51. Ibid., 90.

52. Bruno, *Atlas of Emotion*, 33.

53. Viano, *A Certain Realism*, 85.

54. Ibid., 90.

55. Pierre Sorlin, *Italian National Cinema 1896–1996* (London: Routledge, 1996), 113.

56. Orio Caldiron, *Totò* (Rome: Gremese, 2001), 163.

57. Fo, *Totò: Manuale dell' attor comico*, 86–89.

58. Viano, *A Certain Realism*, 153.

59. Ibid., 154.

60. Bondanella, *Italian Cinema*, 361.

61. Millicent Marcus, *After Fellini*, 289.

62. Wood, *Italian Cinema*, 132.

63. Stefano Masi, *Roberto Benigni: Superstar* (Rome: Gremese, 1999).

64. David Denby, "In the Eye of the Beholder: Another Look at Benigni's Holocaust Fantasy," *The New Yorker*, 15 March 1999, 98.

65. Pamela Kroll, "Games of Disappearance and Return: War and the Child in Roberto Benigni's *Life Is Beautiful*," *Literature Film Quarterly* 39, no. 1 (2002): 29–45.

66. Giorgio Agamben, *Means without End: Notes on Politics*, trans. Vincenzo Binetti and Cesare Casarino (Minneapolis: University of Minnesota Press, 2000), 59–60.

67. Ibid., 78.

68. Adam Lowenstein, *Shocking Representations: Historical Trauma, National Cinema, and the Modern Horror Film* (New York: Columbia University Press, 2005).

69. Daniele Costantini and Francesco Dal Bosco, *Nuovo cinema inferno: L'opera di Dario Argento* (Milan: Nuova Pratiche, 1997), 60.

70. Della Casa, *Storia e storie*, 102.

71. Ibid., 102.

72. Kim Newman, "Profondo rosso," *Monthly Film Bulletin* 52, no. 610 (1984): 349–350.

73. Chris Gallant, ed. *Art of Darkness: The Cinema of Dario Argento* (Godalming, Surrey: FAB Press, 2001), 210; Maitland McDonagh, "The Elegant Brutality of Dario Argento," *Film Comment* 29, no. 1 (Jan./Feb. 1993): 55.

74. Jean-Baptiste Thoret, *Dario Argento: Magicien de la peur* (Paris: Cahiers du Cinéma, 2002), 24.

75. Ibid., 110–111.

76. For a discussion of the material preservation of films as well as a revaluation of the history and constantly altering character of the moving image from the past to the present, see Paolo Cherchi Usai's controversial *The Death of Cinema: History, Cultural Memory and the Digital Dark Age* (London: BFI, 2001).

Epilogue

1. Stephen Gundle, "Television in Italy," in *Television in Europe*, ed. James A. Coleman and Brigitte Rollet (Exeter, Devon: Intellect, 1997), 74.

2. Rinella Cere, *European and National Identities in Britain and Italy: Maastricht on Television* (Lewiston, N.Y.: Edwin Mellen, 2000), 89.

3. Gundle, "Television in Italy," 74.

4. Barbara Corsi, *Con qualque dollaro in meno: Storia economica del cinema italiano* (Rome: Riuniti, 2001), 140–141.

5. Vito Zagarrio, *L'anello mancante: storia e teoria del rapporto cinema-television* (Turin: Lindau, 2004), 114–120.

6. D. N. Rodowick, *Gilles Deleuzes's Time Machine* (Durham, N.C.: Duke University Press, 1997), 6.

7. Steven Shaviro, *The Cinematic Body* (Minneapolis: University of Minnesota, 1993), 32.

A Postscript

1. Paul Ginsborg, *Silvio Berlusconi: Television, Power and Patrimony* (London: Verso, 2004), 110.

2. Ibid., 111.

3. Stephen Gundle, "Television in Italy," in *Television in Europe*, ed. James A. Coleman and Brigitte Rollet (Exeter, Devon: Intellect, 1997), 74.

4. John Ellis, *Visible Fictions: Cinema, Television, Video* (London: Routledge and Kegan Paul, 1982), 97.

5. Richard Dyer, *Stars* (London: BFI, 1986), 39.

6. Ginsborg, *Silvio Berlusconi*, 110–111.

7. Gilles Deleuze, *Cinema 2: The Time-Image*, trans. Hugh Tomlinson and Robert Galeta (Minneapolis: University of Minnesota Press, 1989), 265.

8. Ellis, *Visible Fictions*, 128.

Bibliography

Agamben, Giorgio. *Means without End: Notes on Politics*. Trans. Vincenzo Binetti and Cesare Casarino. Minneapolis: University of Minnesota Press, 2000.

Alonge, Giaime, Giulia Carluccio, and Federica Villa, eds. *La Valle dell' Eden*. Turin: Carocci, 2004.

Alovisio, Silvio. "The 'Pastrone System': Itala Film from the Origins to World War 1." *Film History* 12, no. 3 (2000): 250–262.

Andrew, Dudley. "André Bazin's 'Evolution.'" In *Defining Cinema*, ed. Peter Lehman. New Brunswick, N.J.: Rutgers University Press, 1997. 73–96.

Anile, Alberto. *Il cinema di Totò, 1930–1945: L'estro funambolo e l'almeno spettro*. Genoa: Le Mani, 1997.

Aprà, Adriano, and Jean Gili. *Naples et le cinéma*. Paris: Fabbri, 1994.

Aprà, Adriano, and Patrizia Pistagnesi. *Comedy, Italian Style, 1950–1980*. Turin: Edizione Radiotelevisione Italiana, 1986.

———. *I favolosi anni trenta: Cinema italiano 1929–1944*. Milan: Electa, 1979.

Argentieri, Mino. *Risate di regime: La commedia italiana 1930–1944*. Venice: Marsilio, 1991.

Bachmann, Gideon. "Marcello Mastroianni and the Game of Truth." *Film Quarterly* 46, no. 2 (Winter 1992–1993): 2–7.

Balmain, Colette. "Mario Bava's Evil Eye: Realism and the Italian Horror Film." *Post Script* 21, no. 3 (Summer 2002): 20–31.

Baudet, François. *Fashion in the Twentieth Century.* New York: Universe, 1999.

Bazin, André. *What Is Cinema?* Vol. 1. Berkeley: University of California Press, 1967.

——. *What Is Cinema?* Vol. 2. Berkeley: University of California Press, 1972.

Ben-Ghiat, Ruth. *Fascist Modernities: Italy 1922–1945.* Berkeley: University of California Press, 2004.

Benjamin, Walter. *Origin of German Tragic Drama.* Trans. John Osborne. London: Verso, 1998.

——. "The Work of Art in the Age of Mechanical Reproduction." In *Illuminations,* ed. Hannah Arendt, trans. Harry Zohn. New York: Schocken Books, [1968] 1976.

Bergfelder, Tim. "The Nation Vanishes: European Co-Productions and Popular Genre Formulae in the 1950s and 1960s." In *Cinema and Nation,* ed. Mette Hjort and Scott Mackenzie. London: Routledge, 2000. 139–152.

Bergman, Ingrid, and Alan Burgess. *Ingrid Bergman: My Story.* New York: Delacorte, 1972.

Bertellini, Giorgio. "*Profondo rosso/Deep Red.*" In *The Cinema of Italy,* ed. Giorgio Bertellini. London: Wallflower, 2004. 213–225.

Bertini, Francesca. *Il resto non conta.* Pisa: Guardini, 1969.

Bettetini, Gianfranco, ed. *Sipario!: Storia e modelli del teatro televiso in Italia.* Turin: RAI, 1989.

Bondanella, Peter. *The Films of Federico Fellini.* Cambridge: Cambridge University Press, 2002.

——. *The Films of Roberto Rossellini.* New York: Cambridge University Press, 1993.

——. *Italian Cinema: From Neorealism to the Present.* New York: Continuum, 2002.

Borsatti, Cristina. *Monica Vitti.* Palermo: L'Epos, 2006.

Bosworth, R. J. B. *Mussolini.* London: Arnold, 2002.

Brooks, Peter. *The Melodramatic Imagination.* New York: Columbia University Press, 1985.

Brunetta, Gian Piero. *Cinema italiano tra le due guerre: Fascismo e politica cinematografica.* Milan: Mursia, 1975.

——. "In the Name of the Diva." In *Passion and Defiance: Silent Divas of Italian Cinema,* ed. Angela Dalle Vacche and Gian Luca Farinelli. Milan: Olivares, 2000.

——. "Italian Cinema and the Hard Road to Democracy, 1945." *Historical Journal of Film, Radio, and Television* 15, no. 3 (1995): 343–348.

——. "The Long March of American Cinema in Italy: From Fascism to the Cold War." In *Hollywood in Europe: Experiences of a Cultural Hegemony,* ed. David E. Ellwood and Rob Kroes. Amsterdam: VU University Press. 139–155.

——. *Storia del cinema italiano: Dal miracolo economico agli anni novanta 1960–1993.* Vol. 4. Rome: Riuniti, 2001.

——. *Storia del cinema italiano: Dal neorealismo al miracolo economico, 1945-1959.* Vol. 3. Rome: Riuniti, 2001.

——. *Storia del cinema italiano: Il cinema del regime, 1929–1945.* Vol. 2. Rome: Riuniti, 2001.

——. *Storia del cinema italiano: Il cinema muto 1895–1929.* Vol. 1. Rome: Riuniti, 2001.

——. *Storia del cinema mondiale.* Vol. 1. Venice: Giulio Einaudi, 1999.

Brunette, Peter. "*Deserto rosso/Red Desert,*" in *The Cinema of Italy,* ed. Giorio Bertellini. London: Wallflower, 2004. 153–163.

——. *The Films of Michelangelo Antonioni.* Cambridge: Cambridge University Press, 1998.

———. *Roberto Rossellini*. New York: Oxford University Press, 1987.

Bruno, Giuliana. *Atlas of Emotion: Journeys in Art, Architecture, and Film*. New York: Verso, 2002.

———. *Streetwalking on a Ruined Map: Cultural Theory and the Films of Elvira Notari*. Princeton, N.J.: Princeton University Press, 1993.

Buccheri, Vincenzo. *Stile Cines: Studi sul cinema italiano 1930–1934*. Milan: Vita e Pensiero, 2004.

Buck-Morss, Susan. *The Dialectics of Seeing: Walter Benjamin and the Arcades Project*. Cambridge, Mass.: MIT Press, 1997.

Buckley, Réka C. V., "National Body: Gina Lollobrigida and the Cult of the Star in the 1950s." *Historical Journal of Film, Radio, and Television* 20, no. 4 (2000): 527–547.

Buonanno, Milly, ed. *Imaginary Dreamscapes: Television Fiction in Europe*. Luton, Beds.: University of Luton Press, 1998.

Butler, Jeremy G. *Star Texts: Image and Performance in Film and Television*. Detroit: Wayne State University Press, 1991.

Caldiron, Orio. *Totò*. Rome: Gremese, 2001.

———, ed. *Totò a colori di Steno: Il film, il personaggio, il mito*. Rome: Edizione Inter-cultural, 2003.

Campisciano, Antonina. "Body As Text: Lyda Borelli in *Malombra*." In *Pagina, Pellic-ola, Pratica: Studi sul cinema italiano*, ed. Rebecca West. Ravenna: Longo, 2000. 57–68.

Canosa, Michele. "Febo Mari Vigilò l'esecuzione." In *A nuova luce*, ed. Michele Canosa and Antonio Costa. Bologna: *Fotogenia* 4/5 (1999): 149–165.

Canosa, Michele, and Antonio Costa, eds. *A nuova luce*. Bologna: *Fotogenia* 4/5 (1999).

Cantatore, Lorenzo, and Giuliano Falconi. *La signora Magnani: Antologia di Ritratti e conversazione*. Rome: Edilazio, 2001.

Caprara, Valerio, "L'evoluzione del cinema comico; dal cinema autarchico alle paro-die." In *Storia del cinema italiano: 1945–1948*, ed. Callisto Cosulich. Vol. 7. Venice: Marsilio, 2003. 288–299.

Cardinale, Claudia, Vittorio Gassman, Sophia Loren, Marcello Mastroianni, Stefania Sandrelli, and Ugo Tognazzi. "Acting Italian Style." *Film Comment* 19, no. 2 (April 1983): 46–47.

Cardullo, Bert, Harry Geduld, Ronald Gottesman, and Leigh Woods, eds. *Playing to the Camera: Film Actors Discuss Their Craft*. New Haven: Yale University Press, 1998.

Carrano, Patrizia. *La Magnani*. Milan: Rizzoli, 1982.

Casadio, G., E. G. Laura, and F. Cristiano. *Telefoni bianchi: Realtà e finzione nella so-cietà e nel cinema degli anni quaranta*. Ravenna: Longo, 1991.

Casetti, Francesco. "Cinema in the Cinema in Italian Films of the Fifties: *Bellissima* and *La signora senza camelie*." *Screen* 33, no. 4 (Winter 1992): 375–393.

———. "The Place of the Observer." *Cinema et Cie: International Film Studies Journal* no. 5 (Fall 2004): 10–18.

Casetti, Francesco, and Mariagrazia Fanchi, eds. *Cinema et Cie, International Film Studies Journal* no. 5 (Fall 2004): 52–63.

Castello, Giulio Cesare. *Il divismo: Mitologia del cinema*. Italy: Edizione Radio Italiana, 1957.

Cavell, Stanley. *The World Viewed: Reflections on the Ontology of Film*. New York: Vi-king, 1974.

Celli, Carlo. *The Divine Comic: The Cinema of Roberto Benigni*. Lanham, Md.: Scarecrow, 2001.

Cere, Rinella. *European and National Identities in Britain and Italy: Maastricht on Television*. Lewiston, N.Y.: Edwin Mellen, 2000.

Cherchi Usai, Paolo, *The Death of Cinema: History, Cultural Memory and the Digital Dark Age*. London: BFI, 2001.

———. *Giovani Pastrone*. Rome: La nuova Italia, 1986.

Chieffa, Marco. "Plebeo Impostore e inabilie: Da *I soliti ignoti* a *Brancaleone*." In *Vittorio Gassman: L'ultimo mattatore*, ed. Fabrizio Deriu. Venice: Marsilio, 1999. 147–157.

Chion, Michael. *The Voice in Cinema*. Ed. and trans. Claudia Gorbman. New York: Columbia University Press, 1999.

Cimmino, Giovanni, and Stefano Masi. *Silvana Mangano: Il teorema della bellezza*. Rome: Gremese, 1994.

Codelli, Lorenzo. "Alberto Sordi 1920–2003: Nôtre 'Albertone.'" *Positif* (June 2003): 56–61.

Coleman, James A., and Brigitte Rollet. *Television in Europe*. Exeter, Devon: Intellect, 1997.

Comuzio, Ermanno. "De Sica o della doppia constante: Il sorriso e il tarlo segreto." *Cineforum* 15, no. 140 (1975): 29–37.

Corsi, Barbara. *Con qualque dollaro in meno: Storia economica del cinema italiano*. Rome: Riuniti, 2001.

Costa, Antonio. "*Malombra* sul schermo: da Gallone à Soldati." In *Antonio Fogazzaro. Filologia Veneta* IV. Padua: Esdra, 1994. 231–250.

———. "Muto di luce." In *A nuova luce*, ed. Michele Canosa and Antonio Costa. Bologna: *Fotogenia* 4/5 (1999): 8–27.

———. "Risotto con i tartufi: Soldati, Fogazzaro e il calligrafismo." In *La bella forma: Poggioli, I calligrafici, e dintorni*. Venice: Marsilio, 1992. 95–105.

Costa, Nicolò. *Il divismo e il comico*. Turin: RAI, 1982.

Costantini, Daniele, and Francesco Dal Bosco. *Nuovo cinema inferno: L'opera di Dario Argento*. Milan: Nuova Pratiche, 1997.

Cosulich, Callisto, ed. *Storia del cinema italiano: 1945–1948*. Vol. 7. Venice: Marsilio, 2003.

Creed, Barbara. "The Cyberstar: Digital Pleasures and the End of the Unconscious." *Screen* 41, no. 1 (Spring 2000): 79–86.

Crowdus, Gary. "The Lack of Historical Memory: An Interview with Gianni Amelio." *Cineaste* 28, no. 1 (Winter 2002): 15–19.

Curle, Howard, and Stephen Snyder. *Vittorio De Sica: Contemporary Perspectives*. Toronto: University of Toronto Press, 2000.

Dall' Asta, Monica. "La diffusione del film a episodi in Europa." In *Storia del cinema mondiale*, ed. Gian Piero Brunetta. Venice: Einaudi, 1999. 277–315.

Dalle Vacche, Angela. *The Body in the Mirror: The Shapes of History in Italian Cinema*. Princeton, N.J.: Princeton University Press, 1992.

Dalle Vacche, Angela, and Gian Luca Farinelli. *Passion and Defiance: Silent Divas of Italian Cinema*. Milan: Olivares, 2000.

Damico, James. "Ingrid from Lorraine to Stromboli: Analyzing the Public's Perception of a Film Star." In *Star Texts: Image and Performance in Film and Television*, ed. Jeremy Butler. Detroit: Wayne State University Press, 1991. 240–254.

De Berti, Raffaele. *Dallo schermo alla carta: Romanzo, Fotoromanzi, rotocalchi, cinematografici: il film e suo paratesti.* Milan: Vita e Pensiero, 2000.

———. "La signora di tutti e l'avvento del divismo italiano." In *Light from a Star,* ed. Elena Mosconi. Cremona: Persico, 2003. 31–43.

Decaux, Emmanuel, and Bruno Villein. "Entretien avec Monica Vitti." *Cinématographe* no. 84 (Dec. 1982): 22–26.

de Grazia, Victoria. *The Culture of Consent: Mass Organization of Leisure in Fascist Italy.* Cambridge: Cambridge University Press, 1981.

———. *How Fascism Ruled Women: Italy, 1922–1945.* Berkeley: University of California Press, 1992.

Deleuze, Gilles. *Cinema 1: The Movement-Image.* Trans. Hugh Tomlinson and Barbara Habberjam. Minneapolis: University of Minnesota Press, 1986.

———. *Cinema 2: The Time-Image.* Trans. Hugh Tomlinson and Robert Galeta. Minneapolis: University of Minnesota Press, 1989.

Della Casa, Stefano. *Storia e storie del cinema popolare.* Turin: La Stampa, 2001.

Delli Colli, Laura. *Monica Vitti.* Rome: Gremese, 1987.

Denby, David. "In the Eye of the Beholder: Another Look at Benigni's Holocaust Fantasy." *The New Yorker,* 15 March 1999, 96–99.

Deriu, Fabrizio. *Vittorio Gassman: L'ultimo mattatore.* Venice: Marsilio, 1999.

Dewey, Donald. *Marcello Mastroianni: His Life and Art.* New York: Birch Lane, 1993.

Doane, Mary Ann. *Femmes Fatales: Feminism, Film Theory, Psychoanalysis.* New York: Routledge, 1991.

Duggan, Christopher. *A Concise History of Italy.* Cambridge: Cambridge University Press, 1994.

Dunnage, Jonathan. *Twentieth Century Italy: A Social History.* London: Longman, 2002.

Dyer, Richard. *Heavenly Bodies: Film Stars and Society.* London: British Film Institute, 1986.

———. *Stars.* London: BFI, [1979] 1986.

Eisner, Lotte. *The Haunted Screen.* Berkeley: University of California Press, 1977.

Ellis, John. *Visible Fictions: Cinema, Television, Video.* London: Routledge and Kegan Paul, 1982.

Ellwood, David W. "Un Americano a Roma." *History Today* 46, no. 5 (May 1996): 45–49.

———, ed. *The Movies as History: Visions of the Twentieth Century.* Trowbridge, Wilts.: Sutton, 2000.

Ellwood, David W., and Rob Kroes, eds. *Hollywood in Europe: Experiences of a Cultural Hegemony.* Amsterdam: VU University Press, 1994.

Elsaesser, Thomas, and Adam Barker, eds. *Early Cinema: Space, Frame, Narrative.* London: BFI, 1990.

Escobar, Roberto. *Totò.* Bologna: Il Mulino, 1998.

Euromedia Research Group. *The Media in Western Europe: The Euromedia Handbook.* London: Sage, 1992.

Fanchi, Mariagrazia, and Elena Mosconi, eds. *Spettatori: Forme di consumo e publici del cinema in Italia 1930–1960.* Rome: Bianco e Nero, 2002.

Farassino, Alberto. "Margini, attraversamenti, contaminazioni." In *Storia del cinema italiano: 1945–1948,* ed. Callisto Cosulich. Vol. 7. Venice: Marsilio, 2003. 156–171.

———. *Mario Camerini: Sous la direction de Alberto Farassino.* Locarno, Editions du Festival international du film de Locarno; Belgium: Editions Yellow Now, 1992.

——. "Viaggi del neorealismo: Rosa e altri colori." In *Storia del cinema italiano: 1949–1953*, ed. Luciano de Gusti. Vol. 8. Venice: Marsilio, 2003. 203–222.

Farassino, Alberto, and Tatti Sanguinetti, eds. *Gli uomini forti*. Milan: Mazzotta, 1983.

Fava, Claudio G., with Umberto Tani and Enrico Lancia. *Alberto Sordi*. Rome: Gremese, 2003.

Ferroni, Giulio. *Storia della letteratura Italiana*. Milan: Einaudi, 1991.

Fo, Dario. *Totò: Manuale dell' attor comico*. Florence: Vallecchi, 1995.

Fofi, Goffredo. *Alberto Sordi: L'Italia in bianco e nero*. Milan: Mondadori, 2004.

Fogazzaro, Antonio. *Malombra*. Milan: Mondadori, 1978.

Foot, John. *Modern Italy*. Houndmills, Basingstoke, Hants.: Palgrave Macmillan, 2003.

Forgacs, David. *Italian Culture in the Industrial Era 1880–1980: Cultural Industries, Politics, and the Public*. Manchester: Manchester University Press, 1990.

——. *Rome Open City*. London: BFI, 2000.

——. "Sex in the Cinema: Regulation and Transgression in Italian Films, 1930–1943." In *Re-viewing Fascism: Italian Cinema, 1922–1943*, ed. Jacqueline Reich and Piero Garofolo. Bloomington: Indiana University Press, 2002. 141–171.

——. "Space, Rhetoric and the Divided City." In *Roberto Rossellini's* Rome Open City, ed. Sidney Gottlieb. Cambridge: Cambridge University Press, 2004.

Forgacs, David, Sarah Lutton, and Geoffrey Nowell-Smith, eds. *Roberto Rossellini: Magician of the Real*. London: BFI, 2000.

Frayling, Christopher. *Spaghetti Westerns: Cowboys and Europeans from Karl May to Sergio Leone*. London: I. B. Tauris, 1998.

Gallagher, Tag. *The Adventures of Roberto Rossellini: His Life and Times*. New York: Da Capo, 1998.

Gallant, Chris, ed. *Art of Darkness: The Cinema of Dario Argento*. Godalming, Surrey: FAB Press, 2001.

Gambetti, Giacomo. *Vittorio Gassman*. Rome: Gremese, 1999.

Giacovelli, Enrico. *Un Italiano a Roma: La vita, i successi, le passioni di Alberto Sordi*. Turin: Lindau, 2003.

Gili, Jean A. "Alberto Sordi: J'ai toujours cherché à représenter la vie." *Positif* (June 2003): 59–61.

——. "Être cinéaste en Italie pendant les années du fascisme." *Dossier Mario Camerini. Positif* no. 301 (March 1986): 38–43.

——. "Terzo tempo: retrospective Mario Camerini." *Positif* no. 384 (Feb. 1993): 70–71.

——. "Vittorio Gassman le magnifique 1922–2000." *Positif* no. 476 (2000): 70–77.

——. "Vittorio Gassman: L'homme aux cent visages." *Écran* no. 40 (Oct. 1975): 21–34.

Ginsberg, Terri. "Nazis and Drifters: The Containment of Radical (Sexual) Knowledge in Two Italian Neorealist Films." *Journal of the History of Sexuality* 1, no. 2 (1990): 241–261.

Ginsborg, Paul. *A History of Contemporary Italy, Society and Politics, 1943–1988*. London: Penguin, 1990.

——. *Italy and Its Discontents: Family, Civil Society, State: 1980–2001*. New York: Palgrave Macmillan, 2003.

——. *Silvio Berlusconi: Television, Power and Patrimony*. London: Verso, 2004.

Giusti, Marco. *Il grande libro di Carosello*. Piacenza: Sperling and Kupfer, 1999.

Gledhill, Christine, ed. *Home Is Where the Heart Is: Studies in Melodrama and the Woman's Film*. London: BFI, 1987.

———. *Stardom: Industry of Desire*. London: Routledge, 1991.

Gori, Gianfranco Mino. *Patria diva*. Florence: Usher, 1988.

Gottlieb, Sidney, ed. *Roberto Rossellini's* Rome Open City. Cambridge: Cambridge University Press, 2004.

Governi, Giancarlo. *Vittorio De Sica: Parlami d'amore Mariù*. Rome: Gremese, 1993.

Gramsci, Antonio. *Letteratura e vita nazionale*. Turin: Einaudi, 1972.

———. *Quaderni del carcere*, ed. Valentino Gerratana. 4 vols. Turin: Einaudi, 1977.

———. *Selections from the Cultural Writings*. Ed. David Forgacs and Geoffrey Nowell-Smith. Trans. William Boelhower. Cambridge: Harvard University Press, 1985.

———. *Selections from the Prison Notebooks of Antonio Gramsci*, ed. and trans. Quintin Hoare and Geoffrey Nowell-Smith. New York: International Publishers, 1971.

Grandi, Maurizio, and Franco Pecori. "Neorealismo, Istituzioni e procedimenti." In *Il Neorealismo Cinematografico italiano*, ed. Lino Micciché. Venice: Marsilio, 1975. 192–203.

Grignaffini, Giovanna. "Female Identity and the Italian Cinema of the 1950s." In *Off Screen: Women and Film in Italy*, ed. Giuliana Bruno and Maria Nadotti. London: Routledge, 1988.

Grmek Germani, Sergio. *Mario Camerini*. Florence: La Nuova Italia, 1980.

Guarner, José Luis. *Roberto Rossellini*. Trans. Elizabeth Cameron. New York: Praeger, 1970.

Gubitosi, Giuseppe. *Amedeo Nazzari*. Bologna: Mulino, 1998.

Gundle, Stephen. "La dolce vita." In *The Movies as History: Visions of the Twentieth Century*, ed. David W. Elwood. Trowbridge, Wilts.: Sutton, 2000. 132–140.

———. "Fame, Fashion, and Style: The Italian Star System." In *Italian Cultural Studies: An Introduction*, ed. David Forgacs and Robert Lumley. Oxford: Oxford University Press, 1996. 309–324.

———. "Feminine Beauty, National Identity and Political Conflict in Postwar Italy." *Contemporary European History* 8, no. 3 (1999): 359–378.

———. "Film Stars and Society in Fascist Italy." In *Re-viewing Fascism: Italian Cinema, 1922–1943*, ed. Jacqueline Reich and Piero Garofalo. Bloomington: Indiana University Press, 2002. 315–339.

———. "From Neo-Realism to Luci Rosse: Cinema, Politics, and Society, 1945–85." In *Culture and Conflict in Postwar Italy: Essays on Mass and Popular Culture*, ed. Zygmunt G. Baránski and Robert Lumley. New York: St. Martin's, 1990. 195–224.

———. "Saint Ingrid at the Stake: Stardom and Scandal in the Bergman-Rossellini Collaboration." In *Roberto Rossellini: Magician of the Real*, ed. David Forgacs, Sarah Lutton, and Geoffrey Nowell-Smith. London: BFI, 2000. 64–80.

———. "Sophia Loren, Italian Icon." *Historical Journal of Film, Radio, and Television* 15, no. 3 (1995): 367–385.

———. "Television in Italy." In *Television in Europe*, ed. James A. Coleman and Brigitte Rollet. Exeter, Devon: Intellect, 1997. 62–77.

Günsberg, Maggie. *Italian Cinema, Gender and Genre*. Houndsmills, Basingstoke, Hants.: Palgrave, 2005.

Haarman, Louann. *Talk about Shows: La parola e lo spettacolo*. Bologna: CLUEB, 1999.

Hansen, Miriam. "Pleasure, Ambivalence, Identification: Valentino and Female Spectatorship." In *Star Texts: Image and Performance in Film and Television*, ed. Jeremy G. Butler. Detroit: Wayne State University Press, 1991. 266–299.

Hay, James. *Popular Film Culture in Fascist Italy: The Passing of the Rex*. Bloomington: Indiana University Press, 1987.

——. "Placing the Cinema, Fascism, the Nation in a Diagram of Italian Modernity." In *Re-viewing Fascism: Italian Cinema, 1922–1943*, ed. Jacqueline Reich and Piero Garofalo. Bloomington: Indiana University Press, 2002. 105–141.

Hjort, Mette, and Scott McKenzie, eds. *Cinema and Nation*. London: Routledge, 2000.

Hochkofler, Matilde. *Anna Magnani*. Rome: Gremese, 2001.

——. *Marcello Mastroianni: il gioco del cinema*. Rome: Gremese, 1992.

Hope, William, ed., *Italian Cinema: New Directions*. Oxford: Peter Lang, 2005.

Hunt, Leon. "A Sadistic Night at the Opera: Notes on the Italian Horror Film." *Velvet Light Trap* no. 30 (Fall 1992): 65–75.

Jensen, Paul M. *The Men Who Made the Monsters*. New York: Prentice-Hall, 1996.

Jones, Alan. *Profondo Argento: The Man, the Myths, and the Magic*. Godalming, Surrey: FAB Press, 2004.

Judt, Tony. *Postwar: A History of Europe since 1945*. London: Penguin, 2005.

Kickasola, Joseph. "Contemporary Media and the Evolving Notion of Immediacy." *Quarterly Review of Film and Media* 23, no. 4 (2006): 299–311.

Kleinhans, Chuck. "Notes on Melodrama and the Family under Capitalism." In *Imitations of Life: A Reader on Film and Television Melodrama*, ed. Marcia Landy. Detroit: Wayne State University Press, 1991. 197–205.

Kroll, Pamela. "Games of Disappearance and Return: War and the Child in Roberto Benigni's *Life Is Beautiful*." *Literature Film Quarterly* 39, no. 1 (2002): 29–45.

Landy, Marcia. *Fascism in Film: The Italian Commercial Cinema, 1929–1943*. Princeton, N.J.: Princeton University Press, 1986.

——. *The Folklore of Consensus: Theatricality in the Italian Cinema, 1930–1943*. Albany: SUNY Press, 1998.

——. *Italian Film*. London: Cambridge University Press, 2000.

Lastra, James. *Sound Technology and the American Cinema: Perception, Reception, Modernity*. New York: Columbia University Press, 2000.

Le Fanu, Mark. "No Place like the Present." *Sight and Sound*, July 2006, 34–38.

Ledeen, Michael A. *The First Duce: D'Annunzio at Fiume*. Baltimore: Johns Hopkins University Press, 1977.

Leprohon, Pierre. *Italian Cinema*. New York: Praeger, 1972.

Lovell, Alan, and Peter Krämer. *Screen Acting*. London: Routledge, 1999.

Lowenstein, Adam. *Shocking Representations: Historical Trauma, National Cinema, and the Modern Horror Film*. New York: Columbia University Press, 2002.

Luckett, Moya. "Travel and Mobility: Femininity and National Identity in Swinging London Films." In *British Cinema: Past and Present*, ed. Justine Ashby and Andrew Higson. London: Routledge, 2000. 235–245.

Luzzatto, Sergio. *The Body of Il Duce: Mussolini's Corpse and the Fortunes of Italy*. Trans. Frederika Randall. New York: Henry Holt, 2005.

Mancini, Elaine. *Struggles of the Italian Film Industry during Fascism, 1930–1935*. Ann Arbor, Mich.: UMI Research Press, 1985.

Marcus, Millicent. *After Fellini: National Cinema in the Postmodern Age*. Baltimore: Johns Hopkins University Press, 2002.

——. *Filmmaking by the Book: Italian Cinema and Literary Adaptation*. Baltimore: Johns Hopkins University Press, 1993.

——. *Italian Film in the Light of Neorealism*. Princeton, N.J.: Princeton University Press, 1986.

Martinelli, Alberto, Antonio M. Chiesi, and Sonia Stefanizzi. *Recent Social Trends in Italy, 1960–1995*. Montreal: McGill-Queen's University Press, 1999.

Martinelli, Vittorio. *La guerra di D'Annunzio: Da poeta e dandy a eroe di guerra e "comandante."* Udine: Paolo Gaspari, 2001.

———. "Nascita del divismo." In *Storia del cinema mondiale*, ed. Gian Piero Brunetta. Venice: Einaudi, 1999. 221–249.

———. *Pina Menichelli: Le sfumature del fascino*. Rome: Bulzoni, 2002.

Martini, Andrea, ed. *La bella forma: Poggioli, I calligrafici, e dintorni*. Venice: Marsilio, 1992.

Marwick, Arthur. *The Sixties: Cultural Revolution in Britain, France, Italy, and the United States, c. 1958–1974*. Oxford: Oxford University Press, 1998.

Masi, Stefano. *Roberto Benigni: Superstar*. Rome: Gremese, 1999.

———. *Silvana Mangano: Il teorema della bellezza*. Rome: Gremese, 1994.

Masi, Stefano, and Enrico Lancia. *Italian Movie Goddesses: Over Eighty of the Greatest Women in Italian Cinema*. Rome: Gremese, 1992.

———. *Stelle d'Italia: piccole e grandi dive del cinema italiano*. Rome: Gremese, 1994.

Mastroianni, Marcello. *Mi ricordo, sì, Io mi ricordo*. Milan: Baldini and Castaldi, 1997.

———. "The Game of Truth." In *Playing to the Camera: Film Actors Discuss Their Craft*, ed. Bert Cardullo, Harry Geduld, Ronald Gottesman, and Leigh Woods. New Haven: Yale University Press, 1998. 155–157.

McDonagh, Maitland. "Broken Mirrors/Broken Minds: The Dark Dreams of Dario Argento." *Film Quarterly* 41, no. 2 (Winter 1987–1988): 2–13.

———. "The Elegant Brutality of Dario Argento." *Film Comment* 29, no. 1 (Jan./Feb. 1993): 55–58.

Mendes, Valerie, and Amy de la Haye. *20th Century Fashion*. London: Thames and Hudson, 1999.

Micciché, Lino. *Pasolini nella città del cinema*. Venice: Marsilio, 1999.

———. *Visconti e il neorealismo: Ossessione, La terra trema, Bellissima*. Venice: Marsilio, 1998.

Michelone, Guido. *Invito al cinema di Rossellini*. Milan: Mursia, 1996.

Miller, Mark A. "Barbara Steele: 'Diva of Dark Drama.'" *Filmfax* no. 51 (July/Aug. 1995): 37–44.

Mingozzi, Gianfranco. *Francesca Bertini*. Genoa: Le Mani, 2003.

Mitchell, Tony. "Berlusconi, Italian Television, and Recent Italian Cinema: Re-viewing *The Icicle Thief*." *Film Criticism* 21, no. 1 (Fall 1996): 13–23.

———. "The Construction and Reception of Anna Magnani in Italy and the English-Speaking World." *Film Criticism* 14, no. 1 (Fall 1989): 2–22.

"Monica Bellucci." *Current Biography International Yearbook*, ed. Clifford Thompson and Miriam Helbok. New York: The Wilson Company, 2003–2004.

Moretti, Massimo. "Febo Mari vigilò l'esecuzione." *A nuova luce*. Bologna: Fotogenia, 1997/1998. 149–165.

Moscati, Camillo. *Franco e Ciccio: Due comici venuti della strada*. Genoa: Lo Vecchio, 2000.

Moscati, Italo. *Anna Magnani: Vita, amori e carriera di un' attrice che guarda diritto negli occhi*. Rome: RAI, 2003.

Mosconi, Elena, ed. *Light from a Star*. Cremona: Persico, 2003.

Naremore, James. *Acting in the Cinema*. Berkeley: University of California Press, 1988.

Natale, Richard. "Mastroianni Dead at 72." www.variety.com, 20 December 1996, 2 pages.

Newman, Kim. "Profondo rosso." *Monthly Film Bulletin* 52, no. 610 (1984): 349–350.

Nowell-Smith, Geoffrey. *Luchino Visconti*. Garden City, N.Y.: Doubleday, 1968.

Østergaard, Bernt Stubbe, ed. *The Media in Western Europe: The Euromedia Handbook*. London: Sage, 1992.

Palla, Marco. *Mussolini and Fascism*. Trans. Arthur Figliola and Claudia Rattazzi Papka. New York: Interlink Books, 2000.

Palmerini, Luca M., and Gaetano Mistretta. *Spaghetti Nightmares: Italian Fantasy-Horrors as Seen through the Eyes of Their Protagonists*. Key West, Fla.: Fantasma Books, 1996.

Papotti, Davide. "Amate sponde: L'imagine lacuale in due adattamenti cinematografici di *Malombra* di Antonio Fogazzaro." In *Pagina, Pellicola, Pratica: Studia sul cinema italiano*, ed. Rebecca West. Ravenna: Longo, 2000: 30–55.

Pasolini, Pier Paolo. *Heretical Empiricism*. Trans. Ben Lawton and Louise Barnett. Bloomington: Indiana University Press, 1988. 179–180.

Pellizzari, Lorenzo. "Il cinema pensato: tra liberazione e colonizzazione." In *Storia del cinema italiano: 1945–1948*, ed. Callisto Cosulich. Vol. 7. Venice: Marsilio, 2003. 467–487.

Pescatore, Guglielmo. "Nascita del autore cinematografica." In *Storia del cinema mondiale*, ed. Gian Piero Brunetta. Vol. 1. Turin: Giulio Einaudi, 1999. 199–221.

Piccione, Fabio. *Due cialtroni alla rovescia: Studio sulla comicità*. Genoa: Fratelli, 2004.

Pillittieri, Paolo. *Il cinema tra finzione e falsita: simili, facsimili, quasi falsi, quasi storici, quando il cinema manipola la nostra storia*. Milan: Spiral, 2000.

Pirie, David. *A Heritage of Horror, 1946–1972*. New York: Avon, 1973.

Pistoia, Marco. "Il melodrama e l'eredità del neorealismo." In *Storia del cinema italiano*, ed. Sandro Bernardi. Vol. 9. Turin: Marsilio, 2004. 163–175.

Porro, Maurizio. *Alberto Sordi*. Milan: Formichiere, 1979.

Pugliese, Roberto. *Dario Argento*. Milan: Castoro, 1996.

Re, Lucia. "Il mostro della memoria di Gabriele D'Annunzio: Il Vittoriale degli Italiani." *The Journal of Decorative and Propaganda Arts 1875–1945*, no. 3 (Winter 1987): 7–53.

Redi, R. *Cinema Italiano sotto il fascismo*. Venice: Marsilio, 1997.

Reggiani, Stefano. *Dizionario del postdivismo: Centuno attori italiani del cinema e della TV*. Turin: ERI, 1985.

Reich, Jacqueline. *Beyond the Latin Lover: Marcello Mastroianni, Masculinity, and Italian Cinema*. Bloomington: Indiana University Press, 2004.

———. "Undressing the Latin Lover: Marcello Mastroianni, Fashion and *La dolce vita*." In *Fashion Cultures: Theories, Explorations, and Analysis*, ed. Stella Bruzzi and Pamela Church Gibson. London: Routledge, 2000. 209–221.

Reich, Jacqueline, and Piero Garafalo. *Re-viewing Fascism: Italian Cinema, 1922–1943*. Bloomington: Indiana University Press, 2002.

Restivo, Angelo. *The Cinema of Economic Miracles: Visuality and Modernization in the Italian Art Film*. Durham, N.C.: Duke University Press, 2002.

Ridley, Jasper. *Mussolini*. New York: St. Martin's Press, 1997.

Rodowick, D. N. *Gilles Deleuze's Time Machine*. Durham, N.C.: Duke University Press, 1997.

Rossellini, Roberto. *My Method: Writings and Interviews*. New York: Marsilio, 1992.

Rushdie, Salman. *Imaginary Homelands: Essays and Criticism.* London: Granta Books, 1991.

Russo, Paolo. "Mettere in scene l'angoscia: Dario Argento e l'horror." In *Storia del cinema italiano*, ed. Vito Zagarrio. Vol. 13. Venice: Marsilio, 2005. 442–443.

Ryersson, Scot D., and Michael Orlando Yaccarino. *The Life and Legend of the Marchesa Casati.* New York: Viridian, 1999.

Sabatini, Mariano, and Oriana Maerini. *Intervista a Mario Monicelli: La sostenibile leggerezza del cinema.* Naples: Edizione Scientifiche Italiane, 2001.

Sarris, Andrew. "Notes on the Auteur Theory in 1962." In *Film Theory and Criticism: Introductory Readings*, ed. Leo Braudy and Marshall Cohen. New York: Oxford University Press, 1999. 515–519.

———. "*La signora di tutti.*" *Film Comment* 10, no. 6 (Nov./Dec. 1974): 44–46.

Sartori, Carlo. *La fabbrica delle stele: Divismo, mercato, e mass media negli anni '80.* Milan: Arnaldo Mondadori, 1983.

Savio, Francesco. *Cinecittà anni trenta: Parlano 116 protagonisti del secondo cinema italiano 1930–1943.* Roma: Bulzoni, 1979.

Schifano, Laurence. *Luchino Visconti: The Flames of Passion.* London: Collins, 1990.

Seknadje-Askénazi, Enrique. *Roberto Rossellini et la second guerre mondiale.* Paris: L'Harmattan, 2000.

Shaviro, Steven. *The Cinematic Body.* Minneapolis: University of Minnesota Press, 1993.

Sheehy, Helen. *Eleanora Duse: A Biography.* New York: Alfred A. Knopf, 2003.

Sheil, Mark. *Italian Neorealism: Rebuilding the Cinematic City.* London: Wallflower, 2006.

Sinclair, John, ed. *Contemporary World Television.* London: BFI, 2004.

Sobchack, Vivian. *Carnal Thoughts: Embodiment and Moving Image Culture.* Berkeley: University of California Press, 2004.

Sorlin, Pierre. *Italian National Cinema 1896–1996.* London: Routledge, 1996.

Spackman, Barbara. *Decadent Genealogies: The Rhetoric of Sickness from Baudelaire to D'Annunzio.* Ithaca, N.Y.: Cornell University Press, 1989.

———. *Fascist Virilities: Rhetoric, Ideology, and Social Fantasy in Italy.* Minneapolis: University of Minnesota Press, 1996.

Spagnoli, Marco. *Alberto Sordi: Storia di un italiano.* Rome: Adnkronos Press, 2003.

Steele, Valerie. *Fashion, Italian Style.* New Haven: Yale University Press, 2003.

Stiglegger, Marcus. "Der Zauber von Monica: Anmerkungen von Phänomen Monica Belluccci." *Film-dienst* 48, no. 20 (2005): 6–9.

Tatò, Anna Maria. *I Remember: A film by Anna Maria Tatò.* Mikado and Istituto LUCE in collaboration with RAI, 1997.

Thoret, Jean-Baptiste. *Dario Argento: Magicien de la peur.* Paris: Cahiers du Cinéma, 2002.

Tofetti, Sergio. "Dai telefoni bianchi alle bandiere rosse: genre, filoni, luoghi narrativi." In *Storia del cinema italiano: 1945–1948*, ed. Callisto Cosulich. Vol. 7. Venice: Marsilio, 2000. 269–287.

Toll, Robert, C. *The Entertainment Machine: American Show Business in the Twentieth Century.* Oxford: Oxford University Press, 1982.

Torriglia, Anna Maria. *Broken Time, Fragmented Space: A Cultural Map for Postwar Italy.* Toronto: University of Toronto Press, 2002.

Tournès, André. "Profession: Acteur, Vittorio Gassman." *Jeune Cinéma* no. 90 (Nov. 1975): 16–21.

Tyler, Parker. *Magic and Myth of the Movies.* New York: Simon and Schuster, 1970.

Valentini, Paola. "Il cinema e gli altri media." In *Storia del cinema italiano*, ed. Luciano de Gusti. Vol. 8. Venice: Marsilio, 2003. 103–115.

Verdone, Carlo, with Marco Giusti. *Fatti coati (o quasi)*. Milan: Oscar Mondadori, 1999.

Verdone, Mario. *La Signora Magnani: Antologia di ritratti e conversazioni*. Rome: Edilazio, 2001.

Viano, Maurizio. *A Certain Realism: Making Use of Pasolini's Film Theory and Practice*. Berkeley: University of California Press, 1993.

Viganò, Aldo. "La commedia all'italiana." In *Storia del cinema italiano: 1960–1964*, ed. Giorgio Vincenti. Vol. 10. Venice: Marsilio, 2001. 235–272.

Vincendeau, Ginette. *Stars and Stardom in French Cinema*. London: Continuum, 2000.

Virilio, Paul. *The Art of the Motor*. Trans. Julie Rose. Minneapolis: University of Minnesota Press, 1995.

Vitti, Antonio. *Giuseppe De Santis and Postwar Italian Cinema*. Toronto: University of Toronto Press, 1996.

——, ed. *Incontri con il cinema italiano*. Rome: Salvatore-Sciaccia Press, 2003.

Wagstaff, Christopher. "Cinema." In *Italian Cultural Studies: An Introduction*, ed. David Forgacs and Robert Lumley. Oxford; Oxford University Press, 1996. 216–233.

——. "Marcello Mastroianni." *Sight and Sound* 7, no. 3 (March 1997): 39.

Walker, Alexander. *Stardom: The Hollywood Phenomenon*. New York: Stein and Day, 1970.

Widding, Astrid Söderberg. "Denmark." In *Nordic National Cinemas*, by Tytti Soila, Astrid Söderberg Widding, and Gunnar Iversen. London: Routledge, 1998.

Wood, Mary P. *Italian Cinema*. Oxford: Berg, 2005.

Zagarrio, Vito. *L'anello mancante: storia e teoria del rapporto cinema-television*. Turin: Lindau, 2004.

——. *Cinema e fascismo: Film, modelli, immaginari*. Venice, Marsilio, 2004.

——. *Cinema italiano, anni novanta*. Venice: Marsilio, 1998.

Zavattini, Cesare. "Some Ideas on the Cinema." In *Film: A Montage of Theories*, ed. Richard Dyer MacCann. New York: E. P. Dutton, 1966. 216–228.

Index

Page numbers in italics refer to illustrations.

About the Author

Marcia Landy is Distinguished Professor of English/Film Studies with a secondary appointment in the Department of French and Italian Languages and Literatures at the University of Pittsburgh. Her books include *Fascism in Film: The Italian Commercial Cinema, 1931–1943*; *Italian Film*; *The Folklore of Concensus: Theatricality in the Italian Cinema, 1930–1943*; *Cinematic Uses of the Past*; *Stars* (edited with Lucy Fischer); and *Monty Python's Flying Circus*.